BULLION

Andrew Hogg is editor of the *Sunday Times* 'Insight' team, which specializes in investigative reporting. Educated in East Africa and Sussex, he began his career in journalism on a weekly newspaper in the Home Counties before moving north to join the *Journal* in Newcastle. He began his Fleet Street career as a general news reporter on the *Evening News*, followed by three years on the *Evening Standard* where he specialized in investigations. His first book, *Secret Cult*, of which he was co-author, followed a year's research into the controversial British religious cult, the School of Economic Science. He joined the *Sunday Times* in 1984 and, as crime reporter, took part in the award-winning 'Insight' investigation into drug running and corruption in the Bahamas. He became Home News Editor in 1986 and was appointed 'Insight' editor a year later. Andrew Hogg is married to travel writer Carole Stewart.

Jim McDougall was producer of *Gold*, a BBC1 documentary about the Brink's-Mat Raid first shown in 1987. He began his career in journalism as a provincial newspaper reporter until joining the BBC in Plymouth as a researcher for the *Nationwide* programme. He then worked as a television newsroom journalist as well as producing documentaries, including *Angel of the Snow* – filmed in the Canadian Arctic – which accompanied his first book by the same title. Following a spell producing *Spotlight*, the BBC's nightly magazine programme in the South-West, together with a news-based documentary series, Jim McDougall went on to become a features producer for the BBC in the Midlands, making documentaries such as *Sibonga: A Name of Destiny*, about the Vietnamese boat people, which was networked on BBC2. Since 1980 he has been an assistant news editor in Bristol producing the *Points West* programme and, latterly, has been concentrating on current-affairs documentaries.

Robin Morgan is features editor of the *Sunday Times*. At the age of sixteen he entered journalism in the West Midlands and joined the *Sunday Times* in 1979, travelling extensively on major international assignments. A former editor of the 'Insight' team, he was awarded a 1982 British Press Award for a series of articles that proved the innocence of a man jailed for multiple murders. In 1983 he was named Campaigning Journalist of the Year for an investigation that revealed how the authorities had covered up the deaths of scores of British tourists killed in death-trap apartments abroad. His first book, the bestselling *Falklands War*, was written with the 'Insight' team, and his second, *Rainbow Warrior*, investigated the French attack on Greenpeace. He has since edited and written the text for *Manpower*, a book of photographs by his colleague Sally Soames. Robin Morgan is married with three children and lives in Hertfordshire.

BULLION
BULLION
BULLION

BRINK'S-MAT: THE STORY OF BRITAIN'S BIGGEST GOLD ROBBERY

Andrew Hogg

Jim McDougall

Robin Morgan

PENGUIN BOOKS

PENGUIN BOOKS

Published by the Penguin Group
27 Wrights Lane, London W8 5TZ, England
Viking Penguin Inc., 40 West 23rd Street, New York, New York 10010, USA
Penguin Books Australia Ltd, Ringwood, Victoria, Australia
Penguin Books Canada Ltd, 2801 John Street, Markham, Ontario, Canada L3R 1B4
Penguin Books (NZ) Ltd, 182–190 Wairau Road, Auckland 10, New Zealand

Penguin Books Ltd, Registered Offices: Harmondsworth, Middlesex, England

First published 1988

For permission to reproduce the photographs in this book grateful acknowledgment is made to the following:
Associated Press, 25; BBC, 1; Patrick Haggerty, 9; *Illustrated London News*, 15; London Express News Service, 5, 22; Metropolitan Police, 8, 10, 16; Photo News Service, 12, 17, 18, 19, 20; Popperfoto, 24; Press Association, 3, 11, 14; Syndication International, 4; Topham Picture Library, 2.

Made and printed in Great Britain by
Richard Clay Ltd, Bungay, Suffolk
Filmset in Linotron Melior by
Rowland Phototypesetting Ltd, Bury St Edmunds, Suffolk

Gold has a strange effect on many people. Gold has no conscience. And some people who deal in it have no conscience either.

Detective Chief Superintendent Brian Boyce, after the Brink's-Mat raid

Contents

Preface

The Brink's-Mat raid was not just the biggest robbery in British history. It also presented Scotland Yard with incontrovertible evidence that the most professional armed robbers in the country, a gang based in south-east London, had links with international organized crime.

That relationship between a group of 'traditional' armed robbers and those more at home discussing offshore tax havens and money-laundering schemes led to a far-reaching change at Scotland Yard, where a specialist operations task force was set up to tackle organized crime.

The bullion robbers and the money launderers, however, were not the only members of the criminal fraternity to become involved in the Brink's-Mat case. For the businessmen called in to help dispose of the bullion soon showed that they were equally unscrupulous. Once their involvement was revealed, police knew that there could be no relaxing of their efforts to get back the gold or its cash proceeds. Otherwise, they feared, those enjoying their sudden illegal wealth would use property and other investments to obtain real power within the establishment. 'If a group of criminals have £26 million of gold in their coffers, they have probably got more power than some Third World countries. That makes them a very potent danger to our society,' warned Detective Chief Superintendent Brian Boyce, from the task force.

Evidence of how the gold was sold back on to the open market, and the money then banked, also forced the government to take action. Banks admitted that they handled millions of pounds in cash, much of it handed over the counter in plastic carrier bags, with no questions asked. In the USA failure to report such transactions to the appropriate authorities is illegal, and by late 1987 Whitehall had drafted laws intended to prevent such transactions involving illegal profits from ever taking place again in Britain.

This book does not purport to tell the whole story of the Brink's-Mat raid. Further court cases will take place in 1988, and the likelihood is that the investigation will continue for years to come. Instead we set out to tell the story of the robbery and its immediate aftermath as accurately as possible. Given that much of the evidence later presented in court was fiercely contested, we have also endeavoured, where possible, to remain impartial. In the words of one detective, however, 'Sooner or later you have to decide whose side you are on – and journalists always hate to do that.' At the end of the day we make no apologies for coming down firmly on the side of those officers who confront armed robbers as part of their everyday duties and whose bravery generally merits no more than a paragraph in the national press.

This book could not have been completed without valuable assistance from a number of quarters. Some sources, for obvious reasons, cannot be named. Among those that we can mention, however, are former Deputy Assistant Commissioner Brian Worth of the Metropolitan Police and Commander Jeremy Plowman of the Flying Squad, and his officers.

We are also grateful to Detective Constable Neil Murphy for agreeing to talk to us, and to Assistant Chief Investigation Officer Jim McGregor, from HM Customs, for his guidance.

A number of journalists also merit special thanks. They include Stephen Davis, David Connett and Tony Rennell of the *Sunday Times*, as well as freelances Nigel Bowden in Marbella, Paul Eddy and Sara Walden in Florida, Valerie Cottle in the Isle of Man and Richard Palmer in London. We would also like to thank Gordon Beckett of the *Sunday Times* for the illustrations.

Andrew Hogg
London
December 1987

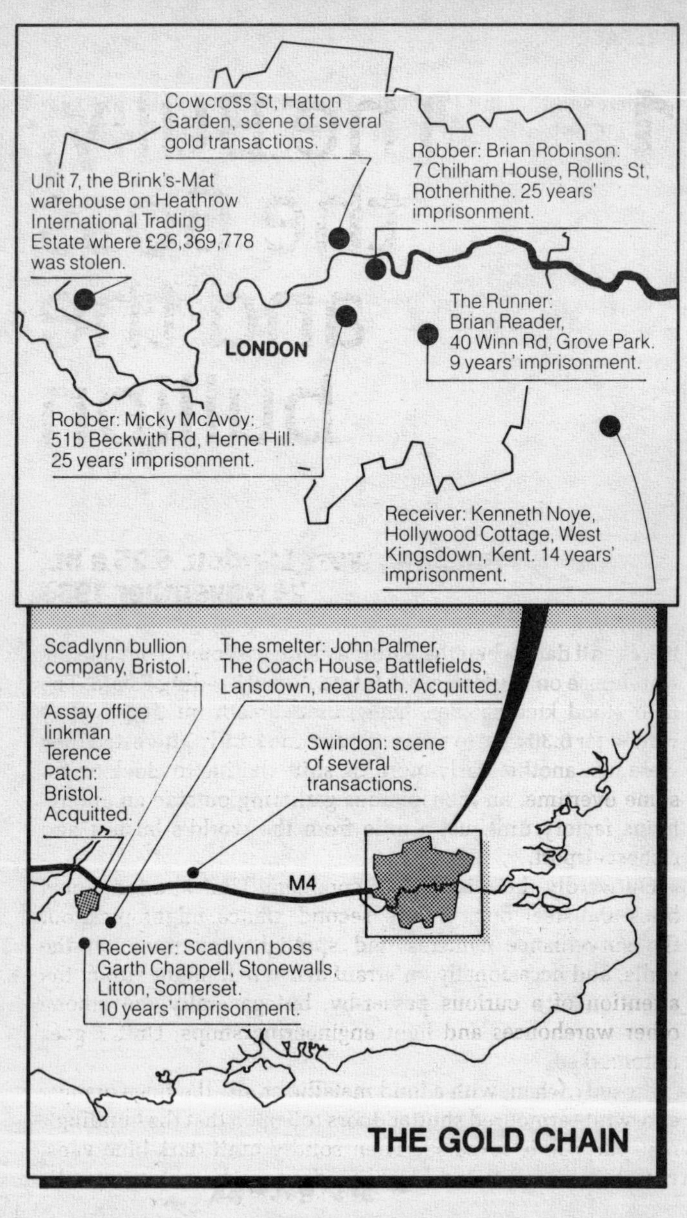
Cowcross St, Hatton Garden, scene of several gold transactions.
Unit 7, the Brink's-Mat warehouse on Heathrow International Trading Estate where £26,369,778 was stolen.
Robber: Brian Robinson: 7 Chilham House, Rollins St, Rotherhithe. 25 years' imprisonment.
LONDON
The Runner: Brian Reader, 40 Winn Rd, Grove Park. 9 years' imprisonment.
Robber: Micky McAvoy: 51b Beckwith Rd, Herne Hill. 25 years' imprisonment.
Receiver: Kenneth Noye, Hollywood Cottage, West Kingsdown, Kent. 14 years' imprisonment.
Scadlynn bullion company, Bristol.
The smelter: John Palmer, The Coach House, Battlefields, Lansdown, near Bath. Acquitted.
Assay office linkman Terence Patch: Bristol. Acquitted.
Swindon: scene of several transactions.
M4
Receiver: Scadlynn boss Garth Chappell, Stonewalls, Litton, Somerset. 10 years' imprisonment.
THE GOLD CHAIN

1. The Bully, the Boss and the bullion

Hounslow, west London, 6.25 a.m., 26 November 1983

It was still dark when the Saturday shift assembled outside the warehouse on the Heathrow International Trading Estate. The men stood kicking their heels, their breath misting as they waited for 6.30 a.m. to arrive. To anyone faintly interested they were just another early-morning shift waiting to clock on for some overtime, an inauspicious gathering outside an anonymous factory unit just a mile from the world's busiest and richest airport.

Outwardly there is little to commend Unit 7, a functional brick-and-steel box. A rare second glance might pick out the surveillance cameras and spotlights mounted on the walls, and occasionally an errant alarm bell might attract the attention of a curious passer-by, but generally, set among other warehouses and light engineering shops, Unit 7 goes unremarked.

It's only when, with a loud metallic crank, the huge orange-and-white armoured shutter doors roll open that the building's real purpose is revealed. Then solidly built dark-blue vans, with barred and tinted black windows and a gold portcullis motif painted on each side, can be seen either entering or leaving a well-protected loading-bay.

The Brink's-Mat security vans are a familiar sight on the trading estate, where the jokes and dreams about their cargoes were worn out long ago. For Unit 7, although not Fort Knox or the Bank of England, is one of Britain's biggest safes, used to store hugely valuable cargoes of currency, precious metals and other high-risk consignments generally, although not always, *en route* through Heathrow Airport.

The cargoes are stored in the vault, containing three large safes, that lies on the ground floor of the unit. Above is the manager's office, the radio-control room where the movement of the vans around London and its environs is constantly monitored, a rest room that doubles as the canteen and a locker room for the thirty or so guards who usually work at the unit.

That Saturday the men waiting outside were forced, as usual, to wait until precisely 6.30 a.m. Only then would the automatic timer neutralize the sophisticated alarm system, allowing the keys to be inserted without triggering flashing lights, bells and alarms linked with the local police station and other security companies.

Security guard Richard Holliday had been the first to arrive in his beige Ford Consul; he was quickly followed by another guard, Ron Clarke, on his moped. Guards Peter Bentley and Robin Riseley pulled up moments later, and the four men mumbled greetings to one another. A fifth guard rostered for duty, Tony Black, was late and still hadn't arrived when the man who would supervise the day's work drove up. Michael Scouse, 37, a former special constable, was the longest-serving guard on duty that day, with twelve years on the Brink's-Mat payroll. His seniority singled him out that morning as the 'keyman'.

Arriving at the unit, Scouse sat in his car until the 6.30 a.m. news bulletin started on Capital Radio. After listening for a few moments he left the vehicle, walked over to the warehouse door and inserted his keys. The routine security procedure required him to enter the unit alone and lock the door behind him, leaving the crew outside while he collected from the safe in a downstairs office another key with which he could switch off the alarm system covering the perimeter walls and windows.

That accomplished, Scouse went back to the main door to allow the crew in. The outside door was relocked from the inside, then Scouse reactivated the alarm system, climbed the stairs and walked through to the radio-control room to look through the paperwork for the day's duties. Meanwhile the four guards had gone into the rest room to take off their coats, Holliday pausing briefly to switch on the radio-room aerials and the surveillance cameras before joining his mates.

Then, as the kettle boiled and Bentley rinsed the pot, the men began discussing the day's load. They already knew it was bullion – they had been told as much the previous afternoon – but now they needed to know the size and weight of the consignment before deciding which vehicle to use. Riseley, who would be crew leader on the run, walked into the control room to consult with Scouse. 'What's the tonnage?' he asked.

Scouse shuffled the documents, mentally adding up the metric weight of the shipments and converting it into its Imperial equivalent. 'It's gold. Three ton. Gatwick Airport for the Far East via Cathay Pacific Airways. It's got to be there by 8 a.m.,' he replied.

It was a regular weekend trip for the Brink's-Mat crew. Although the cargo rarely matched that day's consignment, such is the nature of the work that even the mention of 3 tons of bullion made little impression on Riseley. His response was a practical one: 'We'll need the Mercedes then.'

Riseley walked back to the rest room to discuss the run with the other guards. He would ride in the front of the van, with Bentley driving. Richard Holliday would travel in the back with the bullion and, as added security, Ron Clarke would follow behind in a Brink's-Mat Ford Escort van. Riseley checked through the papers – airway bills, delivery notes, airport security passes. All seemed in order, although Bentley was concerned that the gross weight might be too much for the

Mercedes, which technically had a 2.5-ton payload limit. At that point the doorbell rang. It was Black, not unusually ten minutes late, and the guards heard Scouse go downstairs to let him in.

'You look a bit rough,' called Bentley as Black walked into the rest room. The 31-year-old guard did indeed look pale, unkempt and apprehensive, as if he had just clambered out of bed and raced to work; he confirmed Bentley's suspicion that he had overslept, then, mumbling something about having to use the toilet, he disappeared downstairs again.

'Get on the floor or you're fucking dead.' The masked figure filling the doorway of the rest room spat out the words in a harsh Cockney accent, motioning urgently to the stunned guards with his 9 mm Browning automatic pistol. A stint in the British Army sharpens a man's reflexes, and Riseley was no exception. He had learnt to recognize the voice of authority and to react. He did so now, diving from his chair to the floor, quickly followed by Clarke and Holliday. Only moments before, Riseley had glanced at his watch, a casual reaction to the arrival of Tony Black. It was 6.40 a.m.

The shape in the doorway took one step into the brightly lit room. From his position on the floor Riseley could see a white man, perhaps 5 feet 8 inches tall and clean-shaven, wearing a trilby and a dark car coat or anorak over a black blazer, black trousers and a black tie. The gunman might have been dressed for a funeral but for the yellow balaclava that he quickly hitched up to cover all but his eyes.

For a second or two nothing seemed to happen, then the gunman made the move that was to earn him the nickname 'the Bully' among the guards. Without a word he jerked his gun arm upwards and then, a silver blazer button glinting in the light, smashed the weapon down on the back of Peter Bentley's head. Standing by the sink making the tea, the guard had been slow to react when the door crashed open, believing it to be a colleague playing one of their regular practical jokes. As he fell, Bentley's head hit the table and then the floor, dazing him momentarily and opening two bloody gashes in his scalp. The attacker's gun arm then beckoned through the open door to someone waiting outside, and another three, maybe four, robbers rushed into the room.

'Lie still and keep quiet,' ordered the Bully, as his henchmen began to immobilize the terrified guards, yanking their arms behind their backs and handcuffing them, then locking their legs together at the shins with heavy-duty tape. Cloth bags with drawstrings were then pulled down over the guards' heads and fastened around their necks.

Bentley could feel rough hands pulling at the house and car keys on his belt, then his watch was snatched off and thrown across the room. Blood from his throbbing head wound was trickling down his face and neck. His discomfort must have been evident, for a moment later a voice, sounding almost sympathetic, asked if he was okay and loosened the drawstring a little. It was a crazy thought at a time like this, but the figure that had confronted him during the split-second after the door burst open, he realized, had reminded him of Inspector Clouseau, the bungling detective played by Peter Sellers. But there was nothing comical about the guards' predicament.

Richard Holliday had also taken a close look at the gunman, close enough to distinguish the herring-bone pattern of the tweed hat and the crispness of a starched white shirt. He had even seen a lock of fair hair protruding from the balaclava before the bag was placed over his head. Now he was finding it increasingly difficult to breathe. Thrashing about on the floor, he managed to attract the attention of one of the robbers, who bent down and untied the drawstring, pulling the bag back to clear his upper lip. To ease his discomfort further he was turned on to his back. Ron Clarke was similarly treated, first roughly bound, then casually asked if he was in any distress.

Moments passed, then the guards heard another man speak –this time a well-spoken man, with no discernible accent, who was obviously used to giving orders. 'Get that radio tuned in. If you hear anything, tell us,' he commanded. Later, when they relived their ordeal, the guards agreed that this man was the Boss.

The order was followed by the sound of several men leaving the room, but as the radio crackled through the frequencies, the guards knew they had not been left alone. Seconds passed, then the guards heard the radio tune in to a Metropolitan Police wavelength. It seemed that there was precious little happening outside the Brink's-Mat warehouse: two officers could be heard discussing a spot-check on a vehicle but nothing more. To all intents and purposes, London was waking to a relatively peaceful day.

The guards were not left to consider their position for long. Obviously wary that the four of them were together in the same room, even if they were immobilized, several members of the gang returned and hauled Holliday to his feet, dragging him down the corridor into the locker room. There he was lowered to the floor and pushed back against a girder. But the gang's plan to handcuff him to the steel strut failed when they discovered it was too large for his arms to encircle. Instead he was handcuffed to a radiator where, moments later, he was joined by Ron Clarke. They were left to listen to the noises now echoing in the vault directly below them.

Michael Scouse, one of the six keymen at the unit, had not known when he arrived for work that morning that he would be supervising the movement of 3 tons of gold. It was only when he looked at the worksheets to discuss the day's duties that he realized how much was to be taken to meet the Cathay Pacific flight. Even then he didn't work out the value of the shipment, and there was no indication of its worth in his paperwork. He couldn't know that it was gold in its purest form – worth a staggering £26 million at the previous afternoon's price.

After letting Black into the unit he had returned to the radio room where, after using the toilet downstairs, the late arrival joined him. Black had just started to roll a cigarette when the commotion broke out in the rest room. As they turned towards the door to see what was going on, they were confronted by three men, two of them brandishing Colt 45s and the third a .38

revolver. Like Riseley, Scouse recognized the weapons immediately; he was a member of the Marylebone Rifle and Pistol Club and knew the real thing when he saw it.

Out of the corner of his eye Scouse saw Tony Black drop voluntarily to the floor and did likewise, lying face-down on the carpet. An instant later the cold barrel of a gun was pressing into his neck and a voice was ordering him to put his hands behind his back. He was handcuffed; a cloth bag was placed over his face; and then a boot thudded into his ribs. 'Are you Scouse?'

His answer brought a prompt reaction. He was hoisted to his feet and dragged outside into the corridor, where he was thrown against a wall.

'Breathe in,' ordered the same voice.

Scouse felt his shirt pulled up to his chin and then a hand tugged violently at his waistband.

'Breathe in deeply or you'll get cut.' It was a strange request, made more absurd by the knife that sliced through his belted jeans from the buckle to the crutch. As Scouse filled his lungs he became aware of an overpowering smell. A rag had been waved under his nose.

'Do you recognize the smell?'

It was unmistakable. The next instant he could feel the petrol being poured over his genitals.

'You'd better do as I say, or I'll put a match to the petrol and a bullet through your head. I know where you live. You live in a flat in Ruislip High Street above a television rental shop. We've been watching you for nine months and setting this up for twelve. Now, let's go through the procedure. You have two numbers.'

Scouse was shocked by the knowledge displayed by his attacker. The robbers clearly knew that, for security reasons, each Brink's-Mat keyman was allowed to know only half of each of the combinations for the vault and the three safes inside. The other halves of the combinations were known only to crew leaders, on this occasion Robin Riseley.

The man confronting Scouse seemed in no hurry as he continued to display his intimate knowledge of Unit 7's security system, in particular the alarms; perhaps he wanted to impress upon Scouse that any attempt to thwart the intruders' plans with false information would be spotted instantly. Eventually the raider came to the point. 'What are your combination numbers?'

Scouse hesitated and the gun barrel was pushed up under his chin.

'Tell me or that's it,' threatened the gunman.

The supervisor realized this was no time for false heroics and shouted the numbers. '45-75-55-85.'

The sequence opened one of two locks on the vault door, but the vault door itself was guarded by another door, which, like all those downstairs, was padlocked. The gunman demanded the keys, and Scouse told him where he could find them. Moments later a bunch was rattled under Scouse's nose and the bag pulled off his face.

'Are these the ones?' The gunman held up the brown pouch that contained keys to every door on the ground floor of Unit 7, and Scouse nodded.

Back in the rest room Robin Riseley was receiving the same treatment. He too had been singled out by name, then a knife had sliced through his trousers, pullover and T-shirt, and he smelt petrol as it was poured on to his chest, running down his abdomen into his groin and pooling in the chair he was sitting on.

'Right, Riseley, what's your job?'

The crew leader was petrified, realizing immediately that it was the vault and his knowledge of the combinations that the robbers were after. It never occurred to him to wonder either how the intruders knew his name or, as the questions continued, how they could have known that he possessed half the combinations. Convinced that he would be set alight unless he co-operated, when asked the vital question he responded without hesitation, '50-90-30-55.'

Riseley then tried to describe the dial on the vault but was too nervous to make himself understood. It was a wasted effort anyway, for the intruders had other plans. They cut the tape binding his legs and marched him downstairs to join Scouse.

The former special constable, still with the gun at his neck but with his hood removed, was facing the door leading from the loading-bay into the vault. It was padlocked and protected by an individual alarm that had to be dealt with. Without prompting Scouse reached out for the padlock but realized that the gang had beaten him to it. It was already undone, but the robbers, clearly aware of the alarm, had gone no further.

Turning then to the alarm box on the left of the door, Scouse fiddled with the two dials. The combination had been changed four weeks earlier, and only he and the other supervisors knew the new number, 11-11. The alarm, patched into the headquarters of the Group 4 private security firm, was deactivated, and two bolts securing the door were released. Swinging it open, Scouse moved inside, then, selecting a key from the brown pouch, turned to another box on the left-hand side of the entrance. Inserting the key, he switched off yet another back-up alarm system.

Before them stood the door to the vault itself. There was just one dial to contend with, and Scouse deftly fed in his half of the combination, then turned to find Riseley, now bareheaded, behind him. The crew leader was told to give his combination to his superior, who quickly reeled it off. But the mechanical click that should have indicated that the door was unlocked was surprisingly elusive. Riseley's handcuffs were removed, and he was pushed forward to try it himself. 'No tricks or he's dead,' warned the gunman guarding Scouse as he moved up to the door. This time it worked, and Scouse was again pushed forward to a wall-mounted dial to deactivate a secondary alarm with the combination 5-5.

So far, so good – but now there was a new set of obstacles to overcome. The first, the cage that barred the way to the inner sanctum, was opened by Scouse with a second set of keys from his pouch. Then two further alarm systems had to be deactivated, one connected to Modern Alarms, a London-based alarm-control system, the other to Group 4.

It was all over in moments. Still with a gun in his back, Scouse looked over his shoulder and declared that the alarms were now neutralized. They were in.

*

Hollywood has developed a celluloid cliché over the years, but the image of a bank vault illuminated by the dull buttercup glow of neatly stacked ingots drawing sharp intakes of breath from greedy, gold-crazed villains is incorrect. In Unit 7's vault, shortly before 7 a.m. that morning, the fluorescent lighting revealed only a carpet of drab grey containers, no bigger than shoeboxes, bound with metal straps and bearing handwritten identification codes.

They were there principally on the instructions of Simon Churchill, Assistant Manager (Bullion Instructions) for Johnson Matthey Bank. Churchill was responsible for the movement of all precious metals held by his employers and had received routine instructions the previous Wednesday. Three large orders had been placed by overseas customers. The Republic Bank of New York in Singapore required 1,000 kilos; the Sumitomo Corporation in Tokyo wanted 500 kilos, with the possibility of two further shipments; and the Eastern Trade Corporation of Dubai wanted 470 kilos. Two other orders were awaiting confirmation: the giant Mitsubishi Corporation in Japan was expected to want at least 200 kilos, while the DG Bank in Frankfurt had indicated that it might purchase 500 kilos.

Churchill telephoned London's Brink's-Mat headquarters and asked for security escorts from the Johnson Matthey vaults in Hatton Garden, central London, to Singapore, Tokyo and Dubai. The shipments were to be collected from Hatton Garden on Friday, 25 November. The next day Churchill called Brink's-Mat again. It was short notice, but the two further shipments had been confirmed: Mitsubishi had made up its corporate mind and had placed the expected order, and the West German bank wanted its bullion too.

Brian Avent supervised the consignments' preparation in the bullion-weighing room in Hatton Garden. His instructions, handwritten by Churchill, gave him the shipment numbers, customers' names and locations and, naturally, the size of the orders.

Order number BD8334 for Singapore was packed, fifty kilobars to a box, in twenty boxes, identified by serial numbers

JM427 to JM446. There were ten boxes for Sumitomo (JM447–456) and ten for Frankfurt (JM417–426). Mitsubishi wanted its gold in half-kilo ingots, packed 100 to a box (JM473–476), but the Dubai company wanted its 470 kilos of gold in even smaller sizes: 4,000 bars, each weighing 3.75 troy ounces, packed 250 to a box (JM457–472). Avent completed his task by mid-morning on Friday, and when the Brink's-Mat van arrived at 3 p.m. the sixty boxes, containing altogether 2,670 kilos of gold, were ready for loading. Such was the size of the shipment that two runs had to be made from Hatton Garden to the Heathrow trading estate.

But even before they arrived the vault at Unit 7 had begun to fill up with other consignments. Several hundreds of thousands of pounds in used banknotes arrived and were locked in the three safes. Then, shortly after 1 p.m. on Friday, Unit 7 accepted three boxes of gold ingots and four drums of precious-metal residue. At 5.35 p.m. another van pulled into the loading-bay to offload sixteen boxes of gold bullion, each containing twenty-five kilo-bars, worth a total of £3.6 million. The van also carried two boxes of platinum ingots weighing 20 kilos and worth £160,000. Two pouches were also accepted, one containing traveller's cheques worth $250,000, the other polished and rough diamonds valued at £113,000. By 9 p.m., however, all sixty of the Johnson Matthey shipment boxes had finally been stored in the vault. When Andrew McLaughlin, the late-duty keyman, finally locked his vault at 11 p.m. it held riches totalling £26,369,778 as well as the money in the safes.

Michael Scouse had left work that Friday afternoon at 4.50 p.m. The vault was filling up but at that stage contained perhaps no more than £750,000 in gold and other metals. Scouse had been informed at 3.30 p.m. that he would be working overtime the next day and had been told to recruit a crew from the guards on duty. He knew that, as a routine security measure, he would not be informed of the size and value of the shipment until he arrived for work on Saturday morning.

The men he approached that Friday afternoon were predictably reluctant to work the following day, but none refused. Robin Riseley was single, so had no wife at home to bemoan his absence. He understood that security, flight times and the whims of customers dictated not only unsocial hours but also scant warning. Peter Bentley agreed to work only if no one else could be found, while Richard Holliday, who was married, initially refused but eventually relented. Clarke agreed immediately, as did the final guard recruited, Tony Black.

Riseley left the warehouse at 6 p.m. that evening with Peter Bentley, both men driving to the nearby Waggoners pub on the A4, where they drank until 8.15 p.m. At home in Slough, Riseley cooked himself a meal, put on a record and was in bed by 10 p.m. Clarke took his wife shopping; later, while he was out walking the dog, his wife took a call from Brink's-Mat to confirm that he would be working. Black, meanwhile, went out for a hamburger with his wife and then drove home to bed.

None of them had any inkling of the fortune they were due to handle the next day, and neither did the men who were about to torment and rob them. The gang expected rich pickings but not fabulous wealth. Their audacious plot, ruthless in its conception and brilliant in its execution, was about to land the biggest haul in British criminal history.

At first the shoeboxes were of little interest to the gang. After neutralizing the alarms and opening the vault Scouse and Riseley instantly recognized the size of the potential haul. The gunmen, however, ignored the boxes, stepping over them in their eagerness to reach the three safes that, they believed, would contain items of real value. Perhaps they might have left with the contents, leaving the gold untouched on the floor, if they could have opened the safes quickly, but there was an unexpected setback.

The three safes had to be opened by yet another dual system of keys and combinations. Michael Scouse had the keys and knew which ones to use, but he didn't know the combinations.

Riseley had been entrusted with the numbers but did not know which keys to use. In addition, the safes had a third line of defence: magnetic plates over the locks that, when pulled off, activated an alarm system. Incredibly, the robbers knew about these too.

'Take off those magnetic shields,' ordered the gunman covering Scouse, who did so. He was pushed away from the three strongboxes to allow Riseley to enter the combinations.

But Riseley was in a panic. The combinations had been changed recently; he had not yet memorized them fully and had left at home the diary in which he had recorded them. Ten minutes passed as he tried to remember the correct sequences, fumbling every now and then with the dials.

The robbers controlled their impatience with difficulty. Eventually it was the Bully who spoke, quietly but with unmistakable menace. 'Son, don't fuck me about,' he warned, then, turning to one of his accomplices, he sneered, 'It looks like we've got a hero.'

'It's a shame we're going to have to do him in,' came the reply.

Then, convinced that Riseley was stalling, they began plaguing the hapless guard, one robber pulling his nose while another lit matches close to his petrol-sodden clothing. A knife was produced, and Riseley was told that if he didn't open up, his penis would be cut off. The appalling callousness of their actions terrified Riseley further. As his ordeal continued and the correct figure sequence became even harder to recall, a voice outside the vault issued an ultimatum. 'I'm going by 7.30 a.m. and if they're not open by then, you're a dead man.'

In the outer vault Scouse, hooded again and sitting on a metal chest, tried to help his colleague. 'Look, leave him alone. He's like this in the week,' he pleaded.

It was then, in growing desperation, that one of the gang turned to him and demanded to know what was in the boxes. Scouse, aware that the tension was close to breaking-point, had no hesitation in telling him. There was a moment's silence, and then feverish activity as the gang began ripping at the boxes to see if he was telling the truth.

They quickly found out that he was, and, as box after box was opened, an El Dorado lay revealed. The atmosphere became electrified as, with scarcely contained excitement, the gang turned their attentions from Riseley to the job of moving the gold out to the side of the loading-bay.

'Who knows how to work the shutter door?' Scouse was asked. He gave Tony Black's name.

Black, lying in a pool of petrol upstairs where Scouse had stood, heard the footsteps first and then felt the kick. 'Who's Black? Which one of you is Black?'

Two men grabbed him and marched him into the control room, from where the shutters could be opened automatically. His handcuffs and mask were removed, and he looked down to see a long-bladed knife prodding his chest. Told to open the doors, he did so instantly. A vehicle drove in, and he was ordered to close them again.

Upstairs the guards who had played no part in the gunmen's plans had followed their activities through sounds coming from the area of the vault. They heard the shutter's familiar vibrating judder as the gears slipped before catching; they heard the trolley, loaded with gold, give its distinctive rattle as it rolled into the loading-bay. They heard one robber shout, 'We're gonna need another van,' and listened as the doors opened again and another vehicle drove in. And they heard Riseley scream.

It had been heavy work, but the floor of the vault was soon cleared. Yet still the gang was dissatisfied with their haul and began looking eagerly again at the three safes. Riseley still found it impossible to remember the combinations. A final attempt was ordered – 'And then we're off' – but again Riseley failed. 'Okay, let's go. What are we going to do with him?' said one of the gang.

'Get him upstairs with the others,' replied the Boss.

Riseley's tormentor manhandled him upstairs, pushing him into the cupboard where Black was already cowering. 'I'll fucking teach you,' the gunman said furiously, and with that he punched the guard violently in the stomach. Riseley's scream filled the other guards with dread. But after one blow the gunman dismissed Riseley with the words, 'It's a good job it's Christmas.'

Scouse too had been taken back upstairs, where he was again hooded and handcuffed, and his mouth and legs were taped.

Now, after the terror, came an indication that the nightmare was ending, as one of the gunmen went from guard to guard, checking that they were all securely tied but loosening bonds and hoods to ensure that they were relatively comfortable.

'Are you all right, Mick?' Scouse was asked. The supervisor had just one request – for water to be poured over the petrol that still soaked his trousers and shirt. He was anxious to dilute it, for even now, handcuffed and immobilized as he was, he was terrified that a chance spark might turn him into a human torch.

Below there was the sound of engines starting and van doors banging. One of the gang reappeared at the door of the locker room. 'Merry Christmas,' he mocked, and then, when the sound of the van engines had died away, there was silence.

2. 'We've been turned over'

Alan Bullock kept getting the engaged tone. For the tenth time he dialled the number. He was determined to get through – by now the noise outside was really getting on his nerves. It was Saturday morning, about 8.20, he later told police officers, when the alarm on the Brink's-Mat Ford Transit van that his mechanics were servicing suddenly went off, the wailing making it impossible to think, let alone speak, anywhere near the vehicle.

Bullock, the workshop manager at Norman Reeves Trucks in Dawley Road, Hayes, west London, had groaned aloud. It had happened so often before. A Brink's-Mat van would arrive for a vehicle inspection so that some fault or other could be cured. One of his mechanics would begin poking around in the engine compartment or wiring looms and *bingo*! Somehow the sensitive alarms built into the security vehicle would be triggered.

When that happened there was nothing to be done but to step back and endure the shrieking siren while someone telephoned the Brink's-Mat warehouse at Heathrow to plead for assistance. Then a key holder would drive over to deactivate the alarm before the mechanics' work could resume. It happened with monotonous regularity.

This time Bullock was having trouble calling the Heathrow number. He had dialled so often that one attempt resulted in a wrong number. Finally, however, the connection was made. The dialling tone ended abruptly, and a voice answered. But it wasn't the response Bullock expected. 'Phone the fucking police. We've been turned over.'

There was hardly a moment's hesitation. Bullock slammed down the receiver and dialled 999. 'I've just called the Brink's-Mat warehouse at Heathrow,' he shouted. 'They've been robbed.'

When he eventually put the receiver back on the hook he turned to his workmates to explain his excitement. The alarm on the van continued to shriek.

Inside the warehouse the guards had lost little time in freeing themselves. Peter Bentley had used his teeth and some keys to rip through the tape that bound his hands and legs. That still left him handcuffed to the pipes, but by brute force, after lifting his feet up to the wall and gritting his teeth, he had managed to exert enough strength to snap the chain linking the manacles. Jumping up, he ran into the rest room to free Scouse.

'Get me the phone, quickly,' ordered the supervisor.

Scouse, still cuffed to the pipes, was standing in a puddle of petrol that had dripped from his clothing. Bentley pushed the upturned desk aside, brushed the clutter away and found the telephone wire. He gave it a sharp pull, and the telephone emerged from the debris. As Scouse dialled 999, Bentley responded to an appeal from the cupboard, where Riseley and Black were imprisoned. Although both were handcuffed, Riseley had managed to pull Black's hood off, and Black had been able to kick the cupboard door open.

Rushing downstairs in search of keys or tools to prise open the handcuffs, Bentley stopped suddenly at the bottom of the staircase. It occurred to him that the gang might still be inside the vault or loading-bay. His head was throbbing, but the bleeding had stopped. Peering nervously around the door, he satisfied himself that the raiders had indeed left, then went instantly to lock the outside doors in case they returned. Then, throwing open a toolbox, he grabbed a hammer and a screwdriver and dashed back to help his colleagues.

Bounding back up the stairs, Bentley was forced to check himself momentarily. The adrenalin was flowing, and the blood-rush to his brain made him reel. The feeling passed, and, once back at the cupboard in the rest room, he speared the screwdriver blade into the chain binding Black and hammered the links open. As he turned to Riseley, he heard Scouse complaining that he could not get through to the emergency operator. Bentley, however, realizing that the telephone had not been patched through to an outside line, moved quickly to flick the switch on the console.

This time Scouse was able to get through – but the events of the past hour proved too much for him. He couldn't make himself understood. The operator fired questions at him, but he was too confused and excited to answer coherently. Eventually he was forced to slam the receiver down in exasperation. The phone rang immediately. It was Bullock on the line from Norman Reeves Trucks. This time Scouse got the message over loud and clear. Once the alarm was raised, the rest of the guards were freed; dazed and numbed, they sat back to wait for the sound of sirens. Someone waved a wet handkerchief in Bentley's face, and he mopped his bloody head wounds. Scouse had dialled 999 again to ensure that the police had been alerted by Bullock. This time he was able to control his emotions and to explain what had happened. To make absolutely certain that help would soon be at hand, he then attempted to get into the radio room, where the panic button was located, but the thieves had locked the door. It didn't matter. In less than a minute the first ululating wail could be heard approaching.

There are few occasions when the need arises to disturb the top brass over breakfast on a Saturday morning, but Deputy Assistant Commissioner David Powis, the bullish, ruddy-faced head of London's detectives, a man who had joined the police service originally as a shorthand writer, had no qualms about ringing Assistant Commissioner Gilbert Kelland. Both men were rarely seen on the job outside New Scotland Yard. Theirs was an administrative command role; they were the generals of the Metropolitan Police force. The odd occasions when the press and the public did get to see them were usually times of exceptional crisis or tension. Whenever the IRA or Colonel Gadaffi brought their wars to the streets of London the two men might be seen on television, flanked by the field commanders, at a press conference. Equally, they would handle sensitive matters, such as kidnappings, when any mention in the press might endanger the victim. It was Kelland and Powis who would make the high-powered appeal for silence to reporters quietly summoned to the Yard. Generally, however, they stayed out of the limelight, working directly to the Commissioner himself and implementing his policies and orders, through the command structure, with the aid of the battalions on the ground. Powis had decided to call his chief, a slim, silver-haired and bespectacled man who resembled a dapper City broker in his pin-striped suits, after hearing about the raid from his wily junior, Commander Frank Cater.

The streetwise commander, the man in charge of the colourful and elitist Flying Squad, needed the Brink's-Mat job like he needed the proverbial hole in the head. Months earlier another 'firm' – disguised in monkey masks – had coolly taken £6 million in used banknotes during an Easter raid on the Security Express depot in London's East End. On that occasion too a guard had been doused with petrol. The robbery had been billed as the 'Crime of the Decade'. Was the same gang now also responsible for what was possibly the 'Crime of the Century'? After all, the previous holder of the title, the Great Train Robbery, near Leighton Buzzard in Bedfordshire in 1963, had netted only £2 million.

It was to prevent Powis from first hearing of the Brink's-Mat job through radio news or papers that Cater had called his immediate superior, and, likewise, Powis preferred that Kelland should hear it first from him. Kelland was a solid, upright professional, a no-nonsense (some would say humourless) man who would not take kindly to choking on his breakfast at the shock of an excited broadcaster announcing the haul at Heathrow.

Powis gave Kelland a brief outline of Cater's knowledge so far. The Flying Squad boss was on his way to Unit 7 at that moment, and Powis would be joining him there shortly.

The conversation was brief, and Kelland asked to be kept informed. It went without saying that Cater would immediately begin screening the guards on duty that morning. It didn't take the fabled copper's nose but simple common sense to tell him it had to be an inside job. No one just unlocks a door and walks into a warehouse like the Brink's-Mat building unless someone inside has shown him how.

Cater and his detectives moved fast, and by the time the commander arrived at the scene the standard procedures were already being implemented, with policemen crawling all over the warehouse collecting the minutiae that might prove invaluable, first as an aid towards the identification of the raiders and second to build up a prosecution case against them.

Scene-of-crime specialist Tony Phillips quietly picked his way from room to room collecting abandoned clothing, four hoods, six sets of handcuffs and the keys that unlocked them. He labelled each in turn with his initials and marked them Exhibits AWP/25 to AWP/43. The industrial tape that had been used to secure the guards was found by fingerprint officer Brian Rice. He too used his initials to label four pieces of tape before beginning, with others, to dust the outside door, the stairwell, vaults and safes. Police photographer Robert Isted set up his tripod and camera and filled twenty-seven frames with the crucial areas of the warehouse interior, and Constable Myrddin Jones, the official plan-drawer, painstakingly reconstructed a large-scale map of the unit's layout.

David Stickland, the Brink's-Mat depot manager, who just the previous day had logged the contents of the vault and informed the six guards of his weekend staffing requirements, arrived and took his checklist into the vault to make an inventory of the remaining items. There were the empty pouches, which had contained banknotes, traveller's cheques and other valuables, and there were three drums of precious-metal waste – but little else.

In the meantime the guards had all been whisked off to hospital for check-ups. Bentley needed his head wounds seen to, and both Scouse and Riseley had suffered blistering and soreness where the petrol had come into contact with their skin. May Tun, the casualty officer at Ashford Hospital who examined Bentley, found that the gashes on his head were superficial and needed no stitches. The swelling and bruising warranted nothing more than aspirin. Bentley was given a tetanus booster injection and advised to admit himself to a ward for twenty-four hours' observation. Dr Tun was concerned that he may have lost consciousness during the attack and thought it wise to be cautious; he might be suffering from concussion and, if allowed home, could later experience a delayed reaction.

But Bentley was adamant that he was going home. The doctor then turned her attention to Riseley and found everything normal except skin irritation where the petrol-soaked clothing had rubbed the skin. She told him to wash the area with soap and water and discharged him. Scouse was seen next; a red, blistering patch of skin matched exactly the outline of his petrol-sodden underwear. He also was advised to wash and given a course of Piriton tablets to ease the rash. All three men might later have wished that they had stayed in hospital. For within a couple of hours of the raid they were reliving it in police interview rooms, and the questioning grew increasingly uncomfortable.

It began cheerily enough. A little idle banter to put the guards at their ease, a quick run-through of the events and then down to detail. At first the questions seemed eminently reasonable. The detectives wanted to know if any of the guards had seen anything suspicious when they arrived for work that morning; they asked if the raiders' faces had been seen and took copious notes as the guards responded; they asked for estimates of the crucial time between the raiders' appearance and their departure, for descriptions of guns carried, clothing worn and accents used. The guards' memories were probed incessantly.

But then the question-and-answer session grew more intense. The officers wanted to know when each guard had learned that he would be working overtime that Saturday, when they had discovered the size of the vault's contents, what they had done on Friday night and if their colleagues had behaved in any way out of the ordinary. It wasn't long before the guards realized that they themselves were regarded as prime suspects.

The detectives had good reason to probe. The facts, as they emerged, strengthened the conviction that somehow an insider had helped. The raiders had made mistakes and had sown the seeds of their own destruction. Whatever the success of the operation, the Brink's-Mat job never mounted a challenge for the title of the 'perfect crime'.

Cater took stock as each of his interrogating officers briefed him on the sessions with the guards. Nobody knew how the robbers had entered the premises, and there was certainly no sign of forced entry. The first possibility – that a door had been accidentally left open – was highly unlikely. An alarm would have alerted the guards inside if such had been the case. Instead one of two other possibilities had to have occurred: either the early-morning visitors had been let in by a guard, or they had somehow acquired copies of the keys.

Nuggets of information gleaned from the guards gave added support to the 'inside-job' theory. The robbers had known the names of the two men on duty who could help them gain access to the secure areas, bypassing the alarm systems. They had also known exactly where each guard would be in the first few minutes of their working day. In addition they had known that Saturday morning was a worthwhile time to raid the warehouse and, what's more, they had known the precise time at which they had to strike before the shipment was due to leave. Had the robbers disguised their knowledge by using the same brutality to extract the names of the combination-holders that they had used to get the numbers, and had they disguised the ease with which they had entered the building, Cater might have been thrown off the scent or at least been persuaded to question his instinct. But by Saturday evening he was sure not only that one of the guards was involved but also that he knew which one it was.

Of the six guards three were considered to be 'prospects' by the detectives. Riseley and Scouse were initially suspected because they knew the combinations, but the third man stuck out like a sore thumb. He was the guard who had been out of the sight of the others in the minutes before the raid, and now the humming computers and buzzing telephone lines produced some damning intelligence. This guard had a brother-in-law, who, in the jargon often written for television detectives, was 'tasty, very tasty' indeed. The brother-in-law had a sizeable criminal pedigree, including two convictions for assaults on policemen. He was also believed to have been involved in armed robberies, although it had never been proved. In the past three years he had beaten two armed-robbery charges. One was thrown out by a magistrate because of insufficient evidence; the other, for handling money taken in an armed raid, was dropped when the Director of Public Prosecutions (DPP) decided that there was not enough evidence to offer to a court.

Finding out exactly what this man was doing now became the prime concern of Cater and his detectives. As the forensic examination of the warehouse continued long into the night and spotlights illuminated the exterior, Cater called his squad together and told them to start squeezing their informants.

It was a 'softly, softly' approach at first. The guards were allowed to go home, and no indication was given that the police knew the identity of the inside man. By now the press were clamouring for information, and Cater willingly obliged. He knew that the more coverage the raid was given, the greater was the chance that a witness might come forward who had seen the raiders' vehicles leaving the warehouse.

Gareth Parry, writing for the *Guardian* on the following Monday, was the first to hint darkly that the robbers 'had access to inside sources'. Having quoted Commander Cater's belief that the robbers had already disposed of the gold, the report went on to claim that the detective was convinced that it had already been melted down and smuggled out of the country. Privately, Cater was not so certain. He knew that the robbers had 'stumbled' on the haul and were unlikely to have a tailor-made plan for the disposal of gold ingots that, if stacked together, would have equalled the size of a small cupboard 6 feet by 3 feet by 2 feet. None the less, police forces throughout Britain had been alerted to check ship, rail and air terminals, and foreign police forces had also been notified.

The next bit of information to fire the interest of the press was the record reward money that was announced. Lloyd's of London were prepared to pay £2 million for information leading to the return of the gold. Some 70 per cent of the risk had been placed with about eighty syndicates at Lloyd's, the rest with a number of other major insurance companies.

One breakthrough for the detectives occurred relatively quickly. Members of the public who had driven past the industrial estate on the morning of the raid had reported seeing a white estate car, followed by a blue Transit van, leaving the area. The car fitted the description of a Hillman Avenger, owned by a suspect whom Cater had in mind.

The clue was important enough for Cater, on the Tuesday after the raid, to call a press conference at Scotland Yard. Some sixty journalists crowded into a ground-floor briefing room where he described the two vehicles that he was looking for. One of them, he said, 'appeared very heavily laden and was riding very low upon its suspension'. Its engine sounded 'very laboured and under stress'. Asked if it would be difficult to dispose of such a large amount of gold, Powis replied, 'It would not be difficult, knowing the amount smuggled on the international scene.' There were, he said, 'no-questions-asked markets' around the world.

By Wednesday the insurance payouts had started, the first payment going to Johnson Matthey. A spokesman for insurance brokers Stewart Wrightson said, 'Lloyd's have a tradition of paying out quickly on big losses. Two and a half days is not bad.' Meanwhile the robbers' haul had leapt in value; gold that morning was fetching £277.190 per troy ounce, nearly £20 more per ounce than on the previous Friday afternoon. Public interest in the raid was intense, and, from at least one quarter, criticism began to be heard about the police hunt for the robbers. That Wednesday morning Scotland Yard had to weather a considerable broadside from Britain's largest-selling newspaper, the tabloid *Sun*, then selling 4.7 million copies daily. 'Imagine the frenzy of activity there would have been among the guardians of the law and order in the United States, France or any other major country if the crime of the century had been committed on their patch. When it happens here, there is about as much urgency as if someone had booked the Commissioner's car for illegal parking,' blustered an editorial in the paper's inimitable style. 'Days pass. Leisurely press conferences are held to keep in touch . . . There are no arrests, apparently no clues. A massive consignment of gold has vanished as completely as a feather in a hurricane.'

The *Sun* had got this one wrong. In fact, considerable resources had been deployed in following up inquiries, and Cater was increasingly optimistic.

As well as interviewing the guards, detectives had spent days taking scores of statements from anyone who could conceivably be of help. Calls were received from people all over the country who claimed to have seen heavily laden vans and lorries that might have been carrying the gold. Each sighting was logged and examined. In addition, everyone working on the estate on the day of the raid had been interviewed. Most had seen nothing, heard nothing and knew nothing.

On a more off-beat note, four clairvoyants had contacted the police, claiming to have seen everything in their crystal balls, tea-leaves or log fires. A retired Metropolitan Police clerk had dreamt of seeing the robbers burying their gold in the cellar of a famous East End pub on the Wapping waterfront. A taxi-driver wondered if two businessmen, who had casually asked him to drive them from the Ritz in London to Blackburn at 4.30 on Sunday morning, might have something to do with the robbery. They had paid the fare of £416 in cash. Another man had overheard in a pub a conversation in which, he swore, the words 'Heathrow' and 'gold' had been used. There was even a call from Littlehampton, where three heavily laden vans had been seen heading for the beach nearby. The caller was wrongly convinced that there was a connection.

Cater's major breakthrough, however, occurred when he gave the go-ahead for the investigation to take an unprecedented turn. A young detective sergeant on his team had the bright idea of videoing a reconstruction of the events during the raid to highlight any flaws that might exist in the guards' statements. It was the first time such a filmed reconstruction had been used by the Yard, and it was an immediate success, as one guard was shown to have lied in his statement. The events that he had described were generally accurate, but there was one outright lie. And, surprise, surprise, it was the guard whose brother-in-law had a 'tasty' record.

Six days after the raid Cater was more convinced than ever that he had found the gang's weak link. By now a weighty file of information had been compiled on the suspect guard, the brother-in-law and his known associates. If his suspicions were right, Cater knew not only the identity of the Boss but also who the Bully and at least one other member of the gang were likely to be. It was time to show his hand.

At 8 a.m. on Sunday, 4 December, eight days after the raid, his detectives arrived, unannounced, on the doorsteps of all six guards' homes. They explained to the perplexed men that they were required at Hounslow police station to answer further questions. Five of them were to be questioned methodically and respectfully about their statements; the sixth was to be interrogated.

That duty fell to Detective Inspector Tony Brightwell and Detective Sergeants Nicholas Benwell and Alan Branch. They returned with their charge and sat down to re-examine his earlier statement. The questions continued for more than six hours, and the young guard sitting across the table from the three officers tried to hide his growing anxiety.

Eventually, at about 3.15 in the afternoon, Brightwell rose to his feet. 'There are certain points which have arisen as a result of the original statement which you made, the video reconstruction of the events and during this interview . . . To put it bluntly, we are not happy with your story. We will leave you to have a re-think.'

The detectives let him sweat for more than an hour while they discussed his story over coffee in the canteen, eventually returning to the interview room at 4.52 p.m. They were sure of their ground, and Branch delivered what they hoped would be the *coup de grâce*.

'I am arresting you for armed robbery,' he announced and cautioned the prisoner, who was then taken to the charge room, searched and locked in a cell. Again he was left to sweat. So far he was showing no signs of weakening, although it was plain that he was frightened.

More than two hours passed before the prisoner was taken back to the first-floor interview room.

'We have now been right through your version of the story on two separate occasions and had the television reconstruction,' said D S Branch. 'It is very obvious to us that you are lying and have a lot to hide.'

'I am not lying. I've told you the truth,' responded the prisoner, dolefully.

'We are going to go through your diary and personal affairs such as your bank accounts. Okay?' said Branch.

'Yeah,' replied the prisoner. He described the joint accounts he and his wife held: two bank accounts with Lloyds' Twickenham branch and three building society accounts, two with the Leeds and one with the Abbey National.

'Now I want to go through your diary and ask you about some numbers,' said Branch.

Brightwell, who had been leafing through the book, took over. 'This entry on 26 November 1983, the day of the robbery. When we first saw your diary you had written in there "06.30". Why did you write that in?' he asked.

'That was the time I was due to start.'

'Is it not right that you have worked a lot of Saturdays this year? Is it not also right that Saturday work normally starts at 06.30?' The prisoner nodded twice in confirmation. 'But you have never written a start-time down for any Saturday this year. Why did you write it down this Saturday, the day of the robbery?' No explanation was forthcoming, and Brightwell continued. 'Since we first saw your diary you have written in "01.30" after the "06.30". Why did you do that?' The prisoner responded that there was no particular reason, and Brightwell rounded on him. 'That's rubbish, isn't it? You realized the significance of the "06.30" so you tried to cover it up by adding "01.30"?'

Branch now took over, asking the prisoner to explain yet more numbers in his diary. The prisoner answered the questions calmly, sticking to his story, refusing to budge. He had been nervous, anxious even, but if this was the worst they could throw at him, then perhaps he would be home sooner than he had thought.

'Okay. That covers your diary. Do you drink a lot?'

It was a strange question to conclude with. Branch seemed uninterested in the answer. The prisoner relaxed and tried to finish a sentence about his occasional light ale with the lads, but Brightwell brought him back to reality. The information that now dropped from the detective's lips was delivered in the casual manner that generally requires rehearsal, but it had an explosive effect on the prisoner's confidence.

'What does your brother-in-law think about the robbery?'

The cat-and-mouse game was not yet over. That the police knew about his 'tasty' brother-in-law had come as a shock to the prisoner. For on paper they weren't related. His sister was the man's common-law wife.

Brightwell and the two sergeants again decided to sweat the prisoner. They called a uniformed officer to escort him to the cells and, as he sloped out of the room, the detective called after him.

'You know a lot more than you are telling us. You'll be detained until the morning.'

On Monday, at 11.32 a.m., the interrogation resumed. But, instead of returning to the question of the brother-in-law,

Branch began probing the prisoner's account of the night before the raid. It was soon established that his story did not match the statements given by his wife and a friend, who had both described his movements.

The detectives were travelling down a well-worn path. What they needed was a confession. If the prisoner stuck to his guns, the evidence so far gleaned would not be enough to make the charge stick, but by broadening the questions to suggest a far greater knowledge of the prisoner's guilt they hoped to drive a wedge into the fissure already appearing in his resolve and crack it wide open.

Branch interrupted the prisoner's answers to questions about his movements that Friday night.

'Stop right there and listen to me. Yesterday we pointed out to you inconsistencies in your story. We have only just started today with mundane matters and it is immediately obvious that you are trying to cover somebody or something up. If your mate and your own wife don't support your story . . .'

At this point the prisoner paled visibly and mopped his brow. 'Can I have a cup of tea?'

D S Benwell left the room and returned moments later with a plastic cup from the vending machine outside. The prisoner took a sip and looked up.

'Where do I start?'

3. Going fishing

Anthony John Black had always thought highly of himself. He was a slim, dark-haired man of 31, with a broad moustache and a ready wit. He was quick to smile, quick to womanize and painfully slow to grow up and accept responsibility. On paper his record seemed impressive, at least as far as a job guarding Brink's-Mat property was concerned, but it hid a wild, impulsive streak, which regularly prompted his enthusiasm to override what little judgement he possessed.

Brought up in south London's dockland, he had escaped the gloom and decay of that area by joining the Army. As a lowly trooper in the 17/21 Lancers he was posted to Northern Ireland and, eager to acquire the trappings of adulthood, had married young and foolishly. He had been in Ulster only a few months when he met Vivien Sorrie. They were married according to the rites of the Church of Ireland, in Omagh, Co. Tyrone, on 5 May 1973. He was just 21 and she 18. Within weeks he was posted to Cyprus and, because his wife was pregnant, she went with him. Their daughter Clare was born on 5 December, and mother and child returned home to Omagh a month later.

Black stayed on as Turkey and Greece fought over the divided island, first as a British soldier and later under the flag of the United Nations peace-keeping force. In the space of a few months he had left home, fought subversion, married, fathered a child and found himself caught in the cross-fire of another war. But now, with his wife and child back in Ulster, his desire to settle down seemingly deserted him. It was to be two years before Black returned home, in December 1975, and then the young family had barely finished celebrating Christmas before he moved on again. This time the posting was West Germany, with his regiment of light reconnaissance tanks. Again Vivien and Clare went with him. But within weeks Black was disappearing from the family's married quarters to sleep with his new-found West German girlfriend, Suzanna Jahnke.

Vivien soon found out, and in May 1976, again just a few months after arriving in a foreign country with her husband, she was on her way home, this time to consult her solicitor. She returned to West Germany in June, as Tony had pleaded for a second chance, but she soon realized she was wasting her time. He was still seeing Suzanna Jahnke. Dejectedly, his wife and child trekked back to Ulster for the third time in three years.

There was never any real hope of mending their fences, yet the couple tried just once more when Black was posted back to Northern Ireland. He turned up on the doorstep of Vivien's parents' home in Omagh, where she and his child were living. It was agreed that a final attempt was to be made: Tony would buy himself out of the Army, and they would get a council flat in London.

At first their prospects looked good. He was a regular soldier with six years' service in a regiment with fine traditions, had seen some action in two troubled areas and was married with a daughter. Such an apparently solid citizen had little trouble acquiring a job with Brink's-Mat as a driver/guard at their Arnold House depot in the City.

It lasted just six months. Black was still receiving letters from West Germany, and when Vivien found out she threw him out. Within weeks he had resigned from his job at Brink's-Mat and was back in a flat in Hansegin, living with Suzanna and the child she had had by another man. She helped him to find casual work with a friend, oddjobbing on removals and painting and decorating, until he obtained his work permit. Then he found a full-time job as a driver, but the work, in his own words, was 'too gutty'. He started at 2 a.m. and finished at 5 p.m. It lasted only three weeks, and when he quit Suzanna kicked him out. Once again his charm came into play, and he successfully persuaded her parents to put him up. He then tried to sign on at the local social security office, but the West German officials rebuffed him, finding him another job instead. It involved nothing more than collecting the empties from the municipal bottle banks, but within weeks he was out of work. He had, he claimed, pulled a muscle in his leg, but the time he took off resulted in the sack.

Black returned to England and went straight to his parents' home in Bromley, south-east London. The following day he walked into the Brink's-Mat office and asked for his old job back. It was unusual to be rehired, but his former supervisor relented. He started work on 29 January 1979.

For the first time Black showed signs of maturity. He performed his duties satisfactorily, apart from the odd late start, and he began re-establishing links with his family. He was the youngest of four, and his elder sister Jennifer proved invaluable when it came to looking for accommodation close to his work in the City.

Jennifer's common-law husband 'knew of a place which could be had for key money, perhaps a couple of hundred'. In the event, Black never paid the key money, but the flat, above a parade of shops on a gaunt post-war council housing estate in Ben Jonson Road, in the East End of London, was his for the asking. When he moved in it was his sister's boyfriend and another man who drove him there in a Rover 3.5.

Soon two colleagues from Brink's-Mat moved in with him, and for six months Black was untroubled. He paid his rent regularly and worked overtime whenever he could. But while he was settled in his work, his domestic life remained a mess. By now Vivien had filed for divorce, and it came through in April 1980. Black was ordered to pay £12.50 a week maintenance and, surprisingly, kept the payments up. There was a fright, one Saturday morning, when two detectives rapped on his door. They were, they said, from Rotherhithe murder squad and were looking for a man called Stokes who, according to their paperwork, was the registered tenant of Black's flat. After searching it thoroughly, they left without ever explaining their interest. Soon afterwards Black moved out to live with a girlfriend who worked at Brink's-Mat, but the relationship lasted only a few months.

When it ended he went to live with his parents again and picked up with an old flame. He found another flat in Dulwich, and for a year he seemed settled. Then, during a delivery to Lloyds Bank in Twickenham in June 1981, he met bank clerk Lyn Halliday. He invited himself to her home in Ashford, close to Heathrow Airport, for dinner one night and, three weeks later, moved in. Six months after they met they were married in Ashford Register Office. Then, having bought a maisonette in Kenilworth Road, 2 miles from the airport, Black successfully applied to Brink's-Mat for a transfer to the Heathrow warehouse, which was nearer his home.

Black was a popular workmate, playing the odd practical joke and fixing his colleagues' cars when they went wrong. He was never going to make supervisor – his commitment to the job wasn't up to scratch – but he performed his duties to the satisfaction of his superiors. He was still impulsive, however, his principal weakness being his craving for attention. He would keep an audience spellbound with yarns about the kings' ransoms he had guarded. Men in his position were expected to watch their words, but Black would gossip idly about the Brink's-Mat security procedures and the precautions that were taken.

And, despite his position as security guard with a highly reputable company, his recklessness encompassed dabbling in petty crime. On one occasion he gave his cheque book and card to his brother-in-law, Brian, who then went on a shopping spree. Later Black travelled to the City Road police station, reported his cheque book and card stolen during a visit to a leisure centre and sauntered home to wait for his co-conspirator. The brother-in-law duly turned up, having signed twenty-six cheques, but instead of the £5 Black had been promised for every cheque successfully tendered, he received a lawnmower, a black-and-white portable TV, some groceries and liquor. It mattered nothing that the cheques were drawn on the Lloyds branch where his unsuspecting wife worked. It was a slick and common deception against which the banks are virtually powerless to act.

Although he didn't participate in the racket again, Black went on to receive a number of generous 'gifts' from his brother-in-law, who seemed to practise the cheque fraud as regularly as others pop down to the corner shop for a packet of cigarettes. To the brother-in-law the racket was little more than an amusement and about as significant as the small change in his pocket. But the ease with which he operated impressed the Brink's-Mat guard and tempted him to seek the company of his sister and her husband more frequently. He soon became hooked on the free gifts that would intermittently appear, taking a childish delight in the ease with which they were obtained. It never occurred to him that there was a price to pay.

Brian Robinson never really liked his wife's younger brother Tony, but Jennifer got on well with him, and as he was always popping round to their council maisonette in Chilham House, Rollins Street, New Cross, it was necessary to put on an act. So Black was tolerated, and Robinson pretended friendship and proved generous for the sake of the family. But the two were like chalk and cheese. Robinson was a hard case, a quiet man with a violent streak, not given to idle boasts, whose organizing abilities had earned him the nickname of 'the Colonel' among the criminal fraternity of south-east London. Like many of his contemporaries, he had served several prison sentences, but they had failed to have a salutary effect. For it didn't matter how intelligent, sharp and streetwise he was, Brian Robinson was part of a recognized phenomenon, a man to whom crime was a way of life, in which to pay for anything was considered weak.

It was shortly after the cheque-book incident that Black, who was then still working at the City Brink's-Mat branch, had his first inkling of the stakes for which Robinson was prepared to play.

Could he, asked Robinson, help out with a favour for a

friend? The man in question had a very particular need: he wanted photographs of the insides of Brink's-Mat vans, both the Ford A series and the D series. Just pictures, nothing more than that. So Black obliged, borrowing Robinson's Polaroid and returning a few days later with three poor-quality prints. He and Robinson left the flat behind New Cross Station and walked around the corner, where they met a man who was introduced only as Mick. Mick asked if a Land Rover with a makeshift ram welded to the front would be strong enough to burst open the back doors of a Brink's-Mat van. Black scoffed at the suggestion. 'No way! Those vans are impregnable, the best on the market.'

He didn't really know whether such a plan would work, but he wanted to appear knowledgeable. The conversation ended abruptly. The man called Mick disappeared with the photographs in his pocket, and Robinson took Black back to the flat. Soon afterwards, in December 1980, a Brink's-Mat van with £811,000 on board was stopped and robbed in Dulwich, south-east London. Its armoured rear doors were rammed open by the jib of a mobile crane, but the police were lying in wait after a tip-off. They were armed, and, with a video camera set up in a near-by comprehensive school to capture what happened, a fight developed in which detectives fired five shots. The gang was arrested, although the informant, one of the robbers, was allowed to escape. Later he alleged that he had tried to warn detectives that there might have been an inside man in Brink's-Mat but was ignored.

Some days later Black saw his brother-in-law and asked the inevitable question.

'No, Tony. I wasn't on that job. I had a feeling it was a set-up,' said Robinson. And there he left it.

More than two years passed before Robinson put Black on the spot again, and when he did so it quickly became clear that this time he wanted more than a few Polaroid photographs. He had been generous to Tony Black, and he expected Black to be generous in return.

*

It took Detective Sergeant Benwell more than eight hours to take down Black's twenty-one-page statement. That Monday morning, 5 December 1983, ten days after the raid on the warehouse, Black had finished his cup of tea and DS Branch set the ball rolling. 'Okay, Tony, why don't you start at the beginning? We won't interfere. We'll just sit here and listen.'

Black outlined his involvement in general until, shortly after noon, Branch suggested a break for lunch. Black had got much off his chest, but his fear of the police had been replaced by a very real fear for his and his family's safety. 'I'm feeling much better now,' said Black. 'It's like a weight off my mind. It was just too big – I couldn't handle it. There's one thing, though. I'm worried about these people, what they're going to do. Can I see your boss, Mr Cater, and talk to him about it?'

'He's very busy, but we'll try and arrange that for you,' replied DS Benwell, for the three officers who had taken him from his home more than twenty-four hours earlier had stayed with him throughout the interrogation. At 1.10 p.m. Black was taken back to his cell, where he was served lunch, and at 2.12 p.m. he was brought back to the interview room to face the three officers again.

'If you want to, Tony, you can write your own statement, or I will write it for you,' said Benwell.

'No, you write it, please,' asked Black. 'I want to tell you everything, but I'm a bit worried that I might leave some things out.'

'Take your time,' advised Benwell. 'There's no hurry.'

'It started about a year ago, maybe less but certainly no more. I think I was round Brian's house when he asked what it was like at Heathrow. He wanted to know if there were any good deliveries to the airlines, things like that. I told him there was nothing specific, so he asked if there was anything "we could walk in on".'

Black did take his time. Brightwell, Benwell and Branch listened intently as the prisoner recalled his rapid descent into his present predicament. He never went into his motives for making the raid possible, but he didn't have to. The seeds of his destruction lay in his character; the impulsive, irresponsible streak that had wrecked most of his relationships had plunged him headlong into Robinson's plot. It was obvious from the story he told that he had been oblivious to the consequences all along.

All he could say now about his reasons for getting involved was that it 'stimulated' him. He surprised detectives with his couldn't-care-less attitude to his share of the spoils. He had embarked on the disastrous escapade on the basis of nothing more than a promise that 'something would be put by' for him in a numbered Swiss bank account, which he wouldn't be able to touch for at least five years. Black was not only stupid; he was recklessly trusting too. It never occurred to him that his brother-in-law's generosity might not extend to honouring the agreement.

Soon after Robinson's new approach the two were meeting regularly to discuss the prospects of profiting from Black's inside track, for the guard did know of something that Robinson could 'walk in on': the regular Dublin-to-London Aer Lingus currency flight that he met once or twice a week at Heathrow in order to collect banknotes. To avoid saying too much in front of their wives, the two men would go fishing together at weekends to weigh up the opportunities. One Sunday, while driving to a favoured stretch of the Thames at Laleham, on the outskirts of west London, Black took Robinson through Heathrow's sprawling canton and pointed out the Aer Lingus buildings where the banknotes were exchanged.

Days later the two men met again at Robinson's flat. Black's sister, Jennifer, was out, so Black asked if Robinson had thought any more about the job.

'I've been back to have a look, but it's not on,' he replied. 'The Aer Lingus building is next to Egypt Air, or one of those Middle East airlines, and they always have the Bill round there,' he said, using the London slang word for the police. 'It's no good. Don't you get anything back at your base?'

For more than an hour they discussed the Brink's-Mat depot

on the industrial estate. Black had worked there for nearly a year now, and he had discovered that there was much that was routine about its operation.

He was able to detail precisely what kinds of valuable were stored in the vault and for how long. He could predict the arrival of banknotes, diamonds, traveller's cheques, gold and other precious metals, for, although routine is often the soft spot of the security business, Brink's-Mat was dependent on the dictates of its customers, who worked normal office hours, and of the airlines, which stuck rigidly to schedules.

Black was surprised to find that Robinson already knew quite a lot about the warehouse. He had obviously kept vigil outside it on numerous occasions, timing the comings and goings, looking for the loopholes that might guarantee entry. He had noticed that one vehicle regularly arrived back late at the depot, at about 11 p.m., after collecting first from the banks and then from the late arrivals at Heathrow. But he wanted to know more. Robinson was thorough and meticulous. Black answered every question thrown at him.

No, it wasn't possible to follow a van through the shutter doors because there was a guard standing at the entrance ready to padlock them from the inside. Intruders in a vehicle or on foot outside could not overpower those inside before the panic button was punched.

But, yes, there was one night, above all others, that could guarantee rich pickings. Friday was the best night to hit the warehouse; there were often large hauls stored there for delivery to the rich, gold-hungry Far East. Sometimes there was as much as £1 million, even £2 million, to be had. The KLM flight 808 from Amsterdam, in particular, disgorged large sums every Friday night into the hold of a Brink's-Mat vehicle.

'That's it, then,' said Robinson. 'It's got to be Friday night. But how?'

Some weeks later, in midsummer, three to four months before the raid, Robinson contacted Black and said they must meet. There were some people he wanted to introduce to Black. It was obvious that their earlier conversations were not idle chatter, for Robinson was taking precautions. He named a garage outside London and told Black to be there, at a set time, the following Sunday morning.

When he pulled up outside Gibb's showroom at Bedfont on the A30, close to Heathrow, Robinson was waiting. There were two other men in the car. He knew them as Mick, the man to whom he had given the Polaroid pictures taken inside the Brink's-Mat vans, and Tony, the man who, some years earlier, had helped him move into the flat in the East End.

Mick, the youngest of the three, had a malevolent presence. In his early thirties, he was a stocky man 5 feet 8 inches tall, with short fair hair and a plump, clean-shaven face. He emanated violence.

Tony was a huge, dark-haired man, close on 40. The first thing that struck Black was his immense build. He had broad, muscular shoulders that were out of proportion to the rest of his body.

To start with it was a re-run of the question-and-answer sessions that he had had with Robinson. Then, having convinced themselves that a Friday night was, as Robinson had told them, the best night for a raid, the newcomers turned their attention to the warehouse itself. 'It was along the lines of "Could you do this and could you do that?",' Black told his interrogators. 'They wanted to know precisely how the unit was operated.'

Black obliged. He ran through the procedures in great detail, from the moment the guards arrived for work to the moment they left. He missed out nothing, detailing the alarm procedures, the locks and those who knew the combinations, the internal layout of the building from loading bay to vault and upstairs to the office. He told them who held the keys and on what occasions they might be left unattended.

The meeting then adjourned, with instructions to Black to continue providing information. This he happily did, arranging meetings with Robinson every time he had something new to impart, often using the pay phone inside the warehouse to make the arrangements.

Sometimes they would meet outside Gibb's Garage, at others at Hatton Cross Underground station, the next stop down from Heathrow. On one occasion it was a dead-end road, on another the car park of the Bulldog public house in Ashford. Sometimes the three men would meet him in Robinson's Renault; on other occasions they would turn up in Mick's BMW. Always Black arrived in his Opel.

Every time they met, Robinson would ask Black to detail precisely what had been in the vault the previous Friday night. At one meeting, on the river bank at Laleham, Black described how the previous Friday there had been twelve boxes of gold, worth perhaps £2 million. Sometimes, he insisted, there was more. The next step in Black's downfall came when Robinson handed him a self-winding, auto-focus camera and instructed him to photograph all the rooms inside the warehouse. Once again he complied, taking the necessary pictures when, in between deliveries, he was given the job of painting the inside of the vault.

The first day he photographed the vault. The next evening he stood inside the shutter door and photographed the delivery bay and stairs leading to the first floor. Then he went upstairs and photographed the rooms. There was little risk attached. He chose moments when all the other guards were out on deliveries and there was only one keyman on duty with him. When he had finished he handed the camera, with the film still inside it, to Robinson.

The next meeting, after the gang had analysed the photographs, was arranged by Robinson. Black duly arrived at his sister's home, then the two men went out on the pretext that Black was to fix a rattle in Robinson's car. Robinson drove straight round to another house, a terraced council property in Greenwich, south-east London. 'We went in through a gate to the back garden and walked through a bead curtain into the kitchen. Brian led the way through a second door into the sitting room. Mick and Tony were already there. They had the photographs out on the floor and a plan I had drawn to show the warehouse layout. They were big colour shots, professionally developed, not like snapshots. They kept asking me questions about the map and the photos, like "What does the keyman do when he opens this door?" or "What does the keyman do when he opens the vault?"'

Black pointed out every wall-mounted alarm and lock and ran through the procedures and timing for the umpteenth time. The Achilles heel of the warehouse was the side door through which the guards passed at the beginning and end of their shifts, but even that was protected by an alarm, and the keyman had the only key to unlock it. Eventually the plotters broke up. Robinson drove Black back to his flat, leaving Mick and Tony to tidy up. Some days later Black was called to another meeting. The three men had decided that the only way in was through the side door, and Mick handed Black a piece of cuttlefish and several pieces of Plasticine, all individually wrapped in plastic bags. Mick took a Chubb key from his pocket, unwrapped a ball of Plasticine and demonstrated how to make an impression of the key.

The next day Black went to work. It was not uncommon for the keyman, when up to his elbows in paperwork, to hand his bunch of keys to another guard to let a colleague into the building. Black bided his time. Sure enough, during a late-duty shift, he was handed the keys to open the back door. On his way downstairs he took out both the cuttlefish and the Plasticine and pressed the brass key into every piece. After handing over the keys he went to the payphone and called Robinson. 'I've got 'em.'

The two men met the next day, and that same week Robinson returned with three copies of the key and several small files. 'Try these. If the keys don't work in the lock, then use the files to take a little bit off and square them up.'

So far it had been all too easy. Black was enjoying his role; it excited him to be the centre of so much attention. He revelled in the knowledge that to Brink's-Mat he was just another guard but to his new-found friends he was linch-pin of a masterly and audacious plot. Black had seen too many movies; just as the big screen produced moments of nerve-jangling drama, so too did the plot he was now involved in.

It was during a quiet lull in the day's activities that Black took the keys downstairs. Glancing over his shoulder to ensure that no one was watching through the observation window in the control room upstairs, he walked across to the side door and pushed the first copy into the lock. He turned it no more than a fraction of an inch before it stuck. It had been badly cut – that much was obvious from the look of it – and it wouldn't come out.

Black didn't need to paint a picture for the engrossed detectives. They could imagine the panic that must have gripped him when the lock jammed tight around the key and refused to release it. If it didn't come out, it would be a matter of no more than hours, perhaps even minutes, before it was discovered. There could be only one explanation for the existence of a spare key and a rough copy at that; the company's internal security would descend on the warehouse, bringing the police with it. Black's fingerprints, and perhaps Robinson's or Mick's too, might be lifted off the shank. Even if they weren't, it might be possible to trace the locksmith who had cut it, and amid the ensuing investigation Black's relationship with Robinson could emerge. Certainly the keyman would be able to remember who had used the master key recently, and it wouldn't be difficult to identify Black as the guard who had worked most late duties when all was quiet, and copies could be made and later tested. Black felt blind panic setting in as he wrenched at the obstinate piece of brass. It wouldn't budge, and he kept looking over his shoulder, growing increasingly fearful. He was sweating now, and his fingers began slipping as he tugged and wrenched for what seemed like hours but was probably no more than a minute. Wiping his hands on his trousers, he tried again; this time it broke free. That's it, he thought. I'm not trying the others.

But he was still anxious. Perhaps the lock had been so damaged that a locksmith would have to be called in? Would he discover any telltale signs that could betray Black?

The end of the shift brought him considerable relief. The lock worked smoothly as he and his colleagues left the building, and he immediately called Robinson, who went straight over to

Black's flat. There they discussed other ways in which the robbers might gain access to the building. There was a window on the ground floor. Could it be left open? Could the window stays be sliced through with bolt cutters? Was it big enough, for he and Tony were big men? What alarms were wired to the window, and could they be bypassed?

Black was unhelpful, his answers too vague. He was still unnerved by his experience and made it obvious that the window was a problem.

Then for a short period, during the first two weeks in September, Black managed to escape the double life he was leading. He took his wife to Corfu, where his parents had a mobile home near Bukari Beach, and forgot about Brink's-Mat and Robinson.

It was a brief respite. As soon as he returned – before he had even gone back to work – he was summoned to another meeting. It was an excited threesome that met him in the car park of the Bulldog pub. Tony was anxious to do the job the following Saturday morning.

Black was worried. It was apparently crunch-time, but he had been away for a fortnight. What if the procedures had been modified or the flights changed to make another night of the week more lucrative? Black didn't even know if he would be working that Saturday; he never did until the last minute. As it turned out, he was, and for the first time he faced the possibility that he would become caught up in a raid that he had helped to instigate. On arriving at the warehouse, he left a downstairs window ajar, waiting nervously throughout the shift for something to happen.

It was an anticlimax. The day passed off without incident, and when he next met up with Robinson and his friends, he was told that they hadn't been able to prepare for the raid in time. In reality, it was probably a dry run to test whether Black would be prepared to go through with the raid.

Now, Black having passed the test, it was evident that the gang were even more impatient to go into action. From now on, everyone was on stand-by. Black was told that every Friday Robinson would be near a telephone, expecting a call from

Black to let him know what might be arriving at the unit that night and whether he would be on duty the next day. A code had been worked out to enable Black to use the payphone in the unit to set the ball rolling. The words 'I'm going fishing tomorrow' would mean he was working.

Three weeks passed, then Black phoned Robinson with bad news. For the past eighteen months, at times when the warehouse wasn't holding too much of value in the vault, a local contractor had been called in to carry out refurbishments. These had included the installation of the elevated offices and control room on the first floor above the delivery bay. The programme was close to completion when the warehouse manager, David Stickland, decided that the time had come to enhance the new look with a complete change of alarms and locks and an extra external security camera to cover the door and window. Robinson swore, thought for a moment, then asked Black if it was at all possible to get hold of one of the new keys. This time, however, he didn't want an impression taken; he needed it in his hands, so that a locksmith could cut a proper copy.

Robinson was in luck, said Black. Stickland was off sick, and he had seen a bunch of three keys lying on his desk. He knew they fitted the front door, and, provided Stickland did not return the next day, he could 'borrow' them for an hour or so at lunchtime.

'Okay, where do you want to meet?' asked Robinson.

Black suggested the car park of the Beaver pub in a shopping precinct near the warehouse between noon and 1 p.m.

He arrived at 12.30, having taken one of the keys off the ring, and Robinson, wearing a suit and a tie, walked over to his car and climbed into the passenger seat. Then Mick appeared, bending down to Black in the driver's seat and collecting the key, which he took to Tony waiting in a near-by car. Both men then drove off and Black turned worriedly to Robinson. It struck him that the key might not be returned.

'Don't worry,' he was assured. 'We've found a place in Hounslow High Street that can do a copy. I've had one or two of my own done, and it's a proper key shop.'

Mick returned fifteen minutes later with three copies. They had cost him £4.50, he said, handing all four to Black.

'Try them, and mark the one that's the best fit,' he said and left.

In fact, the robbers could have taken longer ensuring that the copies were as good as possible, for Black didn't get an opportunity to return the master key until late the next day.

An opportunity also arose that afternoon to try the three copies. None of them worked, but at least none of them stuck either. Checking that there was no one watching, he took a piece of emery cloth from his pocket and rounded the rough spots on one key. It slid into the door lock and turned with a soft click. He put the key back into one pocket. The remaining two he left untried in another. Back in the office, Black took a piece of Sellotape and wrapped it around the shank of the key that had worked.

It was late October, and at last the robbers knew they were ready to go. All that remained was for Black to tip them off next time he was asked to work overtime, for that would be the signal that a big shipment was due in. From then on he called every Friday.

It was approximately midday on 25 November when Robinson's telephone rang. The message was the same as it had been for weeks now: no overtime, no big shipment. After imparting the bad news, Black put the receiver down and went to lunch.

It was two hours after his return that he was told that he would, after all, be required to work the next day. He knew from experience that meant a run to Gatwick to catch Cathay Pacific and that, in turn, meant gold. When the coast was clear he walked downstairs to the payphone and dialled Robinson's number. He was, after all, going fishing the next day. Was it possible to alter the arrangements? His brother-in-law wasn't sure; the team had been stood down and it would take time to reassemble them. He asked Black what time he finished and told him to drive directly to the Bulldog car park.

'If I'm not there, go home and I'll ring you tonight.'

Black left on time after completing a run to Heathrow and drove to the pub, but Robinson was not there. Back home, he sat and chatted with his wife until, at 7.15 p.m., the telephone rang. It was Robinson.

'Can I see you? I'm round the corner.'

Black made an excuse to his wife and left. He drove to the Bulldog and climbed into the passenger seat of a black Ford Escort driven by Mick. The other two were in the back. The door had been opened for him, and the second he climbed in he was handed a piece of tissue paper.

'Use this. Don't touch the motor,' said Mick.

Robinson asked if Black had any idea of what might be inside the vault overnight.

'I don't know exactly. There might be two boxes; there might be twenty, plus whatever might have been cleared through customs tonight.' Throughout the meeting they discussed the boxes, but not once did it occur to Black to tell the others that they would be placed on the floor of the vault. They had assumed that the boxes would be locked in the safes. They were more interested anyway in what cash would be available. What they really wanted was banknotes – easy to transport, easy to hide and easy to spend. Black estimated the potential haul at perhaps as much as £2 million.

He ran through the security procedures and alarm system one more time and gave Robinson the name of the keyman and the crew leader. 'It's Scouse and Riseley, they have the keys and the combinations,' he said. They talked about the personal panic alarms that Scouse carried and decided that if he had time to hit the button, then the robbers would 'scarper PDQ'.

Then they discussed who would be on the raid. Black was concerned that his association with Robinson would be discovered in the aftermath, so Mick and Tony assured him that his brother-in-law would not be required. He would instead be 'away establishing an alibi'. Mick described how they would use petrol, watered down, to frighten the guards who held the secrets to the vault and asked if the guards were the type to 'have a go'. 'No,' replied Black, 'they'll be too frightened. They'll do as they are told.'

'It doesn't matter,' said a voice in the back, 'we have a right nutter on the team.' It was a humorous reference to Mick in the driver's seat, the man who, hours later, the terrified guards would label 'the Bully'. He turned in his seat to share the joke with the men in the back, and one of them added: 'There'll be no trouble. He'll stick a soldering iron up their arses if there is.'

All that was left to decide was the timing. Black was asked what he thought, and he replied: 'I'll come down and signal you through the window when I'm ready. Give me two or three minutes to get back upstairs and come on in.'

He climbed out of the car, using the tissue paper to handle the door and walked back to his Opel. Later that night he and his wife Lyn went out to buy some take-away food, then, after watching television, they went to bed. But Black couldn't sleep. His brain was working overtime, and when he finally fell asleep it was early morning.

He woke with a start at 6.20 a.m. He had slept through the alarm and had no more than ten minutes to wash, dress and drive to work. He jumped up, grabbed his uniform off the bed and struggled into it on the run. Tearing through the suburbs he arrived at the industrial estate shortly before 6.40.

The robbers were waiting nearby, breathing fire and damning Black. The minutes had ticked by after 6.30 and they wondered if he'd 'lost his bottle'. He hadn't – but could he keep it?

'Mick Scouse came downstairs to let me in and locked the door behind me. I went upstairs and took my coat off in the radio room. There was a conversation about vehicle weights. I made an excuse about going to the toilet and went downstairs. I had a look round and then went to the door. I couldn't see anything through the window because it was still darkish outside and the light was on inside. I just put my arm up and waved. I had no way of knowing whether they had seen me or not. Then I went back upstairs and into the rest room. I rolled myself a fag.

'A couple of minutes later they came upstairs. I saw one directly in front of me and another pass behind him. The one in front was Mick, I think, because he had a yellow balaclava on and later he pulled it up when I was lying on the floor and whispered, "It's all right. We've got the lot."'

Black ran through the raid. It was, generally, as he had told the police in his earlier statement. He had discussed what to say with Robinson before the raid and was told: 'Just tell the truth, but leave out the naughty bits.'

Now he admitted the section on the video reconstruction that had helped catch him out. When dragged into the control room to operate the controls of the shutter door, he had, contrary to his earlier denials, been able to see through the observation window into the delivery bay. There he had seen the van, bright blue in colour, being loaded up.

In conclusion, Black turned again to the question of his cut. 'There was never any discussion about how much I would get. Nothing was said about percentage or cut, just that I would have to go on working for Brink's-Mat for another five years or so before I collected it. They were to make the arrangements. It could go in a Swiss bank account, they said.'

Benwell sat back. It was 10.12 p.m., almost eight hours after he had started writing down Black's statement, and he was exhausted.

'Would it be possible for me to see Mr Cater now?' asked Black.

'I'll find out,' said Detective Sergeant Branch.

Minutes later Commander Cater entered the room and waved the three detectives out. They believed that they already knew the identity of Robinson's accomplices. Black had said that he thought the surname of the big man, Tony, was White. Criminal intelligence had already confirmed that a Tony White and a younger man, Mick McAvoy, were known acquaintances of Robinson. It was also known that White owned a vehicle similar to the white car seen leaving the estate shortly after the robbery. The detectives went downstairs to collect the mug-shots they had already put to one side from police files. There were two folders, each containing twelve photographs of various individuals. In each batch they had placed mugshots of McAvoy and White. Shortly before midnight, after Commander Cater had finished with Black, D S Branch pushed the folders under Black's nose. The first file was opened, and the pictures were spread across the table. Black immediately pointed to one.

'That's Mick,' he said. He had confirmed the detectives' suspicions. The photograph he pointed to was of the Bully, McAvoy.

They pushed the second folder over the table and Black again picked one out immediately. 'That's Tony,' he declared. It was a photograph of a man called Tony White.

In the early hours of Tuesday, 6 December, Black was led back to his cell.

4. Cops and robbers

The speed with which Cater and his detectives were able to establish the identities of at least some of the men believed to have carried out the Brink's-Mat raid was testimony to the vigilance that Scotland Yard exercises in combating armed crime. It was also evidence of the incestuousness of the world inhabited by London's top-class armed robbers.

For the Brink's-Mat story is not the stuff of popular fiction – the slick robbery carried out in isolation by vaguely glamorous villains determined to live out the rest of their days in ease. The truth is far more prosaic, and far more alarming.

In reality, the Brink's-Mat raid was just one more encounter in a war in which the battle lines are well established, and the participants on both sides are often known to each other, if not personally, then at least by reputation.

On one side are some of the best detectives that Scotland Yard can muster and, on the other, men who regard leaping across a pavement, masked and carrying a pistol or sawn-off shotgun, as part of a day's work. Whether the target is a middle-aged security officer or a young girl working behind the counter in a building society office, they will generally use whatever violence is required to achieve their aims.

Two specialist operations branches are Scotland Yard's

main weapons against the armed robber, SO8, the Flying Squad, and SO11, the criminal intelligence branch. (At the time of the Brink's-Mat raid the prefix SO had not yet come into use. The branches were part of C Department and hence used the prefix C.)

Flying Squad detectives are a particular type, self-motivating officers with a proven record of being good thief takers, skilled in interviewing suspects and running informers. On the street experience and initiative are vital, as well as a large dose of straightforward bravery, for the chances are high that sooner or later a detective will find himself looking into the barrel of a sawn-off shotgun or a pistol. Sheer physical bulk is an extra asset. That doesn't preclude women Flying Squad officers, but they are generally used for surveillance purposes.

Major surveillance operations, however, are carried out by detectives from SO11, the branch that compiles information about top-class criminals by monitoring their activities and checking their acquaintances. In the case of SO11 detectives, the ability to remain anonymous and, later, to record accurately what they have seen, a job far more difficult than it sounds, are fundamental prerequisites.

Of the two branches, the Flying Squad is the older, having been in existence so long that the Squad's nickname in Cockney rhyming slang, the Sweeney (from Flying Squad/Sweeney Todd, the notorious Fleet Street barber who turned his customers into meat pies), is generally regarded as a cliché.

The Squad was set up at the end of the First World War, when London experienced a crime wave as large numbers of men recently released from the armed forces emerged on to the streets, many of them hardened to violence after the carnage of the Western Front. At the same time the use of motor vehicles in the course of crime began to increase.

A month before the war ended twelve especially selected detectives at Scotland Yard were informed that they were to become an experimental crime-fighting force. No longer would they be bound by regulations that prohibited police officers from crossing the border of the division in which they were based to tackle crime. Instead theirs was to be a roving commission – they were to become the first mobile police squad in the country.

The words were grand enough, but initially the reality was rather different. Instead of cars, or even motorcycles, transport for the fledgling group consisted of a covered horse-drawn wagon hired from the Great Western Railway. Such was their success, however, that after the first year the group was permanently established and by 1920 had been provided with two ex-Royal Flying Corps Crossley motor tenders, capable of a top speed of 35 m.p.h. (The speed limit at the time was just 20 m.p.h.) The vehicles were proof of the importance attached to the group's work – the entire Metropolitan Police force vehicle fleet at the time numbered just two cars and four dispatch vans.

Two months after the vehicles arrived, a *Daily Mail* journalist named W. G. T. Crook deemed the group worthy of a write-up, in the process referring to them as a 'flying squad of picked detectives'. The name stuck, and by 1921 Flying Squad had become their official title. As well as being the first motorized police squad in the country, in the early 1920s they soon became the first in radio contact with base. The step was so novel that their equipment was frequently used by British intelligence agencies to eavesdrop on unauthorized transmissions emanating from Britain. It was literally the only equipment capable of doing this, and a copious amount of intelligence was collected.

As the years passed, and technical advances produced faster cars, the Flying Squad endeavoured to keep pace, although it was frequently reminded by the Yard's top brass that its vehicles were intended simply as a means of transport to the scene of a crime, not as pursuit vehicles. The reminders were seldom heeded, and the squad slowly but surely came to drive a succession of famous British models, including Bentleys, Jaguars and Wolseleys.

From the outset the men of the Flying Squad, with their swooping-eagle tie motif, were regarded by the general public as something special. In the 1920s Edgar Wallace wrote a play about them; soon afterwards J. Ord Hume, a well-known composer, wrote a brass-band march for the squad. Their exploits went on to figure in a number of British films, and as late as the mid-1970s the squad was being eulogized in a television series called *The Sweeney*.

During the late 1960s, however, the image of Scotland Yard's detectives as courageous men dedicated to upholding the law without fear or favour began, in the eyes of the public, to undergo something of a change. To understand the story of the Brink's-Mat raid, it is important to understand why, in less than twenty years, a climate had arisen in which Scotland Yard detectives were sometimes viewed with as much suspicion as the criminals they dealt with. Quite simply, it was the activities of a number of corrupt officers that played straight into the hands of London's professional criminals, tainting in the process the Yard's many honest officers.

The question of police corruption was already starting to be aired when Robert Mark was appointed to the post of Assistant Commissioner at Scotland Yard in 1967. Mark arrived after serving as Chief Constable of Leicestershire, where he had distinguished himself by introducing some of the first traffic wardens to be seen in Britain.

The appointment of provincial officers to senior posts at Scotland Yard was unpopular – so much so that only one other outsider had ever been given such a senior posting. But within a year Mark had risen to the rank of Deputy Commissioner, where he found that his only full-time responsibility was internal discipline, and even then he did not have a free rein. The Deputy Commissioner was powerless to act if the accusations against an officer were of a criminal nature. Since 1879 a lower-ranking officer, the Assistant Commissioner in charge of crime, the head of London's detectives, had been vested with absolute authority to deal with that kind of criminal investigation.

On becoming Deputy Commissioner early in 1968, Mark made it plain that he was not prepared to become a mere figurehead or attempt to curry favour with anyone. He would concentrate on weeding out of the force those who in some quarters were beginning to give it a bad name.

His first move was immediately to ban the practice of allowing officers convicted of criminal offences to remain on the payroll while suspended pending the hearing of an appeal. In the case of detectives found during a disciplinary hearing to be unfit to work unsupervised, the sanction of returning them immediately to uniformed duties was introduced.

That achieved, he turned his attention to police cases in which either the DPP had refused to prosecute or officers had been acquitted. Mark wanted to know whether those cases warranted internal disciplinary procedures and possible suspension.

The effect was instant. In Mark's own words: 'It soon became plain that of the increasing numbers of officers being suspended, the majority were from the CID and that the uniformed branch were only too pleased to see someone deal with a department which had long brought the force as a whole into disgrace.' For by the late 1960s a general decline in law and order, coupled with the money being made from the permissive society, notably pornography and drugs, had caused corruption, among detectives at least, to become virtually endemic. This didn't mean that they were in any way intrinsically more dishonest than uniformed officers; they were just far more likely to have temptation thrust their way as they investigated major racketeers.

Public suspicions about the honesty of London's detective force grew in 1969, when *The Times*, a newspaper in those days still very much the voice of the establishment, published a story accusing a detective inspector and two detective sergeants of corruption.

A small-time south London criminal had been visited by two detectives wanting information, and when he appeared reluctant to help a stick of gelignite was thrust into his hands and he was told that if he did not pay £200, he would be charged with possessing explosives. The criminal was furious, particularly as he was already making regular payments to another detective as a 'licence fee' so that he could continue operating.

Instead of handing over the money he went to *The Times*, and a meeting was arranged with the detectives, at which he pretended to submit to the extortion. A tape recorder picked up one of the detectives saying that if the criminal ever needed a problem straightened out, he should get in touch immediately: 'I know people everywhere, because I'm a little firm in a firm. Don't matter where, anywhere in London, I can get on the phone to someone I know I can trust, that talks the same as me.' The article in *The Times* accused the officers of taking bribes in return for dropping charges, giving false evidence and allowing a criminal to continue his illegal activities (known among criminals as being given a 'clear run'). The story, partly because of the newspaper in which it appeared, received enormous attention.

Tackling corruption among the ranks of Scotland Yard's detectives was to prove a lengthy business for Mark, not least because of the blind eye turned by a number of senior officers to transgressions. Following the *Times* exposé, Jim Callaghan, then Home Secretary, ordered a special inquiry into police corruption by one of HM Inspectors of Constabulary. The inspector, Frank Williamson, began collecting information but claimed his efforts were ignored both by the Home Office and by the Yard's Commissioner, Sir John Waldron. In 1971 Williamson, six years away from retirement, resigned, alleging that he had been blocked at every turn.

Later that year, however, with inquiries continuing into a considerable number of detectives, Mark was given an opportunity for overall reform. He claims that during a routine conference the Commissioner, Waldron, expressed concern at the continuing activities of corrupt detectives, claiming that the problem must have arisen because of lack of supervision. Mark immediately replied: 'Nothing of the kind. There isn't a person in this room, except perhaps the C Department representative, who doesn't know perfectly well that the answer lies in the thoroughly unsatisfactory way in which the CID investigates allegations of crime against its members.'

Waldron's response was to tell Mark to do something about it, and within ten days a blueprint had been produced for a new department, to be known as A 10, that would take over the job of criminal investigations into members of the police force. The team, rapidly christened the 'rubber heels squad' within the force, was to be handpicked from both uniformed and detective branches and would report directly to the Deputy Commissioner.

Before A 10 could become fully operational, however, a new scandal broke when, in November 1971, the *Sunday People* ran a series of articles about the men behind London's burgeoning pornography trade, including a leading pornographer called Jimmy Humphreys, accusing them of corrupt dealings with officers from the Obscene Publications branch.

The following February a report in the same paper revealed that Commander Kenneth Drury, head of the Flying Squad, had recently returned from a Cyprus holiday where Humphreys, a man with nine convictions to his name, who had even served a spell in Dartmoor prison, had been his host. The two men, it later transpired, first met early in 1971 at a lunch party that Humphreys had given to celebrate the promotion of a Flying Squad friend, Detective Inspector Alex Ingram, and the police chief and the pornographer had gone on to socialize regularly.

Mark immediately ordered an investigation into their relationship, during which Drury claimed that he made a contribution to the cost of the trip. He had only gone along in the first place, he explained, in the belief that Humphreys could assist him in finding the Great Train Robber Ronnie Biggs (who by that time had settled in Brazil).

Drury's story was not believed, and he was served with disciplinary papers and suspended, but, rather than face the disciplinary board, he resigned. Before he did so, however, he wrote an article for the Sunday newspaper *News of the World* claiming that Humphreys had been one of his informants. The furious pornographer, aware of the effect that such a claim could have on many of his contacts, responded a week later through the columns of the same paper, saying that the opposite was the case – he had never received any money from Drury but instead had wined and dined the police chief on a total of fifty-eight occasions and had always picked up the bill.

Two weeks before Drury's resignation Mark became Commissioner at Scotland Yard and immediately announced to the force at large the setting up of A 10, emphasizing that in future all allegations of a criminal nature against serving police officers would be passed to that department.

In the following months the number of detectives arrested for attempted extortion and blackmail rose sharply; during Mark's rule as Commissioner, which lasted nearly five years, the eventual tally of police officers who left the force either following, or in anticipation of, criminal or disciplinary proceedings amounted to some 478. The simple act of resignation, however, didn't render them immune from prosecution, as Drury was to discover.

In April 1973 Humphreys's wife, Rusty, complained to A 10 about her husband's dealings with corrupt officers, details of which had been recorded in his personal diaries. The pornographer was abroad at the time, having fled to Holland to avoid questioning about an attack on a male friend of his wife as well as a new offensive against Soho pornographers by the newly reformed Obscene Publications Squad, now made up of officers from the uniformed section.

When the diaries were retrieved by A 10 from the Serious Crimes Squad, which had been investigating the attack, twenty-one detectives were identified, up to the rank of commander. The investigation that followed was a lengthy affair, but in 1976 the go-ahead was given to arrest twelve serving or former detectives, including Drury, and two officers who had served in the Flying Squad under him, Ingram and Detective Inspector John Legge.

Humphreys, who had by that time been extradited from Holland, told the court that he had paid Drury £100 a week to 'keep my business smooth'. Apart from cash payments and the Cyprus holiday, Drury was also alleged to have accepted a pair of gold cuff-links and entertainment in the West End. Humphreys also revealed that he had provided workmen to renovate Ingram's house and had later given him a car in appreciation of his services.

Legge's problems had begun when he spent a holiday in an apartment in Ibiza owned by Humphreys, but the detective explained to the court that, on joining the Flying Squad, he had been rebuked by Drury if he did not attend social functions hosted by Humphreys. Then, when Legge was experiencing some domestic difficulties, it was Drury who had suggested the holiday in Ibiza.

In the event, the judge found that Legge had no case to answer, and he was discharged. Drury, however, was found guilty on five charges of corruption and sentenced to eight years' imprisonment, reduced to five on appeal. Ingram was found guilty on two charges and sentenced to four years, reduced to three on appeal.

Whether Humphreys was ever an informant of Drury's is not known. For the running of informants is traditionally one of the most precarious parts of a detective's job. At his trial Drury said that it was 'absolutely essential' for Flying Squad officers to mix socially with people connected with the criminal fraternity. He claimed: 'During my career, I made a point of mixing with criminals. It is essential that you do so. You cannot expect them to give information about crimes if you ostracize them except when you want information from them.'

He had already given a flavour of his defence in the *News of the World* article that had so upset Humphreys: 'A good detective is only as good as his informants. And a copper's informants, by their very nature, are going to be villains or associates of villains. So where do you draw the line?' he wrote. 'You can't talk to a snout only when you want something out of him. He's got to know you and trust you . . . All of which means that you've just got to mix with him socially, in his own surroundings, whether they be a scruffy little back-street caff or a plush restaurant or night club. You've got to be part of the scene.' That, he claimed, was the way it was in the Flying Squad. 'The lads are in and out all the time, getting around, being seen, keeping themselves in the know about what the underworld are up to.'

The problem with that philosophy, however, is that it is a course that can leave a detective wide open to corruption. Criminals, it is known, will sometimes help police in an effort to divert attention from their own activities while at the same time obtaining, through the usefulness of the information given, a degree of protection from prosecution.

It is there that the corruption can occur, in the form of a detective either turning a blind eye to what is going on in return for a cut of the action or, if the information leads to the recovery of stolen property, pocketing some of the reward money that the detective will claim on the informant's behalf.

Those are not, of course, the only possible opportunities for corruption among detectives. A strategically placed officer can, for a fee, try to ensure that bail is granted, hold back evidence and details about past convictions from a court, or pass on to a person under investigation details of the case being made against him or warnings about police operations in which he could become compromised. In a more straightforward manner, corrupt officers can also hold on to a proportion of whatever valuables they recover during an inquiry.

It was the question of reward money that in 1976 kept alive the belief that there was still a fundamental corruption problem involving some Flying Squad officers. The occasion for this was a television documentary about the case of an informant called 'Mary Frazer'.

She, it was claimed, had provided a woman detective constable in the Flying Squad with a valuable lead about the identities of two men who, in 1972, had robbed a branch of Barclays Bank in Wembley, north London. The raid, in which £138,111 had been taken, was one of a series of highly successful bank robberies at the time, and detectives were convinced that the same gang was responsible.

One name soon thrown up was that of Bertie Smalls, later so infamous among London's robbers for becoming a supergrass that 'doing a Bertie' was to enter London slang as a euphemism for turning Queen's evidence. Smalls by then had left the country, but detectives began a dragnet operation to find out who his accomplices might be.

It was 'Mary Frazer' who, within three days of the Wembley raid, passed on to Woman Detective Constable Joan Angell the names of two men: Bruce Brown, ostensibly a respectable property developer, and Bryan Turner, a hardened criminal who owned a supermarket as a front but made most of his money from running an illegal 'kalooki' game in a north London club.

Arrests followed, and after Turner had been charged Angell submitted a formal report claiming a reward for 'Frazer'. By 1974, however, no money had been forthcoming, and the WDC filed a formal complaint to A 10 alleging that the Flying Squad inspector in charge of the case had behaved unethically in his relationship with police informants.

A 10 quickly discovered that Angell's original claim for a reward for 'Frazer' had completely disappeared, although she could produce a photostat to prove it had been submitted. Then it was discovered that the claim had been deleted from the Flying Squad informants register. The inquiry went on to establish that reward money had, in fact, been paid to an informant called 'William Wise', after it had been claimed on his behalf by the detective inspector and a detective chief superintendent who was head of divisional CID at Wembley. The chief superintendent had already been investigated by A 10 following a claim by the wife of Bruce Brown that he had taken £25,000 from a safety box belonging to the robber, who was an old golfing partner. He had been cleared by the inquiry and had retired from the force.

A 10 established that 'Wise' had received a total of £2,175 reward money, much of it paid after the detectives claimed that he had informed them about Brown's and Turner's safe-deposit boxes in which some of the robbery proceeds were found.

In the end A 10 decided that although 'Mary Frazer' might have a moral claim to the reward, the complaints against the detectives were 'unsubstantiated'. None the less, WDC Angell felt sufficiently strongly about the matter to state on television: 'I think that the best thing that could happen would be a public inquiry into the whole system but, in particular, into these sets of circumstances, which are very disquietening.'

By 1977, the year in which Mark retired as Commissioner, it was obvious that the events of the previous nine years had more than slightly tarnished the image of London's detective force. As well as the Drury case, a number of officers from the Obscene Publications Squad had been sent to prison, and a group of Drug Squad officers had been convicted of perjury.

Reform was obviously needed, and, as part of an overall reorganization of the Metropolitan Police, it was decided to decentralize part of Scotland Yard's operational role. At the same time, a long-term objective was agreed for C Department, the aim of which was 'to establish a climate whereby the efforts of both detectives and uniformed officers to prevent and detect crime are properly co-ordinated and subject to effective control'.

In the case of the Flying Squad, a complete change in their terms of reference was ordered. After a review of their role it was decided that instead of dealing with serious crimes in general, they would in future tackle armed robberies only, with the squad's officers forming a central robbery squad that would consist of a co-ordinating unit at Scotland Yard and four smaller groups placed strategically around London.

The newly appointed Deputy Assistant Commissioner, Powis, also ordered a crackdown to stop corrupt policemen from creaming off reward money meant for informants. In future all payments amounting to more than £500 would be handed over by the DAC himself.

The robbery squad proved an immediate success. In its first year on the streets robberies involving firearms dropped from 935 to 734 – but still the spectre of corruption hung over the Yard. For in 1978 another major inquiry, Operation Countryman, started. It began in the City of London force after a supergrass alleged that gangs that had carried out three armed robberies were linked with corrupt police officers. Robbery squad officers had helped City police with their inquiries into the raids, so the investigation soon spread to Scotland Yard.

Before long, senior Flying Squad officers, many of whose colleagues were under suspicion, were making formal complaints about the activities of the inquiry team (made up of policemen from provincial forces), particularly in their dealings with supergrasses. Criminals, claimed the Flying Squad, were being encouraged to trade their way out of lengthy prison sentences by producing allegations of corruption.

By the following year the Countryman team was alleging that its inquiries were being obstructed not just by Scotland Yard but by the DPP itself. The head of the Flying Squad, Commander Donald Nesham, was demoted and later resigned as a result of the claims, although he denied ever hindering the inquiry.

It took nearly four years for the investigation to run its course, and when it did, it ended in successful prosecutions against just three detectives, only one of them from the Metropolitan Police.

To the end the members of the Operation Countryman team claimed their efforts to expose corruption had been 'nobbled'. In the words of one newspaper report when the operation was eventually disbanded:

> They now believe that the network of corrupt detectives known as the 'firm within a firm' still exists and flourishes and resists all efforts to expose it. They believe it involves hundreds of officers and extends to the senior reaches of the London police hierarchy.
>
> They believe detectives have organized crime in London for years, planning and physically carrying out robberies and burglaries as well as stealing rewards and extorting money for bail, privileges and weakened prosecutions.
>
> They believe London has the most corrupt detective force in the country and that the system is oiled by a handful of 'brokers' who link criminals with corrupt policemen and in return receive money and a licence to commit crime.
>
> They can prove in court only a fraction of what they believe.

This was scarcely the stuff to inspire the men of the Flying Squad, but by then they were concentrating on an attack from a very different quarter. For, after the initial success of the robbery squad, they now sometimes found themselves almost literally fighting for control of the streets. Their honesty might be called in question by the media and their integrity attacked in court, but Flying Squad's prime concern was to deal with an astonishing explosion in armed crime. While Scotland Yard had been racked with internal inquiries, the figures for armed robbery had soared from 380 robberies in 1972 to 734 in 1978 and a massive 1,772 four years later. The 336 per cent robbery increase over that ten-year period was even more startling when measured against a 94 per cent rise in other crimes in the capital during the decade. The robbery figures for 1982 alone were 332 up on the previous year, and more than £12 million had been taken at gunpoint from security vans, post offices, building society branches, supermarkets and similar targets. Flying Squad knew how bad the problem had become; they saw it every day, and risked their lives in tackling it head on. They had to – for it had become increasingly evident that unless they caught a team in the act, the robbers would exploit the prevailing suspicions about the Metropolitan Police. They would plead not guilty, claiming, almost as a matter of course, that they were the victims of fabricated evidence – and, given the publicity surrounding the problems at Scotland Yard, juries were increasingly inclined to believe them. Ironically, despite the dramatic increase in armed crime the most vehement critics of the police, both in the press and elsewhere – a number of whom seemed to believe wholesale what they were told by criminals with considerable axes to grind – were still unlikely ever to encounter an armed robber.

It was evident that something drastic had to be done to combat this hugely profitable growth industry, and in 1982 it was decided to expand the Flying Squad's role. Some 200 officers, about 30 per cent of them authorized firearms officers, would now concentrate their efforts solely on the prevention and detection of armed attacks on security vans, banks, building societies, betting shops, post offices and jewellers.

The man chosen to spearhead this new drive, Commander Frank Cater, a former Royal Marine who took over in January 1983, was well used to challenges. Seventeen years earlier he had helped to break the grip of the Richardson gang in south

London – a grip the Richardsons had regularly enforced through the use of torture. He topped that achievement two years later when second-in-command of the police team that smashed the rule of the Kray twins in east London. For a detective force anxious to put the past behind it, Cater had another outstanding credential: under Mark he had been drafted into A 10 to help with the clean-up of the CID. Later, back on the streets again, he had also distinguished himself by smashing the Murder Incorporated contract-killing gang, which numbered among its victims a 10-year-old boy.

Cater, however, had scarcely got his feet under the desk when the Security Express raid took place, to be followed eight months later by Brink's-Mat. When they occurred he turned for assistance, as a matter of course, to the Yard's other battalion in the war against armed robbers, S O 11, the criminal intelligence branch.

SO11 had also suffered during the purges of the 1970s. A detective chief inspector and a detective sergeant were investigated during the Humphreys inquiry, disciplined and required to resign, and later a detective superintendent was fined £500 for breaking the Official Secrets Act by passing confidential papers to a property tycoon who committed suicide. But until the Brink's-Mat case, SO11 was virtually unknown to the public at large. It was a situation very much to the liking of the branch, to which security is everything and headlines are anathema.

The motto of SO11 sums up their role in modern policing – *Sceleratus non scelus*, which, loosely translated, means 'The evil doer rather than the evil deed'. For generally the branch's role is not to make arrests but to watch known professional criminals in the hope of enabling officers from other branches to catch them red-handed when they next embark on a crime.

SO11 was set up in March 1960, when serious crime in London had become increasingly prevalent and it was obvious that behind much of it lay real organization. In the East End that organization was masterminded by the Krays, while in south London the Richardsons were beginning to make their influence felt.

At that time Scotland Yard had no central intelligence department. Shortly after the Second World War an attempt had been made to set one up with the formation of a unit known as the Ghost Squad, which concentrated on criminal surveillance, working hand in glove with the Flying Squad, which would step in to make arrests. That way the anonymity of the Ghost Squad was preserved – criminals did not come to know its officers – and, just as crucially, Ghost Squad officers were not required as witnesses in court, with the attendant publicity that would have brought. Within a matter of months, however, other priorities had developed, and the Ghost Squad was disbanded.

But the lessons that had been learned were not forgotten, and today a similar relationship exists between SO11 and other police departments. Once a major criminal has been 'targeted' by detectives, it is generally officers from SO11 who are drafted in to keep him under surveillance, monitoring his movements and watching his acquaintances. Detectives from other branches then step in at the appropriate time to make the arrests. The only difference is that today SO11 officers can, when it is unavoidable, find themselves in court giving evidence. An earlier practice, that of other officers purporting in court that they had carried out the surveillance, has been discontinued.

Scotland Yard will not divulge the exact number of officers working for SO11, but it is known that their selection is, in the words of one former SO11 officer, a 'tortuous process'. In 1986, out of 220 policemen who applied to join the branch, only eight were selected, three of whom either dropped out or were asked to leave before the end of the initial five-week training period.

Prerequisites for selection include an unremarkable appearance. 'A 6-foot 6-inch policeman with ginger hair would stand out in any crowd – likewise a policewoman who looks like Marilyn Monroe. She can hardly dress down to a Mrs Mopp if the occasion warrants it,' the authors were told.

The hours are long, and much of the work is outside, so great stress is placed on physical fitness. Officers must also be able to demonstrate that they have the confidence and initiative to work effectively on their own, without constant supervision, and they must prove to be highly accurate in recording what they see.

The five-week training course is, in fact, aimed at undoing much of their earlier police experience. Conventional police work usually fits into a routine; the requirements of the job are defined and the activities of a police officer highly regimented. SO11 officers have to be encouraged to think for themselves.

They must also learn to lose any telltale traits that could give them away as police officers. Many aspects of police work result in officers becoming used to attracting attention on the street – the uniform alone is partly responsible – which can lead to a demeanour noticeable even when they are in plain clothes or off duty. But in an age when virtually every professional criminal is, in police jargon, 'anti-surveillance conscious', which means that he will routinely take precautions to avoid being followed, the last thing an SO11 officer wants to do is to attract attention. Instead he or she has to master the art of becoming an anonymous face in the crowd, ostensibly noticing nothing but in reality seeing all. There are tips that make the job easier. When carrying out observations on foot, for instance, 'always look as though you know where you are going'. People who amble seemingly aimlessly tend to get noticed.

SO11 officers are also taught that it is easier to dress down than dress up. When following a suspect who might, on the same evening, visit a pub on the roughest council estate and meet a contact in a plush West End hotel, an SO11 officer would typically wear a polo neck over his tie and don a dirty anorak for the pub. At the hotel the polo neck and anorak can be discarded, but if he goes on duty in a leather jacket and jeans, he might have problems looking as though he belonged in the hotel foyer.

Following the five-week training, a candidate will spend a year on probation with the branch, where his or her performance will be closely watched. A probationer can be removed from the post at any time. But in a police force where most detectives will serve no more than two or three years with one particular branch, a good officer will, after getting through the probationary period, generally remain with SO11 for a minimum of five years and sometimes much longer.

The branch's equipment includes a variety of covert surveillance vehicles, including black taxis complete with 'cabbies' wearing authentic-looking car drivers' licence badges, an arm rest in the back concealing a radio receiver and the cab driver's radio in front tuned in to base.

Another favourite vehicle is the innocent-looking builder's van, seemingly long past an appointment at the scrap yard. Anyone peering in through the back windows would simply see a jumble of builders materials and some green netting. Behind the netting, however, is a mobile observation post capable of seating several officers. Their vantage point on the world is through either the netting or a periscope going up through the roof. Spyholes in the side of the vehicle are no longer used; they are too easily spotted. Dirty overalls and more netting behind the front passenger seat disguise another entrance to the look-out post.

Other SO11 equipment includes the most up-to-date electronic eavesdropping and radio-tracking equipment available to police, about which they will say nothing. And they have direct access to the Home Office, where, theoretically at least, the Home Secretary's signature is required on the warrants that authorize telephone taps, known in police jargon as the 'bell' or 'intercepts', about which they will say even less. It is known, however, that the actual tapping is left to handpicked and positively vetted British Telecom engineers based at 'Tinkerbell', a red-brick, five-storey block called Chantrey House, close to London's Victoria Station.

In the early 1970s the branch was the first in the British police force to become completely computerized. Now computer programs, including some developed for US law-enforcement agencies, are used to analyse incoming information and extract the relevant intelligence. Programs exist that can draw up the psychological profile of, for instance, a mass murderer. Others have been created to plot the movements of suspects, say, in a major armed robbery.

The increase in armed robberies facing the Flying Squad and Criminal Intelligence branch in 1983 can be put down not to any one factor but rather to a combination of circumstances.

Until the 1950s bank raids tended to be carried out at the dead of night, with a master safecracker pitting his wits against whatever security arrangements were in use. Gradually, however, improvements in lock design and other security measures meant that tackling a safe itself was an increasingly difficult proposition. Even the use of gelignite was no longer a sound bet: a device had been developed that, if triggered by the force of an explosion, simply threw extra bolts across the safe door.

Criminals then introduced oxy-acetylene torches to get around this problem, but these proved to be slow and cumbersome and, on occasion, would actually reduce the contents of the safe to charred paper before the door could be forced. In addition, safe manufacturers soon got wise and inserted a sheet of glass against the inside of safe doors. If that was broken, extra bolts would be automatically activated.

Robbers therefore began to turn to 'across-the-counter' bank raids. Old-style attacks on bank safes didn't require any confrontation on the part of the robbers, but going into a bank in broad daylight did, so it was essential for the robbers to be able to guarantee control. Early in the 1960s firearms began to appear with increasing frequency.

By the end of that decade, however, banks had begun installing screens to protect their cashiers. It was also apparent that while the risk in such raids was high, the rewards were generally low, so once again those intent on armed robbery looked for new methods.

Cash in transit was the answer. Despite the predictions of

popular pundits that Britain was fast becoming a cashless society because of the increased use of cheque books and credit cards, the consumer society still needed ready money and plenty of it. As a result, during the 1960s specialized security firms emerged to take on the responsibility of transferring money, with armoured vans replacing vulnerable clerks carrying briefcases. It was these vans and their guards that now became the focus of the robbers' activities. The attacks proved so successful that they soon escalated. By the early 1980s even the biggest raids were hardly regarded as news.

Cash-in-transit raids were not a new concept. A £240,000 raid on a post office van in the West End of London during May 1952 had been the first 'epic robbery', and it had been followed, eleven years later, by the Great Train Robbery. But by the early 1980s, as attacks soared, a new phenomenon had become apparent to detectives. An inordinate number of men convicted for the more professional type of robbery, and a number of others thought to be likely suspects, came from just one area – south-east London.

Today detectives find it difficult to explain the reason for this criminal sub-culture. They point to the fact that different parts of London have traditionally tended to specialize in different kinds of crime: lorry hijackers used to concentrate in London's East End, around Commercial Road, while the Somers Town area of north London was known as a haunt of railway thieves. But in those cases the explanations were geographical. Commercial Road is close to docklands on the River Thames and lies on what used to be a major arterial route to freight terminals at Tilbury and Harwich. Somers Town is less than 2 miles from three major London rail terminals.

South-east London, however, is simply a sprawl of modest or run-down housing developments stretching from the docks on the south side of the River Thames down to the green fields of Kent. Unlike other parts of London, there are few select areas where those with an above-average income are likely to live. It is suburbia pure and simple. The explanations from those who have policed the area are not wholly satisfactory but, in the absence of a full sociological survey, have to suffice.

The core of the problem is said to lie in the widespread disregard for law and order that has existed for centuries among certain families of dockers in the riverside Bermondsey and Rotherhithe areas, where pilfering from cargoes was once a way of life. Family loyalty in such groups was paramount, and the extension of such families through local marriages formed a web of contacts and relationships. Until the very recent dockland developments those ties remained virtually intact. The East End of London might have been decimated by the German airforce in the Second World War and the city planners afterwards, but in the south-east one of London's largest working-class communities, centred on the Old Kent Road, stayed put.

The Great Train Robbery too had a part to play in the process – most of the robbers came from south-east London. The heroic status they were to achieve in the eyes of many was nowhere more evident than on the streets where they grew up. Even though guns were not used on that occasion, armed robbery took on a romantic hue.

Meanwhile the demise of London as a major port was to bring in its wake widespread unemployment among the dockers' community, particularly with the closure in 1970 of the Surrey Commercial Docks and the Grand Surrey Canal in Rotherhithe. The effects were exacerbated in the late 1970s and early 1980s by the decline of British industry generally. Crime was one way out for those determined to stay above the breadline – and armed robbery guaranteed the biggest returns. Today the situation is worse than ever. When, in July 1987, an officer from Scotland Yard's firearms unit shot dead two youths and wounded a third who were armed with a sawn-off shotgun, a pump-action twelve-bore and a Magnum pistol in an attempt to snatch £250,000 from a security van, extra police had to be drafted into the area to prevent a riot. Women shouted at patrolling officers from the balconies of their flats; children taunted them in the street; and seven people near a pub frequented by the robbers were arrested on charges ranging from threatening behaviour to assault.

The police had known what to expect and had even called in the force helicopter, for by then the area was well known as a place where armed robbery was regarded as a legitimate way to get rich quick. Despite Britain's relatively strict firearms regulations, in some pubs guns are as easy to come by as a stolen television set or video recorder. After the 1987 shootings one senior Flying Squad officer said: 'Some 60 per cent of all armed robberies in the country take place in London, and about three quarters of those which take place elsewhere are committed by Londoners. Proportionally, the chances are high that an armed robber is from south-east London.'

It was the direct result of a continuous effort to identify, and combat, the south-east London gangs that, once Tony Black had cracked, enabled Cater and his men to move in so swiftly on other members of the Brink's-Mat team. For when the Heathrow robbery took place an enormous amount of information had already been gathered about individuals in the area from which he had originally come.

An entire C11 operation, code-named Operation Kate, had, during 1981 and 1982, concentrated on building up police intelligence about a hard core of very professional robbers in south-east London who were believed to specialize in 'epic' robberies, while organizing and providing guns and guidance for teams intent on smaller targets. The hard core, who knew and trusted each other implicitly – a number of them had even been to school together – were also into drugs in a big way. The money made from robberies would be used to pay for large cannabis consignments from Amsterdam, the sale of which they were able to control right down to street-level.

The surveillance operation was top-secret; those taking part reported directly to the then commander of C11, Brian Worth. 'We didn't want to take any chances,' he said later. 'We were into a highly efficient and professional core of robbers who had contacts with the judiciary. We were also concerned about possible leaks to the press.' Not even their other colleagues in C11 knew what the surveillance teams were working on as, for nearly a year, suspects were placed under observation, phones were tapped and the legitimate business enterprises of a number of suspects were closely analysed to find out just where their money was coming from.

It was an enormously difficult task. The men the police were up against were professionals who took every precaution against being brought to justice. Among London's armed robbers the law of silence on the streets is just one of a number of safeguards. Even when not about to pull off a robbery, they take routine measures to ensure that they aren't being followed, stopping in cul-de-sacs or driving several times around the same roundabout. They also use highly specialized radio equipment, bought from abroad, which is tuned into the restricted wavebands used by SO8 and SO11 to find out what police team is in the area and what they are up to.

As little planning relating to robberies as possible is arranged by telephone. Codes are used, and before a raid the participants may in some cases vanish from their homes altogether, checking into one of the larger London hotels to make sure that their calls aren't monitored. On the job itself, they go to great lengths to avoid being identified. No telltale evidence is left either in the stolen vehicles used or at the scene of the crime. Alibis will often have been established before the raid takes place, and at the slightest suspicion that something is wrong the robbery is abandoned.

The arms they carry are quickly disposed of. Generally they will have been hired from an underworld armourer (one such figure in the area was known to police and villains alike as Moss Bros., such was the extensive service he offered). The fee is either a straight down-payment (for a time during the early 1980s £500 was the going rate for a sawn-off) or a cut of the actual take. One robber is then specifically delegated to pick up the 'happy bag', the slang term for the holdall or whatever the guns are hidden in. He hands the weapons to his accomplices only minutes before the raid and collects them up again quickly afterwards to return them to the armourer.

After a successful raid few top-class robbers go out and blow their ill-gotten gains. Instead, as in the case of the suspects in Operation Kate, the money is invested in drugs and the proceeds then placed in a legitimate business outlet to disguise its origins. Any improvement in the robber's standard of living can then be explained away as the rewards of honest labour. Meanwhile the robber gets on with planning the next job.

The detectives on Operation Kate were aware that, even if they did succeed in building up sufficient evidence to arrest anyone, there was no guarantee of a successful prosecution. For their targets would simply embark on another way of beating the system – although in this case the only reward would be avoiding a lengthy stay in one of Her Majesty's top-security prisons.

The sequence of events that follows the arrest of top-echelon armed robbers follows a general pattern. As a rule, nothing is said to the detectives interrogating them. Under British law the right to silence while being held by police has long been established. Instead the services of one of a handful of London solicitors who specialize in representing professional robbers are employed, and they in turn engage a barrister sharing the same speciality. From the police's point of view, gaining an admission is vital, for if just one member of the gang can be persuaded to talk, alibis can be exploded and other members of the gang incriminated. But the struggle continues in the courtroom.

As sentences for armed robbery generally range from fifteen years upwards, any reduction a robber can expect for pleading guilty is usually insufficient for him to give up the chance of an acquittal, however slim. As a result, armed robbers invariably plead not guilty, and during the court case will challenge virtually every aspect of the police operation.

It is well known that the problem of obtaining satisfactory evidence has in some cases led disillusioned policemen to collect what little proof they can find, arrest the suspect and attribute to him remarks, partial admissions and sometimes full confessions that have never been made. The process is known as 'verballing'.

When he gets to court the defendant denies that he has ever made the remarks attributed to him and calls the police liars. However convincing he may sound, the police will, at least partially, still benefit. With the permission of the trial judge, the prosecution are generally allowed to tell the jury of the defendant's previous criminal convictions, which the police hope will sway the case their way. One consequence, however, is that detectives who do not resort to 'verballing' are just as likely to have allegations of fabrication levelled against them as those who do, leaving the jury unable to distinguish between honest and dishonest officers and increasing the chance of acquittal for a guilty defendant.

If, as is often the case, detectives deny a suspect access to a solicitor for fear that the inquiries may be hampered, this too will be drawn to the jury's attention as proof of unfair treatment, although the provisions of the Police and Criminal Evidence Act of 1984 ensure that today defendants must have access to a solicitor within thirty-six hours of their arrest.

However, there are a number of factors that work to the advantage of the police in the battle against armed crime. Even if, as in the case of Operation Kate, they are unable to prove their suspicions against certain individuals, the suspects, no matter how much money they make, sooner or later return to crime, which increases their chances of getting caught. For them it is a way of life.

Another factor in the police's favour is that armed robbers don't often stray far from their roots. They frequently associate with each other even when they are not 'working', enabling police to build up an accurate picture of which individuals are likely to operate together. 'Operation Kate was a luxury. We weren't investigating a specific case – we simply wanted to find out who was who in south-east London. We discovered that we have confined in south-east London twenty or so of the most adept, enterprising, violent, ruthless robbers in the entire country,' said Worth.

Luxury it may have been, but as far as the Brink's-Mat raid was concerned it paid off. 'Because of Operation Kate, detectives investigating the robbery had available to them an intelligence package which they simply had to open up,' one of the surveillance team told us.

When it was 'opened up' Brian Robinson's name stood revealed, together with that of Micky McAvoy, a man known to be so suspicious of possible C11 surveillance that at times his caution verged on paranoia.

McAvoy, the Brink's-Mat team knew, would require particularly careful handling. Early in 1983 he had been arrested after his brother and another man were found with £250,000 of cocaine at Heathrow Airport. A search of various premises then revealed a large number of shotguns and pistols, as well as two chain saws. He was not just an armed robber, police believed, but an underworld armourer as well.

5. Questions and answers

As Black slept after making his statement, Cater and his Flying Squad officers prepared to raid the homes of the three men named by the prisoner. Tony White would be first, followed by McAvoy and Robinson. To ensure that the paths of the suspects would not cross and that they would gain no inkling at first that Black was co-operating with police, they were to be taken to separate police stations well away from Hounslow, where Black was being held.

By now, it must have been clear to the gang that he had been picked up and held for nearly forty-eight hours, but they faced a dilemma. If they stashed the gold and disappeared, it would be seen as clear confirmation that they had been on the raid. It was imperative that they stayed put.

In doing so, they pinned their hopes on two factors. The first was the alibis that they had all taken the precaution of establishing to cover their whereabouts when the raid took place. The second was their belief that Black would not talk. The police could have little on him; he had been treated in exactly the same way as the other guards during the raid, and a mere common-law connection with Robinson hardly constituted grounds on which he could be charged. More important, in the world that he inhabited informing was one of the worst crimes anyone could commit. To do so would mean at best wholesale vilification and at worst becoming a marked man for the rest of his life. But although Black moved in that south-east London criminal milieu, he was never really part of it. He was a petty crook, not a hardened professional whose defiance had been tempered by first-hand experience of police interrogation techniques and long years of staring at the grey wall of a prison cell.

At 6.30 a.m. precisely on the Tuesday morning, eleven days after the bullion robbery, the Flying Squad moved in. Detective Sergeant John Redgrave banged on the door of 45 Redlaw Way, a second-floor flat on the run-down Bonamy council estate in south Bermondsey, a stone's throw from the Old Kent Road. Other Flying Squad detectives and uniformed officers, some armed, covered the front and the back of the house.

White answered the door in his pyjamas, and Redgrave calmly explained that he carried a warrant to search the house for stolen bullion.

'Let me read it,' demanded White, snatching it from the detective's outstretched hand. As he scanned the document, Redgrave moved on to the next formality.

'I am arresting you for the armed robbery at Brink's-Mat.' White made no reply. Police officers pushed past him into the hall and began a systematic search of the house, while Redgrave and the other Flying Squad officers ushered White inside and continued the questioning.

'I understand you have a cream Hillman. Is that right?'

White nodded, and Redgrave asked where it was kept.

'In the garage,' said White, sourly.

Redgrave wanted to know where White's lock-up was, but the burly suspect was uncooperative.

It took nearly two hours to search the house before the detectives finally took White, in handcuffs, out to their squad car. He was driven to Heathrow police station, arriving at 9.50 a.m., put in a cell and left to fret.

Redgrave wanted to arm himself with more information before tackling the prisoner again, so he went off to interview White's wife, Margaret.

*

Some twenty minutes after police raided White, Micky McAvoy was awoken by a knock on the door of his home at 51B Beckwith Road, Herne Hill, a flat in a large, Edwardian house in a smart, tree-lined street. He opened it to find Flying Squad Detective Inspector Tom Glendinning on the doorstep and the house covered front and back by armed police. It was an essential precaution, given their suspicions about McAvoy's role as a supplier of weapons to armed-robbery gangs.

'You are being arrested on suspicion of being concerned in the bullion robbery at Brink's-Mat last Saturday,' said Glendinning.

McAvoy pretended bemusement. 'Leave it out! Where did you say you are from?'

He was taken to Chiswick police station and, like White, was left in the cells to consider his position.

Brian Robinson was the last to be picked up. At 6.55 a.m. Detective Chief Inspector Ken John led the Flying Squad team to the door of 7 Chilham House, Rollins Street, a ground-floor flat on a drab housing estate in Rotherhithe, less than a mile from White's address. The suspect opened up, clad only in his underwear. DCI John ran through the formalities, and Robinson replied, 'Come on in. Look around. I've been half expecting you.' At 9.30 a.m. he was arrested and driven to West Drayton police station.

Just as the arrests were staggered, so too was the questioning of the three new prisoners. Tony White, still in a surly and uncommunicative mood, was the first to be seen, at 2 o'clock that afternoon, at Heathrow police station. The police account of his interrogation was to be hotly disputed at the Old Bailey nearly a year later.

Redgrave, who had arrested him, was busy interviewing Margaret White, so the session was conducted by two other Flying Squad officers, Detective Sergeant Robert Suckling and Detective Constable Michael Charman.

According to witness statements that the detectives later made, the session began at 2 p.m., with White asking the whereabouts of 'the ginger-haired geezer who nicked me this morning'. Told that the officer was seeing White's wife, the prisoner was at first angry, then philosophical. According to the detectives, he replied, 'I've got no problem. She's been nicked before. She'll say nothing.'

Suckling, it is claimed, then outlined to White the reasons why he was being held and asked the prisoner to explain his part in the robbery. From that point on, according to the disputed statements, the prisoner grew increasingly aggressive.

'Like I said this morning, that's bollocks. You've got no evidence, nothing, and you just come round to me on the off-chance, hoping to find something. Now you've turned up a blank, you're fucked. Don't waste my time.'

Suckling asked White why there were groceries in the boot of his car and packed suitcases in his bedroom. He also wanted to know why White's young son was not at home and, intriguingly, why the dustbag was missing from the vacuum cleaner (the search was indeed thorough). His theory was that White had been expecting a visit, so had sent his son away and had cleaned the house to remove any forensic evidence that might have linked him with the raid. White, Suckling believed, had himself been preparing to leave the house when the police called.

'Tony, do you think I look stupid?' asked Suckling. 'You know the score. It seemed obvious to me that things were planned around our visit this morning.'

'No, I don't think you're stupid,' replied the prisoner. 'All I'm saying is that if I sit here with my mouth shut, you haven't got fuck-all. I know that.'

The detective then endeavoured to question the prisoner about his movements on the day of the robbery and the evening before it, drawing the reply that White could not remember what he had done on the Friday and was at home in bed with his wife the next morning when Brink's-Mat was raided.

Suckling listened impassively. There was little point in continuing to beat around the bush – he was getting nowhere. It was time to play the trump card. 'Listen to me and I'll tell you what you are facing,' he said forcefully. 'Tony Black has made a full and frank admission about this robbery and the build-up to it, and he has told us about your part in it and Mick McAvoy's and Brian Robinson's.'

White was incredulous. 'What's he said, for fuck's sake? I don't believe it!'

The next move that the detectives claimed to have made was also later to become a matter of fierce debate. For they maintained that, to prove they weren't lying, White was then shown a copy of Black's statement. He allegedly glanced at the front page but was stopped from reading it all. His response after seeing the document was, the detectives said, categorical.

'What do you think I am, another Tony Black? You've got your grass. I'd die for my mates before I'd shit on them.'

He then, according to police, went on to ask if they had 'nicked the rest' and said he wanted time to think things through in his cell. A contemporaneous note of the interview was allegedly shown to him, but he refused a request to sign it.

There the interview was said to have ended: White had at no stage denied that he had been involved in the Brink's-Mat raid.

At West Drayton police station, five minutes after White's grilling had started, Robinson was cautioned by DCI Ken John. He at first refused to answer any questions unless his solicitor was present. Question after question brought the same refusal, until John decided to call a halt and sent Robinson back to his cell.

The interview resumed shortly before 5 p.m. Skirting around the case itself, the two men discussed a few peripheral points about Robinson's family before John delivered his bombshell. Black had told police 'certain things that incriminate you'. Robinson saw the trap: 'I don't know what he's saying,' was his only reply.

Robinson responded to more general questions about his relationship with his brother-in-law and their fishing trips and, when asked if he had fallen out at any time with Black or had discussed Brink's-Mat with him, he replied, 'No. I don't smack his sister about or anything. I don't owe him any money, and I've never asked him about his work.'

Generally, Robinson confirmed much of what Black had told the police about their relationship, such as his help in finding Black a flat, but he left out the 'naughty bits', just as he had advised the guard to do on the eve of the raid.

Robinson also confirmed his friendship with White and McAvoy, but again he kept his answers brief and innocent. He claimed that on the Friday he had played golf, arriving home shortly after dark, and had stayed in for the rest of the evening. For the day of the robbery he was able to detail his movements from the moment he woke.

He had risen, he claimed, at 6.10 a.m., waking his wife Jennifer in the process, and had driven to his mother's home on the Isle of Sheppey. He had stopped for breakfast at the Little Chef restaurant on the M 2 at roughly 6.50 a.m., filled up at the petrol station and bought a bunch of flowers for his mother, who had been ill with glandular trouble. Arriving at his mother's home at 8 a.m., he had found her sitting in the kitchen, where she made him some tea and they chatted. At one point, he claimed, his mother scolded him for not bringing her grandchild to see her. Robinson's brother Vic, who lived with their mother, then came downstairs. During the journey Robinson had noticed that his radiator was overheating, and Vic agreed to empty it and refill it with anti-freeze. The visit, claimed Robinson, lasted until tea-time, when he returned home.

It was a convincing alibi, and John knew that it had to be partly true, but it was the timing of what Robinson had done that interested him. If he could find a flaw in that, the alibi would crumble.

By then there was little doubt in the detective's mind that he had the right man. Officers who had searched Robinson's home had discovered masking tape similar to that used in the robbery, a Polaroid camera to substantiate Black's story and a knife in the bedside-table drawer. The prisoner dismissed them all. The tape was for keeping paint off carpet edges while decorating, the knife was to deter burglars and – he was emphatic – he had never lent the camera to Black. The interview ended at 6.20 p.m. with Robinson refusing to sign the notes the detectives had taken.

At Chiswick police station DI Glendinning was having an equally frustrating time trying to get something out of McAvoy. The questioning started at 3 p.m., and the detectives tried a technique similar to that used on White and Robinson. After a stream of questions related to the robbery brought no response, they would suddenly drop in mundane questions of little significance in an effort to elicit at least one reply and undermine the prisoner's lack of cooperation. It was a standard technique, with Glendinning asking whether McAvoy wore a hat, and other apparent trivialities. The effort failed, for when at last the prisoner was told that Black was helping police, he made no reply.

Eventually McAvoy did speak, but he seemed as far as ever from cracking. 'I'm completely innocent of these allegations put to me. I've had nothing to do with the Brink's-Mat job, and I would like my solicitor present during these interviews.' Glendinning refused the request.

The interview was stopped for five minutes while the officer making notes went to find a refill for his pen, and when he returned it continued in the same vein. Glendinning's questions met with silence. McAvoy was sent back to the cells.

Later that afternoon, according to police, White was again taken from his cell, this time to be interviewed by the 'ginger-haired geezer', DS Redgrave. While White was to dispute the contents of the first interview, he was to deny that this second one ever took place. What the police account purportedly showed was that, within the space of an hour, White's surly bravado had disappeared, and he was clearly a very worried man.

According to the police account, it began with White asking for more time to consider his position. 'I'm facing the next twenty years away. My boy will be in his twenties by the time I come out. Be reasonable. I need more time. I know I've got choices. What I've got to do is pick the right one.

'Firstly, if I do my bird, the biggest problem ain't you people, it's what the animals on the outside will do to my family to get their hands on the gold, so do I give it up or keep it?

'I don't want to do thirty years . . . I done twelve years the last time. If I give you the gold, the chances are I will do less. If I do, then my mates will think I've grassed and I'm not prepared to risk it, I'm not prepared to do it to my mates. Robbo [Robinson] has been my buddy for years, we went to school together for fuck's sake, and Micky is my best mate. If I do a day's bird less than them, then they'll know I've grassed and I'd rather do the whole thirty years than have them think that. My biggest problem is my wife and boy. I've got to take care of them.'

Then he changed tack slightly. 'What if my wife told you where the gold is – would she get the reward?'

Redgrave, according to the police statements later, would not discuss the question of a reward and turned White's attention to the robbery itself, but White refused to cooperate. He was invited to leave his friends out of it and just relate his part in the robbery.

'What! And give you ammunition to shoot me down? I've never pleaded guilty in my life and I don't intend to start now. I've got to sort out what's best for my family. I can't do that in an hour, you'll have to give me more time.'

Again, claimed the officers, White refused to sign the notes of their conversation and the interview ended.

That evening the detectives compared notes. The three suspects had been in custody for the best part of a day. One had politely denied any wrong-doing; another had been aggressively blunt in his dealings with the police; and the third had maintained a stony silence. The first had a detailed alibi, his wife, his sick mother, and a brother who would have to be interviewed. The second man could bank only on the word of his wife to confirm his Saturday morning lie-in. The prisoner in

Chiswick would not divulge his alibi unless his solicitor was there to hear it.

The police had the detailed confession of a guard who claimed that all three were undoubtedly to blame, but so far the only evidence was circumstantial, and there was not much of that. In addition, all three men had refused to sign the contemporaneous notes of the interviews. They knew that the veracity of the unsigned records could therefore be questioned in court. Any mistakes they may have made, any slips that opened up a chink in their armour, could be dismissed as fabrication. Without signatures at the bottom of each page, all the records so far taken could be denied totally as 'verbals'.

From the police point of view, the pressure was on. There were major holes in the case against each of the men Black had fingered, and the prisoners' solicitors were beginning to object to their continued detention. Soon the men would have to be charged or released.

Somehow Cater's men had to convince the men in the cells that their position was hopeless. There were two possibilities. If the guards were to pick out the robbers at an identity parade, that would be enough to charge them. And if they were all allowed to read Black's statement, perhaps one of them would be prepared to talk in the hope of obtaining a lesser sentence.

Cater decided to authorize identity parades and also instructed his officers to show the suspects Black's confession. Others began checking the details that had so far been forthcoming from Black's account and Robinson's alibi. Then began the lengthy process of taking statements from key-cutting shops in Hounslow High Street, the Little Chef restaurant and the person from whom Robinson claimed to have bought flowers. The relatives of the three prisoners were also to be questioned more closely.

The next morning, Wednesday, the detectives were back to see White at Heathrow police station. D S Suckling walked into the incidents room to find the prisoner already sitting at the table. Opposite him was D C Charman, poised over a wad of paper, ready to take notes. The third interrogation began. Once again what took place was later emphatically denied by White.

Suckling began. 'We left you last night on the understanding that you wanted time to think. Have you any more to tell us about the whereabouts of the gold?'

'Yeah. I've thought about it. I've still got the same choices.'

'You've got to make your mind up which way you go about it.'

'I know. You said last night I might be able to see Black's statement. Have you got it?'

Suckling took a copy of the guard's confession and passed it to White, who read it through once, then asked if he could read it a second time because he had not 'taken it all in'. When he had finished Suckling asked him if he agreed with the contents.

'Yeah. It's more or less right.'

'Has it changed your mind about giving more details about the robbery and, in particular, your part in it?'

'All I'm saying is that it's about right. Don't expect me to put anyone in the frame or give any other details.'

Suckling asked White to confirm that he knew both Robinson and McAvoy, and then he asked the crucial question. 'Is it right that you met with Black in the company of Robinson on a number of occasions to plan the robbery at Brink's-Mat?'

'Yeah,' replied White.

He was asked the same question again, this time with reference to McAvoy. It brought the same response, but yet another attempt by Suckling to persuade White to elaborate on the grudging admissions failed. After several more questions about the earlier stages of the plot, White became impatient.

'Look, mates, sorry for interrupting but what you're saying to me goes back some time. I've told you I agree with the fucking thing [the statement]. Now I can't remember who done what, or where. Can't we leave it at that?'

Suckling refused to let go. He took White forward to the night before the robbery and asked about the meeting in the car park of the Bulldog public house.

White confirmed that it had taken place and again he snapped. 'How many times are we going to go over this?

What do you want me to say? Yes, it is fucking right and, yes, I went on it but that's it. I've told you, no more fucking questions about that thing. What I want to talk about is that gold and what can be done for me, all right?'

'Okay,' replied Suckling. 'What do you want to say?'

'I've thought and I've thought but in the end I'm going mad. I want to give you where the gold is but I don't want to grass anyone up. I'm in a right Catch 22 situation. Can we do a deal?'

White explained that he was uninterested in reward money. What he wanted was to get the 'best deal for me, Micky and Robbo'. If lighter sentences could be agreed for all three, said White, then he 'might be able to get the gold back'. Suckling was concerned. He asked what White meant by 'might', and the prisoner explained that the robbers no longer had control of it. Suckling explained that he could not promise a lighter sentence.

'Right. That's it. I'm saying no more,' said White. 'I've given you what I want. Come back when you've made your minds up.'

Suckling invited White to sign the record of their conversation and again he refused.

'You know my position. When you come back and I can see the other two you might get the gold back but not until then.'

The interview ended at 12.40 p.m. White had smoked two cigarettes and sipped two cups of tea, according to the police record of the interview.

As with his earlier interviews, White would later in court entirely dispute this version of events, claiming that he had been verballed. He said he made repeated requests for his solicitor, none of which was recorded in the police version. He also claimed that he was told that if he didn't confess, he would be 'fitted up', and he denied ever being shown the copy of Black's statement, saying he had never heard of the guard until his name was mentioned by detectives.

That afternoon, at West Drayton police station, Brian Robinson was also handed a copy of his brother-in-law's confession. As he read it, he stopped at intervals to comment on its contents, telling DCI Ken John that the cheque-book fraud Black had referred to was 'not his game' and asking, 'Who's George Stokes?' when he came to the reference to the Rotherhithe murder squad's inquiries at Black's East End flat.

At 3.02 p.m., while still in the middle of reading the statement, Robinson put the document back on the table, looked up at DCI John and caved in.

'Okay, guv. I can see he's done the business on me. Is he going supergrass?'

John explained that Black would be giving evidence against the three men and asked Robinson to read the rest of the confession. He resumed reading but stopped after a few minutes to ask if the other two prisoners had seen the statement. John nodded and Robinson asked what their reaction had been.

'I am not sure. I believe one has put his hands up, but I don't know about the other.'

Robinson wanted to know which one had talked, but John refused to answer, telling him instead to read on. The prisoner seemed incapable of finishing the document. Every few minutes he would lift his head and ask another question.

'Tell me, for my own peace of mind, did it take long to crack him?'

He grasped eagerly at that part of Black's statement which related that he had asked that Robinson should not participate in the raid.

'Look, I never intended to go into the place, not even through the window. See, he's got it here. I told you I didn't go on the job. He confirms my story. All I did was introduce Tony Black to some blokes.' He read on. 'Look! I had nothing to do with the petrol; that was someone else's idea, not mine!' Eventually he finished reading Black's words.

'I can't say anything about the Saturday, guv. Believe me, I wasn't there. The vans and all that, I can't help you with. Look, guv, if I could get the gold back, I would help you. I'm looking at a thirty-year stretch. Do you think I wouldn't help you if I could? It all adds up against me, but, honestly, I was only helping some others who were hard-up. They never expected to get all that gold. We expected a good haul but nothing like that gold. My share was just going to be a drink for the introduction, that's all.'

He admitted checking out the Aer Lingus terminal and asking Black to acquire photographs of Brink's-Mat vans before the Dulwich raid but continued to plead his innocence of the robbery itself.

John tried cold logic on his prisoner. 'You don't honestly expect us to believe that, do you, Brian? The only reason you were not on the job, if that is true, is that you knew you would be seen as a result of your family ties with Black and you therefore had to have a cast-iron alibi, which you appear to have. Tell me what you did on Thursday, 24 November.'

'Can't remember.'

'See what I mean, Brian? You know your precise movements for Saturday, the 26th, but you don't remember Thursday.'

Robinson shrugged his shoulders. 'I've told you my part, and if you don't believe me, forget it. You've told me you can't do me any favours, only I can help myself, so that's what I'm going to do. I don't want to discuss this any more until I've seen my solicitor.'

Robinson was returned to his cell at 4.23 p.m., having refused to sign the record of the interview.

'I'm not saying anything about nothing.'

A night in the cells at Chiswick police station had not softened McAvoy's attitude and DI Glendinning left the room to make a telephone call. It was Wednesday afternoon, and getting any kind of answer out of the prisoner was proving an uphill struggle. When Glendinning returned McAvoy again refused to recount his movements on the days before and after the robbery.

'Look! I've got an alibi and I'll give it to my solicitor when I've been charged.'

Glendinning tried to reason with the prisoner, and when that failed he tried to rattle him with the prospect of an identity parade.

McAvoy's reply was dismissive. 'Get on with it then.'

The detective asked him if his attitude would change if he were picked out by witnesses.

McAvoy maintained his frosty lack of concern. 'I'm innocent. If they pick me out, then they'll have made a mistake, won't they? They'll have got it wrong. I wasn't there.'

He insisted that Black was lying about his involvement and, yes, he had thought about the consequences if charged and convicted. 'For £26 million I'll get thirty years. On a normal robbery it would be eighteen, but for that one, it will be topped up to thirty.'

Glendinning persisted, telling McAvoy that Black had detailed his role in the planning and execution of the raid on the warehouse.

The prisoner reacted flippantly. 'Downstairs I'm reading Harold Robbins. Black should start writing stories like that.'

It was useless continuing, and the interview ended at 3.36 p.m., but Glendinning decided to try again later that night. The battle of wits began at 8.30 p.m. McAvoy was again informed of the wealth of evidence against him, then the detective tried to throw him off his guard.

'Look, we believe you made a basic mistake in not wearing a mask for part of the raid. We intend to hold an identification parade in due course. Two of the guards were well placed to see the man with the gun and the description fits you.'

Then Glendinning played the ace up his sleeve. Black's statement was pushed in front of McAvoy and he was told to read it. McAvoy glanced at the first page, flicked through the rest and read the last sheet.

'Read it all. You'll find it interesting,' said Glendinning.

'I'm not reading that. You read it.'

The detective read it out aloud, and when he had finished he asked McAvoy what he had to say.

'He's got some memory, he has.'

'Is it true then?' said the officer.

There was no response.

'Were you involved in the robbery?' he asked.

McAvoy answered the question with another. 'What are the others saying? Have they seen this?'

McAvoy was still stonewalling, so Glendinning dropped another bombshell in his lap.

'Tony White has accepted his part in the robbery, having read Black's statement, but he has indicated that he wants to have a meeting with you and Robinson to discuss the job and the recovery of the gold. I understand he doesn't want to break any loyalties between you.'

The prisoner was still reluctant to open up, but now he was at least responding to questions. He wanted to know what the police might have offered White in return for his cooperation. Then he asked if White had seen Commander Cater.

'How do you know Mr Cater?' asked Glendinning.

'I spoke to him four years ago.'

'Why are you interested in Mr Cater?'

'Well, if White has seen him, then I want to see him.'

Glendinning grabbed the opportunity to repeat his earlier question. 'So you are admitting, then, that you were involved in the robbery?'

'Can I see Mr Cater?'

'There's no point getting Mr Cater along until we know why.'

'You know why,' said McAvoy.

'No, you tell us.'

'If White's done this, then I might help myself as well.'

'Do you mean you were on the robbery?' asked Glendinning.

'It looks like it or I wouldn't be here, would I?'

'Mick. Were you on the robbery?'

'Yes!'

The detective tried to hammer home further questions, but McAvoy retreated again into his shell, refusing to answer any more questions until he had seen the senior detective.

'How well do you know Mr Cater?' asked Mr Glendinning, hoping to pick up the threads.

'I trust him. I don't trust many of you lot.'

The prisoner got his wish shortly before midnight. Cater and one of his deputies, Chief Superintendent Brown, waved

Glendinning and another detective out of the room. It was McAvoy's request that he see the two chiefs alone. It proved to be a complete waste of time.

McAvoy repeated the questions he had asked his interrogators. He wanted to know what White had said, what deal might have been offered for his cooperation, and then requested a meeting with the other two prisoners.

Cater told him he could not do deals, refused to agree to the meeting and told him: 'McAvoy, you are wasting my time. You asked to see me. If you want to indicate where the gold is, then do so. All I will tell you is that whatever you say about the gold will be dealt with at the highest level. Now it is up to you.'

'I can't help you,' said McAvoy.

In the High Court that day another battle was being fought. Tony White's lawyer, Henry Milner, an engaging public-school-educated man who specializes in representing people accused of serious crimes such as armed robbery, had issued a writ of habeas corpus on behalf of seven people held by police in connection with the raid. They were Tony White and his wife Margaret, Micky McAvoy and his wife Jacqueline, Mrs Patricia Dalligan, who lived at 7 Tarves Way, the house where Black claimed the plot had been discussed, and her sons, Stephen, 23, and Mark, 17.

Victor Durand, QC, read to the court a sworn statement by Milner that, in effect, challenged the police to charge the prisoners or release them. At that time the law did not define clearly how long police were allowed to hold suspects in custody without a charge unless it was under the Prevention of Terrorism Act. It stated simply that for a serious offence a person should be brought before a court as soon as was practicable. (Since then the provisions of the Police and Criminal Evidence Act have tightened up the rules, so that today a suspect can be held for only thirty-six hours without charge; then he must be taken before a magistrate. If at that time police are not ready to prefer charges, they must apply for an extension of the time limit.)

Durand informed the judge, Mr Justice Taylor, that all seven prisoners had been denied their right to legal advice, and Milner's statement read that he had repeatedly asked for access to the prisoners but had been stopped from seeing them by the Flying Squad.

When counsel representing Scotland Yard replied that the habeas corpus action would be defended, the case was adjourned until the next morning, but it never re-opened. At 9.30 that night White was charged, followed by Robinson and McAvoy. The others were released. The next morning the three defendants were brought to Feltham magistrates' court and remanded in custody on the charge of stealing gold and other valuables worth £26 million.

The first of the identity parades took place the following Friday, 9 December, at Ealing police station. The first witnesses arrived shortly before lunch. The guards, Scouse and Clarke, were shown into the first-floor superintendent's office to await the identity parades. The blinds were drawn on the windows, and uniformed officers were in attendance to ensure that none of the witnesses caught a glimpse of the prisoners before the parades. Robin Riseley arrived soon afterwards, and at 1 p.m. Bentley and Holliday joined the group.

Downstairs Robinson, McAvoy and White were being held in separate cells. They had each been given the standard form, 620, on which to sign their agreement to taking part in the line-up. Brian Robinson's solicitor expressed his reservations. His client had attended a football match and a wedding reception at which Brink's-Mat guards had been present. He believed the guards about to be called in could recognize Robinson from those events but might mistakenly believe that they remembered him from the raid. After some discussion, however, Robinson agreed to take part.

The first parade was held at 4 p.m. in the charge room, where the lighting was good. Robinson was asked if he objected to any of the nine men chosen to stand beside him and said no.

The prisoner took up his position, fourth from the left, and Holliday was brought into the room. He had been instructed that he was not to touch or point to anyone unless he could be certain that the man he was picking out had been one of the robbers.

Walking from left to right he inspected the line of faces, and then asked each participant in turn to repeat the words he had heard that morning from the robber who had told him to 'shut it' in a loud voice. He followed that by asking each man to bare his top teeth. There was another slow walk down the line, then he turned to the police officer with him and said he could not be certain. Each man was then asked to put on a hat similar to the one worn by the raider he had known as the Bully, but it was hopeless.

Five minutes later Bentley was led into the room. The guard didn't walk immediately up to the line but stood back, peering at each face for about three minutes. Then he walked behind for a rear view, and requested that each man don the hat similar to the one worn by the Bully. Each man was then asked to repeat the words 'Get down on the fucking floor'. After another long look he turned to the police officer and shook his head. 'No, sorry.'

It was the same for Clarke. 'No, I can't identify anyone.'

The fourth guard was Robin Riseley, the man who had been so terrorized by the robbers when he couldn't remember the combination of the safes. As soon as he entered the room, he turned to Inspector Hughes.

'I think one of them is here.'

'Who are you referring to? Touch the person,' said the officer.

Riseley walked up to Robinson and tapped him on the shoulder.

'This one,' he replied, identifying the robber the guards had known as the Boss.

Robinson stayed silent. One guard out of four had identified him and there was still another one to come. Scouse came into the room, walked slowly up and down the line, asked each man to say, 'Are you all right, Mick?' and then touched someone two places to the left of Robinson. The prisoner was taken back to his cell.

Attempts to find enough men who resembled White and McAvoy failed and the parades were postponed until the next day. Before he left, Henry Milner requested that his client White be allowed to exercise in the yard outside, handcuffed if necessary. Hughes passed the request on to DI Glendinning, who refused. He believed it possible that subsequent allegations could be made that witnesses might have seen the prisoner exercising.

By the following day, however, enough candidates had been found to fill the McAvoy line-up, and at 6 p.m. he was given a new form 620 to sign. It was after 6.30 p.m. when the first witness walked into the charge room. McAvoy, wearing a red pullover, had elected to stand on the far right-hand side of the line, in which each man was holding a large card with a letter of the alphabet on it.

Holliday was the first guard again. He asked the men to wear the hat, walked from left to right and stopped at McAvoy.

'This is the one,' he said touching McAvoy's shoulder. The Bully had been found.

Bentley came next. He viewed them from behind, then requested that they each wear the hat and say, 'Get fucking down.' He reached the end of the line, and McAvoy repeated the phrase.

'That's the gentleman I heard on the day,' said Bentley.

Scouse and Clarke failed to identify anyone, but Riseley was as emphatic as he had been the night before. He walked quickly from left to right and, placing his hand on McAvoy's shoulder, said, 'I am making a positive identification.'

At the end McAvoy was asked in front of his solicitor if he wished to comment on the conduct of the parade.

'No,' he said. 'Only that the witnesses who have identified me have made a terrible mistake. I am completely innocent of this charge.'

Again the police had trouble finding men of White's build to line up with him on an identity parade, or men whom his solicitor found acceptable for that purpose, and it was not until two weeks later, on 20 December, that the security guards reassembled at Ealing police station.

Milner at once objected to the line-up that had been selected, saying the chosen eight did not resemble his client at all. By this time the police felt their repeated attempts to find a suitable cast had gone far enough, for each time it involved elaborate security arrangements. Inspector Gareth Hughes, who was in charge, patiently but firmly insisted that they continue.

'I informed Mr Milner that his client would be submitted to a form of identification whether it be by way of a formal parade, an informal one (i.e. by persons mingling) or, failing that, by a confrontation between his client and witnesses, when each witness would be asked, "Is this the man?"'

Milner made a detailed complaint. He said that it would have been easy to arrange a parade in prison, where enough men could be found who resembled White, but he was reluctantly agreeing to the 'mingling' method because both the parade and confrontation methods were unfair to his client. White and fifteen other men formed up in a horseshoe in the charge room; White stood second from the left. One after the other the guards filed into the room and one by one they failed to identify White. Even the previously emphatic Riseley was unsure of himself.

'I'm sorry. I can't make a positive identification.'

6. Ironsides

Nicknames abound in criminal patois, and Anthony Black had earned both of those attributed to him. Reporters eagerly awaited the trial of the 'Golden Mole'. It guaranteed a raft of good stories and, once those were over, they could run carefully researched or outrageously hyped-up background articles free of the constraints of *sub judice* and contempt of court.

To the police, however, Black was 'Ironsides', a not entirely accurate description of the bullet-proof vest he wore at all times outside his cell. This was not melodrama; the word out on the street was that someone, somewhere, was willing to pay £50,000 to shut him up for good. The police had to take the threat of a contract killing seriously. Ironsides had turned Queen's evidence and, despite the length and intensity of the police investigation his evidence played a crucial part in the prosecution case against the three suspected armed robbers.

With £26 million in gold at stake, not to mention the prospect of sentences lasting into old age for anyone directly involved in the raid, no senior officer at New Scotland Yard was going to take unnecessary risks with the star witness. Prison was out of the question while he awaited trial for his part in the raid. Even in solitary confinement in a top-security unit he would still be at risk. Hard drugs are peddled in prison: why not lives? Instead Ironsides was remanded in custody in a bomb-proof police cell normally reserved for terrorists at Paddington Green police station, close to London's West End. His wife, meanwhile, received around-the-clock protection. Punishment for Black was a judicial formality. It was evident that he was not a hardened criminal, while his cooperation, Scotland Yard detectives believed, had proved vital in enabling them to arrest three members of the most savage and professional armed-robbery gang in London. Less than three months after the Brink's-Mat raid Black was driven at high speed, in an unmarked car, to the Old Bailey. There, on 17 February 1984, in the amount of time it takes to hear a shoplifting case, he was arraigned, the case against him was outlined and he was sentenced.

Black, who sat in the dock flanked on either side by prison officers, naturally enough had pleaded guilty, then prosecutor Timothy Cassel outlined the details of the raid, describing it as 'highly organized, ruthless and enormously lucrative'. Commander Cater then informed the Common Serjeant, the late Judge David Tudor-Price, that the prisoner had confessed and was prepared to give evidence against those he had implicated when they appeared in court.

After less than an hour in court Black was sentenced to six years' imprisonment. With remission for good behaviour he would not serve more than four years and was likely to get parole after just two. The sentence was accompanied by a grim warning from Tudor-Price: 'Never again will your life be safe. In custody you will be segregated at all times, and you and your family will for ever be fugitives from those you so stupidly and so wickedly helped.'

Cater then told the court that, for the prisoner's own safety, he would prefer that Black spent the time leading up to the trial of the three alleged robbers in police custody rather than prison. The detective chief was utterly determined that nothing would stop Black from giving evidence when the time came – neither the tight regime of a prison, which can sap a man's resolve, nor intimidatory approaches from other prisoners.

The application, which had been sanctioned at a senior level after talks between Deputy Assistant Commissioner Kelland and the Home Office, was readily granted.

Before a case goes to trial before a jury it has to be heard by a magistrate, who decides whether there is a prima facie case to answer. In many cases the defence do not contend otherwise and the case is committed without evidence being heard. When a defendant intends to plead not guilty, however, the defence are entitled at the committal stage to call for the prosecution to produce evidence, although the prosecution are under no obligation to do so. Such a request is particularly likely if evidence from an accomplice of the accused forms part of the prosecution case. For the defence want to see what the witness intends to say and establish whether he is really prepared to go through with giving evidence. In such cases the prosecution generally agree that the witness should be heard, for they too want to be certain that he is still prepared to cooperate when faced with those against whom he is to testify.

It was on 1 May 1984, at just such a committal hearing, that Black first came face to face with the three men who, he claimed, had been part of the robbery gang. Such was the security that the hearing had to be moved from Feltham magistrates' court, the closest to the Brink's-Mat warehouse, and transferred to Lambeth magistrates' court, the heavily fortified south London court house where most committals for major crimes in London, ranging from gangland murders to terrorist attacks, are heard.

Black, who had left his police cell still wearing his bullet-proof vest and flanked by armed police officers, was naturally the star witness. As he spoke, Robinson, White and McAvoy sat quietly, shaking their heads occasionally and turning once or twice to smile at family members in the public gallery or whisper denials to their solicitors and barristers. The hearing, they knew, could prove crucial if they were to have any prospect of acquittal. On one level it might have appeared a mere curtain raiser for the full-blooded trial to come, but it was also an opportunity for their lawyers to probe for weaknesses in the prosecution case in the hope of finding a thread to pull on that might unravel the entire case against them. It could be a mere technicality, or it could be some confounding blunder by the police. Whatever it might be, they lived in hope.

On the first day no such opportunity arose for their highly paid legal representatives to go into action, but the second offered the first indication that the Flying Squad's investigation was not necessarily flawless. A vital piece of evidence against one of the robbers was suddenly found to be missing. When Tony White had been lifted by the Flying Squad and taken to Heathrow police station he had been interviewed several times. The first had been a surly show of bravado, liberally sprinkled with obscenities. During the second White had appeared to soften, and by the third he seemed to be a beaten man contemplating spending the rest of his 'active' life in prison. It was then, police claimed, that D S Suckling, acting on instructions from Commander Cater, had allowed White to read Black's statement in the hope that the detail would shake him into confessing.

At the committal proceedings Suckling told the court that White had twice read through the statement by Black and had turned the last page with the words 'Yeah, it's more or less right.' The detective had then entered the copy of the statement as an exhibit, marked R S/1.

Now White was denying he had ever been shown the statement and therefore could not have said the words attributed to him. His Q C, John Mathew, the foremost defence lawyer in the land, who twenty years earlier had defended one of the Great Train Robbers and had gone on to become first senior prosecuting counsel at the Old Bailey before reverting to better-paid defence work, asked the prosecution to produce exhibit R S/1. It was, after all, the only material proof with which the police could possibly corroborate the verbal evidence, and Mathew wanted to have the document checked for White's fingerprints. But the next day in court the prosecution was forced to admit the exhibit had been mislaid.

It was a serious oversight for the prosecution. If the exhibit could not be found, then it would be White's word against those of the detectives and Black. Given that none of the guards had identified White in the identity parade, the case against him could be seriously weakened. Mathew had found the weakness that he intended to exploit at a later date.

By the end of the hearing, however, the magistrate was satisfied that the cases against all three defendants were sound enough to send them for trial, and they were committed to the Old Bailey. The remand period would be spent in custody.

Soon after the remand detectives began hearing rumours that McAvoy had no intention of going for trial. Whispers reached them that a gun was to be smuggled in to help him escape, and overnight he was transferred from his overcrowded Brixton prison cell to Winchester jail. There stringent restrictions were placed on his visiting rights. His brother Tony claimed that he was being held in solitary confinement, that his daily visits had been reduced from fifteen to ten minutes' duration and that all his conversations were monitored by three prison guards. The only respite was each Sunday, when he was allowed to see his girlfriend and sister alone.

In protest, McAvoy went on a hunger strike, and by mid-June his brother was claiming that he had shed 2½ stones and was losing his sight in one eye. 'He is prepared to die rather than remain in Winchester jail,' his brother declared. In the event, such a drastic course proved unnecessary. His solicitor, Henry Milner, took the Home Office to the High Court and demanded a judicial review of the circumstances in which he was being detained. The judicial review was not granted, but two weeks later McAvoy was returned to a London prison, and by the time he appeared at the Old Bailey at the end of October, nearly a year after the raid, he had regained the weight he had lost.

On Monday, 25 October, the three prisoners were brought before Judge David Tudor-Price at the Central Criminal Court to answer two counts each, those of conspiring to commit robbery and of robbery itself. All three pleaded not guilty, and the jury was sworn in to await the first witness, Anthony Black.

His evidence lasted nearly two and a half days and was

punctuated with outbursts from the public gallery and warnings from the judge that the public would be cleared from the court if the disturbances continued. Next to be called were the other guards who had been in the warehouse during the robbery. Then it was the turn of a woman by the name of Penelope Dossantos who, a week after the raid, had driven past Unit 7 and seen a police notice asking drivers to report if they remembered seeing anything suspicious the previous Saturday. She certainly had, she told police. At 8 a.m. on the morning of the raid, she had been driving along Green Lane, Hounslow, and had noticed a white estate car coming out of the industrial estate. She had slowed down in case it pulled out in front of her, but instead it had simply halted at the junction, apparently waiting for something. Suddenly, as her own vehicle approached, the estate car surged forward, followed by a blue Transit van, their tyres screeching as the heavily laden vehicles ground their spinning wheels into the tarmac. Save for passing irritation at the manner in which they cut in front of her, Mrs Dossantos had thought no more about the incident until she saw the police notice. Now she repeated to the jury what she had seen.

Mrs Dossantos was followed into the witness box by DS Suckling and a number of the other investigating officers until soon it became apparent, as the defending barristers questioned and cajoled, jockeying for an opening that might shoulder aside the prosecution, that the cases against Robinson and McAvoy were gathering pace but the evidence against White was simply not staying the distance. Suckling in particular had a hard time in the witness box when questioned about Exhibit RS/1.

The pointers to White's involvement were individually flimsy. The guards had failed to identify him, so all that was left was Black's confession, plus the copy he, White, was alleged to have seen, coupled with his disputed verbal admissions and the fact that he owned a Hillman estate car similar to that sighted by Mrs Dossantos. But even there the prosecution were not having an easy time. Mrs Dossantos, the wife of a car-body worker, had been shown White's car in a police pound and had told detectives she recognized it from markings she saw on its side when it pulled out in front of her. When asked in court to identify the vehicle again from photographs taken by police, however, it became apparent that detectives had photographed only one side of the vehicle – the side she could not have seen on the morning of the raid. In the witness box she was unable to make a positive identification based on the photograph.

Now document RS/1 still could not be produced and the court room buzzed with speculation about its provenance and its whereabouts. The prosecution had leant heavily on the fact that White had seen it and had commented after reading it. Detectives presenting suspects with the confessions of alleged accomplices know that if they agree to read the statement, it can be adopted as evidence against them, whether they sign it or not. If a suspect ignores such a confession, its allegations are worthless because they are made by a co-conspirator who, like Black, could be shown to have gained considerably by implicating others.

A signature on such an exhibit, however, is unnecessary, for every page can be tested for fingerprints that would show if a suspect did indeed touch it and therefore read it. Naturally enough, when the prosecution failed to produce the document the defence, who had questioned, even at the committal hearing, whether the document had ever existed, argued that the police could not produce R S/1 because fingerprint tests would show that White had never picked it up to read it. This mistake by the prosecution allowed the defence to home in, arguing further that if White never saw the statement, the words attributed to him were concocted. The defence was not pulling its punches. It was accusing the Flying Squad of framing White.

Commander Cater gave evidence for the prosecution in an attempt to explain the loss of RS/1. He had, he said, ordered the destruction of all copies of Black's confession after the three robbers had been charged, for 'security reasons', and with hindsight, he said, he realized he had been mistaken.

But Mathew was not so easily persuaded. So far he had cast doubt on the police story that White had seen and read the statement. Now he questioned whether the interview at which police were supposed to have produced it had ever, in fact, taken place.

The defence demanded to see the Occurrence Book from Heathrow police station where White had been held and questioned. It would show if the third interview, at which White was supposed to have read the Black confession, was fact or fiction. If the seeds of doubt had already been planted in the jury's collective mind, they must have germinated with the next revelation. Inexplicably, the Heathrow police station Occurrence Book, an important log that has to be strictly kept to account for the movement and treatment of persons in custody, as well as other matters, had disappeared.

It is possible that the jury had already made up its mind that there was enough doubt to suggest White's innocence when the third week of evidence began with White himself in the witness box to open the defence. By the time he and more than twenty defence witnesses had been called, the jury had listened to seventeen days of evidence and spent nearly four weeks under armed guard. There followed sixteen hours of summing up by defence and prosecution counsels before Judge Tudor-Price was ready to marshal the facts and the complex legal arguments and to present a reliable summation upon which the jury could confidently reach a decision.

Tudor-Price began summing up on the morning of Wednesday, 28 November. He explained to the jury that he would be dividing the case into five parts. The first would be the robbery itself and the 'uncontroversial' testimony of the 'five honest guards'. That would be followed by his consideration of Anthony Black's confessed involvement. Parts three, four and five would deal with the case against each of the accused.

Tudor-Price quickly presented the guards' testimony, tracing a coherent picture of the raid, in which Black figured largely as the 'traitor', McAvoy as the Bully and Robinson the Boss, before moving into the next stage of his summary, the star witness, Anthony Black.

'His conduct was disgraceful,' observed the judge. 'Now he

hopes for an early release, even for only two years as a result of parole, but it is to be observed that his punishment may not cease then, for I dare say he will be physically unsafe for many years to come, both for himself and for his close relatives. I say that whether or not he has told the truth in this court. He has either committed the unforgivable sin of being a grass on his fellows, or he has made false accusations against people who, either themselves or through friends and acquaintances, may not be very pleased with Black.'

Tudor-Price quickly got to the point; there are obvious dangers in convicting on the evidence of an accomplice, he said, if it stands alone against a defendant. An accomplice, he continued, may have many reasons of his own for telling a story that is wholly or partly false – self-interest, malice, the settlement of old scores, a desire to excuse himself at the expense of others or, as was suggested during the trial, to protect the whereabouts of the gold and the identity of the 'real' robbers.

In his advice to the jury the judge asked it to consider first if Black's evidence was believable and, if so, to consider next evidence from other sources that confirmed his testimony. He adjourned the court for a short time to let his words sink in, then recalled the jury to hear his account of the evidence for and against the defendants.

There had been submissions from the defence that if one was to be found not guilty, the case against all three must be thrown out of court; after all, if one of the three men Black had named and identified was considered by a jury to be innocent, then surely the case against the remaining two must be tainted also. Tudor-Price was unconvinced by that argument. He told the jury to weigh the evidence against each man in isolation before considering the links between them.

Dealing first with Black's brother-in-law, Robinson ('the Colonel'), Tudor-Price recalled the evidence given by Black's family in favour of Robinson and against the 'errant' son who had grassed. He sympathized with Jennifer Robinson, whose brother's testimony seemed certain to lead to a lengthy jail sentence for the father of her son.

'She was in a most unenviable position; the strain upon that lady of giving evidence was quite apparent to us all. But she spoke of no quarrel and no enmity between Tony [Black] or Brian Robinson, so the question must be: what caused Tony Black to tell the police that Robinson was involved in planning the robbery? The Crown say he told it because it was true. Why else, when he must have known that his accusation would cause great distress to his family and harm to his sister Jennifer? On the other hand, the defence say Robinson was the name put to him and he seized upon it.'

Tudor-Price reminded the jury that Black's own family found him less than reliable. His first wife, Vivien, had been called by the defence and had told the court that Black was 'not a truthful person'. Even his mother said, 'Until his father died he was a good boy. After that he was unreliable and untruthful.'

'First in the case against Robinson is the evidence of his brother-in-law, Black, challenged in cross-examination and his credit generally attacked,' said Tudor-Price. 'We come then to the next piece of evidence, which is both capable of corroborating Black's evidence and also capable of standing on its own as proof of guilt, if believed, namely his identification by Riseley as the "cool boss".' The judge reminded the jury that Robinson had not kept his face covered at all times during the raid and Riseley had twice caught a glimpse of his features. But it was not the only evidence amassed by the police that the jury might consider damning.

First, Robinson's own wife, having signed a statement giving him an alibi for the evening before the robbery – she said he had stayed home all night and therefore could not have gone to the rendezvous with Black and the others at the Bulldog pub – had later made a statement declaring that she could not remember whether her husband had been home that night or not. Robinson's alibi for the morning of the robbery had involved an early start. He had, he claimed, driven to his mother's home on the Isle of Sheppey. On the way he had met a stranger and chatted briefly to him. The defence had traced the man through a private detective agency and Mr Ernie Stallan had given evidence corroborating Robinson's alibi – that he was at the Little

Chef on the Dover Road at Cobham when he was said to be participating in the robbery. But Stallan's evidence had been questioned by the prosecution, as Tudor-Price now reminded the jury. Stallan, he said, 'as recently as this October [1984] was using the false name of Barnes on one occasion and John Barnett on another'.

In concluding his review of the evidence against Robinson, Tudor-Price said to the jury, 'You have Black's evidence; you have the purported identification by Riseley; you have the alleged confession . . . to the police. On the other hand, you have the alibi put forward that he was at home on Friday night and he was at his mother's on Saturday . . . Is it proved by the Crown so that you are sure that he was on the robbery?'

Next Tudor-Price turned his attention to McAvoy – the Bully. Again, in addition to Black's confession, there was the evidence of identification not only by Riseley now but also by two more guards, Bentley and Holliday. All three picked him out on the identity parade, and Riseley and Holliday had constructed photofit pictures of McAvoy which bore striking resemblances to each other. 'In the [photofit] kit there is a choice of eighty-four different noses and ninety-four different mouths, and both Holliday and Riseley happened to pick the same mouth and the same nose,' said Tudor-Price.

As Robinson before him had contested the police accounts of his interrogation, so too had McAvoy, the judge recalled. McAvoy had denied ever calling Commander Cater in the hope of striking a deal and claimed that the third session of questioning had been fabricated by the police. Tudor-Price summed up the dispute over the interrogations in unequivocal terms. 'There is hard lying going on in this case, by one side or the other, and, of course, it involves a great number of witnesses . . . lying for the Crown or lying on behalf of the defence.'

The judge said that as far as the prosecution was concerned, McAvoy's alibi certainly involved hard lying. He had claimed that over the weekend of the raid his car had been booked into a garage to have an engine rattle repaired and he relied on minicabs to get around. The drivers of two cabs he had used, one on the Friday night and the other on the Saturday morning, swore on oath that McAvoy had been travelling in their vehicles at the times when he was supposed to be at the Bulldog pub rendezvous and on the robbery itself. The prosecution claimed that a log-book produced to back up the claim of the first driver was a forgery – it showed trips made to a school during a half-term holiday – while they were able to demonstrate that an invoice produced by the second driver had been clumsily altered to fit the alibi. 'The Crown . . . say there are signs of obvious concoction which poison the whole part of this evidence,' said Tudor-Price.

The final piece of evidence in support of McAvoy's alibi was also strenuously challenged by the prosecution. McAvoy claimed that he had left his home at the time the robbery was taking place at Heathrow to take a minicab to Chislehurst to collect his car. A painter and decorator he had employed was working on his house that morning and, on returning, McAvoy had paid him £300 for his work. In court the decorator stated that he had given McAvoy a receipt for the cash, which he produced as evidence. During cross-examination, however, the decorator had been forced to concede that the notepaper on which the receipt was written had not been printed until May or June 1984, six months or more *after* it was supposed to have been issued.

Tudor-Price was later to order a police investigation into possible perjury offences during the Brink's-Mat trial, but now he turned to the inconclusive and controversial evidence against Tony White. Like Robinson and McAvoy, White had contested the police evidence that he had been shown the Black statement and denied that he had responded with words that could be considered a partial confession. But, unlike Robinson and McAvoy, he had not been identified by the guards, and an important piece of documentary evidence in police hands, RS/1, could not be produced. Furthermore, Black had said it was White who, with Robinson, had driven him to his new flat in Ben Jonson Road five years earlier, but the defence was able to show that White had been in prison at that time. And during the trial a further crucial piece of evidence against him was challenged by his own parole officer. Black, in his confession to the police and later during cross-examination, had described White as clean-shaven on some eight occasions that he met him during the time leading up to the raid. Yet during that same period White's parole officer had observed on at least one occasion that White had a full naval beard. Indeed, he had made a note of it on White's file.

Tudor-Price brought to an end two days of careful and thoughtful summing up on Thursday, 29 November, at 10.42 a.m. 'Members of the jury,' said the judge, 'in this case allegations have flown thick and fast, and it is for you to decide which ones have substance.'

He recalled the jury at 4.59 p.m., asking whether it was close to reaching a decision. If not, he would adjourn the court. 'I am anxious you should not become tired in the long deliberations that are obviously necessary,' he told them. The foreman explained that all felt they needed more time to consider their verdict. 'Well, we will therefore provide overnight accommodation. We have all the necessary equipment, toothbrushes, shaving gear and so on . . . I think it would be desirable if, after you leave the court, you cease to consider the matter because there is danger of becoming tired and stale.'

The court was adjourned until 10.15 the next morning, but the jury had still not reached a decision by lunchtime. Tudor-Price recalled it, for two minutes only, to ask the members to notify him if they felt their deliberations were likely to involve another overnight stay, and the jury duly returned at 5.02 p.m. to report its inability so far to reach a decision.

It was 2.19 p.m. on Saturday when the jury returned, having been out for more than two days. It was obvious that the members had failed to reach a unanimous verdict, and they sought guidance on reaching a majority verdict. The judge informed them that if it was impossible for all twelve to agree, the court could accept a verdict of ten to two or eleven to one for a verdict of guilty or not guilty – anything else would lead to acquittal. The jury retired once again; again it required more time.

The case dragged on into Sunday, and Tudor-Price, believing it possible that the jury might never reach a verdict acceptable to the court, prepared himself for the prospect of discharging the jury and calling for a retrial. At 2.33 p.m. he called the jury before him and told it: 'If there comes a time when agreement is not possible, then please say so. Do not feel you must go on beyond the limit of what is reasonable.' At 2.35 p.m. the jury retired for the last time and, forty-four minutes later, returned with its verdict.

The jury foreman was asked for his verdict on White first, and the answer was direct: not guilty. McAvoy and Robinson, however, were guilty of robbery. All verdicts were delivered with a majority of ten to two.

Tudor-Price adjourned the court after the verdicts were delivered, as it was thought disrespectful to sentence prisoners on the Sabbath. White, meanwhile, had been discharged immediately, after a year in custody, and had left the court in a Mercedes. He apologized to reporters for having no comment to make. Next morning he was recovering from his celebrations when Robinson and McAvoy were brought before Tudor-Price.

'You and I know the sentence in this case must be very heavy,' the judge told the prisoners. 'There are three reasons for that: the first is that this was a highly planned, sophisticated robbery; the second is that a petrol solution was poured over the guards in order to terrify them; and the third is that the haul was the enormous sum of £26 million worth of gold. The sentence must be sufficient to indicate to all that a robbery of this kind is not worth it. In the circumstances I do not see any distinction between the pair of you. The sentence on you both will be the same, and it is one of twenty-five years' imprisonment.'

Without parole, Robinson (aged 41) would be 66 when due for release and McAvoy (aged 33) 58. Yet both men replied to the sentences with a simple and polite 'Thank you.' At home, hearing of the sentences, White at last broke his silence: 'If I'm innocent, then the other two are innocent. The evidence was the same for all of us. None of the three of us were involved. The reason the police pulled us in was because they've wanted us for a long time, and were waiting for something like this to get to us.'

The last word in the Brink's-Mat robbery trial was the judge's direction that the papers be handed to the DPP to consider if there was evidence of perjury or attempts to pervert the course of justice by the two minicab drivers and the decorator who had supported McAvoy's alibi with false documentation. For Black, Robinson, McAvoy and White the Brink's-Mat job was over. For the police it was just beginning.

7. Follow that Rolls!

'Gold: Precious yellow non-rusting malleable ductile metallic element of high specific gravity, used as a fundamental monetary medium'. The *Concise Oxford English Dictionary* doesn't quite capture the magic of the word, nor its ability to fascinate and corrupt. For 6,000 years it has been hewn from veins of quartz and pyrites and panned from rivers and streams. Today those nations lucky enough to count it as a major resource – South Africa, the USSR, Canada, the United States, Brazil and Australia – mine the precious commodity with relentless efficiency. Even in countries where the amounts to be found don't warrant a highly technical approach, gold fever is just as strong.

Only in the last of the sixty centuries that it has been sought have gold's chemical properties been put to uses other than coinage and jewellery. These days it is an essential ingredient in dentistry and the hi-tech industries, providing high electrical conductivity in printed circuits and improving the tonal image of photographic film.

But such is its rarity that even now 90 per cent of all the gold ever produced, estimated to amount to some 2,000 million ounces, can still be accounted for. Forty-five per cent lies in central banks, such as the Bank of England and the Bundesbank in West Germany, where it is kept as a guarantee of economic stability for the governments in question. The Old Lady of Threadneedle Street, for instance, never lets her reserves drop below 500,000 kilogrammes. Another 25 per cent of the world's gold is in private hands – those of either powerful international conglomerates or hugely wealthy individuals – while the remaining 20 per cent has been used in jewellery, religious artefacts and dentistry.

Even the 10 per cent that is missing has not vanished without trace. Much of it is stuck in a time warp, entombed on the ocean's floor in sunken galleons and more modern ships, victims of either the elements or marine warfare, where it waits to be rediscovered.

There was one thing Commander Cater was sure of. The 3 tons, or nearly 250,000 ounces, of Brink's-Mat gold was unlikely to vanish into any kind of time warp. At some stage, probably sooner rather than later, the robbers would seek to cash in their haul by reintroducing it on to the open market. And that necessary course of action could only increase the gang's chances of detection.

Cater was aware that in recent years a large number of London's major criminals had become very familiar indeed with the working of the gold market. The precious metal had become a favourite commodity with which to swindle the British government out of value-added tax (V A T), a 15 per cent premium levied on a variety of goods, including gold, when they are sold. Paid at that time by the buyer to the person selling the gold, it should then have been returned to HM Customs and Excise.

A variety of scams, however, had grown up to deprive the taxman of his share. One was to smuggle gold into the country, then sell it to a reputable dealer. The 15 per cent he would pay as tax would then be pocketed by the smugglers. Another was to draw up documents showing that the gold been exported immediately after its arrival in Britain, which meant it was not liable for V A T. The honest trader, meanwhile, would still have to pay 15 per cent V A T to the 'company' selling him the metal. That 'company', usually based in short-let office accommodation, would fold within a matter of months without making any V A T returns.

Although similar scams could have been worked on other goods that were subject to V A T, gold was particularly suitable because its high value meant large returns with a minimum of delay. It also had an official price, fixed twice daily by the London gold market, so the smugglers did not have to worry about commercial competitors undercutting their prices, and it was compact and easy to transport. At that time V A T frauds in general had one further major attraction – the maximum penalty for indulging in the racket was a paltry two years' imprisonment. Small wonder then, that V A T fraud involving gold had grown increasinly popular among the well-organized, more professional type of criminal.

Cater knew that the first problem the robbers would face was how to disguise the true origin of the ingots and remove identification numbers and assay marks. The Johnson Matthey ingots, for instance, carried an oval hallmark enclosing a hammer and a pick, a set of figures (either 9999 or 999) to signify their purity and, in some cases, a serial number. Absolutely pure gold just does not exist – some contamination is always present, however expertly the metal is refined: 9999 bars are 99.99 per cent pure, the highest level to which the metal can be refined, while 999 bars, known at Johnson Matthey as ten-tola bars (a *tola* being an ancient Indian unit of weight), are only marginally less perfect.

Cater also believed that, as well as removing the identifying marks, it was a safe bet that the robbers, or the receivers to whom they sold, would have to disguise the purity of the bars. Failure to do so would create too great a risk that legitimate traders would quickly become suspicious that the quantities they were being asked to buy were either smuggled gold or stolen bullion.

This alchemy in reverse would require specialized smelting equipment, the sort sold by only a handful of shops in Britain, most of them in the Hatton Garden area of central London, internationally renowned as a centre for the jewellery trade. Such shops were periodically reminded to be on their guard against suspicious customers ordering smelters, and in the days that followed the Brink's-Mat raid Flying Squad officers repeated the warning as a matter of routine.

It was seventeen days after the robbery when through the doors of Charles Cooper Ltd of Hatton Garden walked an amiable Londoner in his late thirties, stocky and running slightly to plump. Introducing himself as Mr Fielding, he told company director Allan Duncan that he wanted to buy a large smelter and would take delivery straight away.

It was an unusual request, and Duncan patiently explained that the largest smelter they sold, which cost £1,047.71, could not be bought off the shelf. It would have to be ordered and would take a week or two to deliver.

The customer, however, was in a hurry. He couldn't wait that long and would have to try elsewhere. In vain Duncan warned that the competition would give him the same reply. There just wasn't that much call for Alcosa GF080/2 WPG gas-and-air blasting smelters capable of liquefying up to 36 kilos of gold at a time.

The customer, however, contented himself with buying a heat-resistant pot, four bottles of acid for testing precious metals and a set of scales before walking out to try elsewhere.

The following day, the Cooper director allowed himself a smug smile of satisfaction when he saw the round frame of Mr Fielding push through the door. No, he had not been able to get the smelter off the shelf and, yes, he would like Duncan to order him one. Fielding, however, would collect it from the manufacturer and avoid the usual delivery delay. After counting out the price in ready cash, the chubby Cockney then gave an address in London Road, Sidcup, an area of south-east London. The address, like the name Fielding, was false. Duncan didn't know that, but even so he had already decided there was something distinctly odd going on. As the door closed behind the impatient client with the wad of cash in his pocket, Duncan reached for the telephone and dialled the number he had been given by the young detective who had asked him to report anything suspicious.

One week later Flying Squad detective sergeants Daniel Conway and Bill Miller were sitting in an unmarked car and keeping watch at the small factory of William Allday & Co. The sign said 'Alcosa Works', and the detectives were way off their regular patch. They had driven up to Stourport, a quiet Worcestershire town on the River Severn, after learning that the fictitious Mr Fielding planned to call that day to pick up his smelter. The Alcosa Works rarely had customers so eager to bypass the usual delivery that they were willing to make the trip themselves. Duncan had been right to call, but was this the lead that Commander Cater had been hoping for?

Micky Lawson was late. He had telephoned Barrie Turner a few days earlier to suggest they get together. It had been some time since they had seen each other, and Lawson would be in his neck of the woods on Thursday, 22 December. The two men had known each other for many years, and Lawson called Turner his uncle, though the title was merely honorary – his mother had married Turner's brother thirty years earlier.

The two of them generally met only once or twice a year, which was as much as their business commitments would allow. In London Lawson owned property and had a garage where he bought and sold motors, while Turner owned Manson Agricultural Finance of Evesham, in the Midlands. More recently, however, Turner had expanded and purchased a garage in the picturesque Cotswold town of Broadway. Inevitably, Lawson, who never missed a trick, was on the telephone at regular intervals to sell off vehicles that he had picked up at auctions or couldn't shift himself.

This time, Lawson explained, he would be travelling up to Worcestershire himself to pick up some machinery; he also had some spark plugs going cheap and wanted to do business. Turner asked him to come to his office at lunchtime, but Lawson was late. Turner decided to go on ahead to the pub, the

Northwick Arms, for a bite to eat with his accountant and left a message with his receptionist: 'If Mr Lawson turns up, send him over to the pub.'

Turner's table at the Northwick Arms was almost full when Lawson arrived, shortly before 2 p.m. Several regulars had joined the lunch party and all were interested in the man driving the gold Rolls-Royce who had come up from the big city that morning.

Lawson enjoyed being the centre of attention. 'I'm picking up a smelter to melt gold and precious metals,' he explained to his lunch hosts. He was, he said, a jack of all trades and was heavily involved in the jewellery business. To prove the point he pulled out a jeweller's roll bag, unravelled it on the pub table and displayed six or seven pieces of gold, including a necklace and bracelets. Naturally he couldn't resist the opportunity to do business and, with Christmas three days away, within five minutes he had persuaded one lunch guest to part with £125 in exchange for a gold chain. The Northwick Arms regulars were fascinated by Lawson's easy Cockney charm, and more than one joke was cracked about the smelter; the general jesting consensus was that Lawson had 3 tons of gold stacked in his garden shed and was the Mr Big behind the recent robbery.

Barrie Turner was enjoying seeing his nephew again, but it was approaching last orders and Lawson would soon have to go if he was to collect the smelter before the factory shut down for the day. Then he had a brainwave. Why didn't they get a local taxi firm to collect the smelter from Stourport and deliver it to his home? Then he could take Lawson back home to see his wife.

Lawson handed Turner the receipt. It was in the name of Fielding, and Turner went off to telephone the Alcosa Works to tell them that a taxi would be collecting Mr Fielding's order. Then he rang the taxi firm but was disappointed. They were up to their eyes in work. He walked back to the table and told Lawson the pick-up couldn't be arranged. It was then that one of their party, a local business acquaintance of Turner's, offered the use of his van and driver.

At 3.35 p.m. that Thursday afternoon Conway and Miller

watched the white Ford Escort van drive into the Alcosa Works yard and load up. They had orders not to let the collection vehicle out of their sight. A radio call and a minute on the police computer identified the van. It belonged to a local family firm.

At 3.43 p.m. it left the factory, and the detectives followed it out of Stourport, south-east down the A 449. It drove over the M5 motorway, passed through Pershore and, a few miles further on, drew up at the rear of 107, The High Street, in the market town of Evesham. The property belonged to an agricultural finance company, and Miller's car slid to a halt beside the kerb opposite. The van had arrived at 4.13 p.m. but the crate had stayed in the back. The policemen wondered how long they might have to wait for the next leg of its journey. They had already spent hours sitting in the car in Stourport and had hoped the journey south-east, in the general direction of London, would continue. They didn't have to wait long. At 4.27 p.m. a gold Rolls-Royce, registration number HPW 977 P, pulled up. Another radio call produced the name of the registered owner – and it wasn't Fielding. Two hours later, at 6.17 p.m., the policemen watched two men lift the crate from the van and heave it into the boot of the Rolls. The lid wouldn't close, so one of the men walked back inside and came out a few seconds later with a piece of string to tie it down. The two men shook hands, then the plump one climbed into the car and it moved off.

Later that night the gold Rolls Royce backed up the drive of 41, Top Dartford Road, Hextable, in Kent, and the plump man got out and went indoors. It had been a long drive. It was now 1.57 a.m. The 'target' had stopped at a house, a petrol station and a pub on the way through the Cotswolds, Oxfordshire and Buckinghamshire to London, but the packing case was still inside the boot. The Rolls's registration number had given the Flying Squad a name, Michael Lawson, and it matched the address the detectives now found themselves parked outside. They had radioed in and been told to stay put. Relief was promised at 7.30 a.m. They settled back in their seats and watched the lights go off inside Number 41.

The following morning four unmarked Flying Squad vehicles converged on the area. They were given a quick run-down over the radio by the overnight team and then took up positions on the roads surrounding the house. The orders were the same as the previous day's: follow the Rolls until the smelter arrived at its ultimate destination. There was just an hour to wait. Shortly after 8.30 a.m. on Friday, 23 December, Lawson came out of the house, got into the Rolls and drove off. He headed south along the A 20 towards its junction with the M 25. Just a few miles short of the motorway, however, the Rolls turned right into a country road leading to the village of Crockenhill and, after a while, turned right again into the driveway of a large house called Wested Meadows.

Flying Squad detective Chris Colbourne gunned his engine, turned the car round at a farm further down the lane and drove back up the lane. As he passed the house, he looked up the drive. The Rolls had gone! He put his foot down and sped back to the A 20. At its junction he was just in time to see the vehicle disappearing into the distance. He gave chase but failed to sight it again.

The other Flying Squad vehicles had fared no better, and twelve hours later, after a series of frantic checks had been made, all to no avail, DCI Tom Glendinning, who had long since written up his notes of Micky McAvoy's interrogation, banged on the door of the expensive house in Hextable and introduced himself to Lawson.

The suspect was taken to Bexleyheath police station, where he agreed that, yes, he had bought the smelter, for a black man whose name he didn't know. He had stopped off at Crockenhill for a few minutes to see a friend who had not been at home and had then driven to a rendezvous near the M 25, where he met the black man in a lay-by. As the interview progressed, the story at times would change. The black man turned out to be a Turk, and he wanted the smelter to take out of the country. He had paid Lawson £1,500 to buy and collect it.

Glendinning was less than happy with the explanation. First Lawson had said that his client was a black man, then that he was a Turk. Lawson said that he thought there might be something dodgy about the deal but had assumed it was to be used in a VAT fiddle or something. He had met the black man/Turk at car auctions. He didn't know where he lived or what his real name was.

And that was that. The smelter had vanished. Lawson had done nothing illegal, and he was released. Police investigating the Brink's-Mat robbery did not, however, forget his name.

8. Costa crooks

Following the arrests of Robinson, McAvoy and White and the conviction two months later of Black, little was heard for some months about the hunt for the bullion. In fact, the investigation started to be scaled down. With four prisoners in the bag, Flying Squad had fulfilled its thief-taking role. Now the more officers there were looking for the haul, the fewer there were tackling the growing number of other armed robberies that were taking place in the capital – an average of more than four a day. Preventing armed crime was the Flying Squad's main function, and once again it became its priority.

A small band of detectives remained on the inquiry, but as they continued interviewing likely suspects and scouring the clubs and pubs frequented by the more professional kind of criminal, it quickly became apparent that even the £2 million reward money was not enough to tempt anyone to talk. The trail grew cold and at times seemed to fade away altogether.

Ironically, it was a very different story for the detectives working on the £6 million Security Express raid that had taken place some months before Brink's-Mat. By an incredible stroke of fate, the Heathrow raid actually led to a breakthrough in their inquiries. Following the Brink's-Mat robbery, an alert had gone out describing the two vehicles that had been spotted leaving the Heathrow industrial estate, but the task of tracing them was hampered when a television news bulletin put out a misleading description of one of the vans involved.

In fact, the van had been speedily abandoned in an east London back street, where it remained undiscovered for some weeks, even after the arrest of the four Brink's-Mat suspects. The details given in the news bulletin seemed to have had more impact than internal police memos about the robbery, for local beat officers did not give the blue vehicle they occasionally passed a second glance. The van used in the raid, they believed, was a different colour altogether. Eventually, however, a school caretaker reported its presence, telling police that some weeks earlier he had seen two men abandon it and hurry away to a waiting Mercedes. On 1 January 1985 police went to check the van over, and forensic evidence later established a clear link with the Brink's-Mat raid. By sheer coincidence, the road in Hackney, east London, in which the vehicle had been dumped was only a couple of streets away from a garage owned by a man suspected of taking part in the Security Express robbery. After the raid he had been spotted, following a tip-off, in a pub with other suspects, and his garage had been put under surveillance. The operation proved fruitless, however, and was called off a few days later.

Now Cater was perplexed. He believed he already knew the identity of a number of the Security Express robbers – but he also knew most of them had been out of the country during the Brink's-Mat raid. Did the proximity of the van to the garage mean that there was a connection between the two raids after all?

There was little time to work out all the implications – a visit to the garage was an urgent priority. A Flying Squad raid was organized, and the garage owner, John Horsley, was arrested. He heaved a sigh of relief when he learnt the detectives were investigating Brink's-Mat and was telling the truth when he said he knew nothing about the robbery.

He relaxed too soon. Immediately the questions about Brink's-Mat finished he was introduced to a second squad of detectives – and this time they wanted to know all about the

Security Express robbery. At first he denied all knowledge of the £6 million raid, but a check on his finances revealed that some months after the robbery, which had occurred over the Easter weekend the previous year, his bank account had suddenly taken a marked turn for the better.

He was at a loss to explain his sudden wealth, which he had spent on new cars and several foreign holidays, and in the face of the evidence he broke. He admitted that all £6 million of the money had been stored in his private garage after the raid, until collected afterwards by three of the robbers in a white hired van. Horsley then took officers to where £279,000 in notes was hidden behind a false panel in a relative's flat. He claimed this was the remainder of £400,000 he had been asked to look after by one of the robbers.

The detectives were delighted. Said one later: 'If we had raided Horsley immediately after Security Express, we would have found nothing. He had sat on his share of the proceeds until he thought it was safe to start spending. The nine-months delay worked entirely to our advantage.'

One of the names that Horsley provided in connection with the raid was that of another garage proprietor called John Knight, who lived in the expensive Hertfordshire stockbroker enclave of Gustard Wood. When he was arrested and his premises were searched, police found evidence that he had bank accounts and property interests in Spain, funded, they believed, by his £250,000 pay-out from the Security Express robbery.

In early February 1984 the British DPP formally asked a Spanish judge for permission to send two Scotland Yard officers to Malaga, on the bustling Costa del Sol. They were anxious to search an unfinished villa that John Knight had purchased for nearly £350,000 at La Capellania, an exclusive residential development, close to the beach resort of Fuengirola, with expansive views of the Andalucian coastline. They also wanted to search an apartment he used in Fuengirola and obtain more details about his bank accounts, one of which, they knew, contained more than £37,000. They were keen too to get their hands on the contents of a safe-deposit box he used and learn more about two cars he had imported from Denmark.

The officers who travelled to Spain rapidly found they had stumbled on more than they had bargained for. For also enjoying the sunshine around the fashionable beach resort of Marbella were five other Britons who, they rapidly concluded, must also have been involved in the Security Express raid – John's brother Ronnie, a man named Frederick Foreman, an East End publican called Clifford Saxe and two other men, Ron Everett and John Mason, who shortly before the Security Express robbery had been seen at a yard in north London owned by another of the Knight brothers, Jimmy. The Spanish connection was a factor that police investigating the Brink's-Mat and Security Express raids had always known would, sooner or later, begin to work against them.

The top echelon of London's professional criminals had for many years fled south to Spain when the heat was on. It was there that Bertie Smalls and other members of his gang adjourned after their string of successful bank robberies in the early 1970s, but since then the situation had got much worse. For the sunny *costas* along Spain's Mediterranean coast had become the perfect bolt-hole, following a diplomatic row between Spain and Britain that, in 1978, culminated in the breakdown of the extradition treaty between the two countries.

Spain abrogated the 100-year-old treaty, claiming that Britain had failed to honour its terms by consistently refusing to hand over people wanted by the Spanish authorities. In all applications for extradition the British insist on hearing the case against the accused in a British court first to ensure that the evidence is valid. In the case of Spain the court rulings had tended to reflect an official reluctance to pander too strongly to the desires of the Franco regime. In Spain the extradition process is more straightforward. Extradition orders are granted providing the foreign minister, justice minister and minister of the interior agree they are warranted.

Franco died in 1975 and, with him, his regime. The situation failed to change, however, and three years later the Spanish were driven to point out that over the previous twenty-five years the British system had led to just one extradition and the rejection of eight other applications, while for their part the Spanish had handed over fourteen people. The figures, the Spanish concluded, did not indicate much faith in their system of justice.

Following the ending of the treaty, a virtual colony of British fugitives sprang up, turning the *costa* into 'the part of Spain that fell off the back of a lorry', to use the phrase coined by one British Sunday newspaper report.

In fact, the group of Security Express suspects that had fled Britain had already attracted the attention of the Spanish police. The Cuerpo Superior de Policia, the branch specializing in detective work, had two years earlier set up in Malaga a unit called the International Delinquency Squad to monitor the activities of foreign residents, primarily in the hope of countering a burgeoning trade in hashish smuggled from Morocco, 50 miles away across the Mediterranean. The squad was particularly interested in foreigners with large amounts of money to spend and, although only four strong, had a formidable string of contacts and informers all over the Costa del Sol. Word quickly reached it about a group of Britons with no visible means of support who seemed to be investing heavily in property.

At virtually the same time that Knight was arrested the Spanish squad sent, via Interpol, a telex to Scotland Yard giving the whereabouts of the five new Security Express suspects. They had all recently settled on the Costa del Sol, explained the Spanish police. Was anything known about them?

The group was indeed known to Scotland Yard. All of the men had sizeable records, and three of them had been before the courts on murder charges.

The detectives had barely arrived before it became apparent that so many fruitful lines of inquiry were opening up that reinforcements were required. Soon some twelve officers, drawn from both the Flying Squad and C11, were ensconced in the Spanish sunshine.

At first it was a highly secret operation. The detectives knew that if word leaked out about their presence, safe-deposit boxes would be emptied and bank accounts closed down and their quarries would start being rather more circumspect about their meetings and telephone conversations.

But, despite the precautions the detectives took and the apparent support of the Spanish authorities, the silence was soon broken. In June that year Santiago Aroca, a reporter on the Spanish weekly news magazine *Tiempo*, was tipped off about the operation. The very name Scotland Yard can, in many countries, make a considerable impression, conjuring up images of grim-faced detectives in trenchcoats and trilbies doggedly pursuing their quarry through a thick London fog. Spain, where old British B-movies perpetuating the image are staple television fare, was no exception.

That such men were conducting a criminal investigation in the country at all was a major story. But it was even more newsworthy when, as *Tiempo* excitedly revealed in the six pages it devoted to its report, the men from the Yard were keeping a close watch on five of Britain's most wanted men.

Using a confidential Scotland Yard report that the British detectives had been required to file with Spanish legal authorities in Torremolinos when requesting the tapping of certain telephone lines, the magazine revealed that the five men were believed to be spending the proceeds from the 'two biggest robberies committed to date', Security Express and, *Tiempo* erroneously claimed, the 'gold and jewel warehouses of American Express'.

Of the five men John Knight's brother, Ronnie, was the best-known. Ex-husband of Cockney actress Barbara Windsor – a one-time favourite of the Kray twins – Knight was himself a former bookmaker, West End night-club owner and past acquaintance of the Krays.

Knight hit the headlines in 1980, when he stood trial at the Old Bailey for the murder of 'Italian Tony' Zomparelli, a well-known figure in Soho, London's clubland. The murder, it was alleged, was the result of a club brawl ten years earlier when Zomparelli stabbed Knight's younger brother, David, to death. Zomparelli served four years for manslaughter, only to be gunned down at his favourite pinball machine in an amusement arcade when he returned to his Soho haunts. Knight was charged with having paid for his execution but was acquitted.

The report in *Tiempo* revealed that, on arriving in Spain, apart from indulging in his passion for golf Ronnie Knight had bought three properties – two flats in the La Alcazaba development, considered to be one of the most luxurious spots at Marbella, for £40,000 each and a villa worth about £150,000 at La Capellania, slightly further down the mountainside from the house of his brother John. He was also said to have purchased a plot of land on which he planned to build eleven luxury apartments. Later he also invested in an Indian restaurant, Mumtaz, decorated in expensive Arabesque style, in Fuengirola.

The unofficial leader of the group, however, was a man referred to by some of the others as the 'big man'. He was Frederick Foreman who, according to *Tiempo*, had on his arrival in Spain bought four apartments in La Alcazaba, each costing £90,000, and a £90,000 house in Puerto Banus, a ritzy marina near Marbella purpose-built as a stamping ground for millionaire yacht owners. Even the graffiti artists use gold paint.

Foreman, who was once well-known in the London boxing world, had been a leading henchman of the Kray twins, assisting in the running of their West End club operations. Eventually, in 1969, when the Krays were finally put in the dock, he was sentenced to ten years for helping to dispose of the body of one of their victims, 'Jack the Hat' McVitie.

Foreman was also charged with the murder of Frank 'Mad Axeman' Mitchell, who was killed on the orders of the Krays after they had organized his escape from Dartmoor prison only to find his presence irksome. Foreman, 36 at the time, was alleged to have been paid £1,000 for the murder – Mitchell was shot four times in the chest and head and the *coup de grâce* was administered after the victim refused to die – but he was acquitted.

Another acquittal followed six years later, when he was acused of the murder of car dealer and small-time crook Thomas 'Ginger' Marks. Marks's body has never been found but is alleged to have been disposed of in the concrete shell of a motorway flyover.

Frederick Foreman, now turned teetotaller, did not excite the interest of the authorities again until 1982, when he received a two-year suspended sentence for conspiring to supply cannabis in the south of England.

Clifford Saxe, despite the erroneous claims of *Tiempo* that he was the brains behind the Security Express raid, was not in the same league as his four companions. He had, however, been a partner, with John Knight, in the Fox public house in London's East End, which he tended to run as a private club, on occasion ordering most of his customers to leave well before closing time while he had a private get-together with his cronies.

On the Costa del Sol he had bought two villas close to the Knight brothers' at La Capellania. One, worth £71,000, he rented out and later sold. The other, worth £94,000, he lived in; a brass fox's head decorated the back door for old times' sake. Despite his wealth, however, he appeared to the Spanish police to act as a 'gopher' for the rest of the group.

Both Everett and Mason had rather more modest tastes than the rest of the group, which belied their reputation at Scotland Yard as men who had for many years managed by and large to remain one step ahead of the law. They both bought ground-floor flats in Parque Marbella, an expensive apartment block in the centre of Marbella, complete with private, palm-shaded swimming pools and, on a clear day, a view of the North African mountains from the roof. The flats had only cost in the region of £30,000 each, but they turned out to be good investments. Just three years later they were each said to be worth £120,000.

Everett, an east London property developer, had been sentenced to seven years in 1952 for a wages snatch, then ten years later was sent to prison for three years for conspiracy to rob a bullion van containing £122,000. In 1970 another conviction followed, this time for six years, after he attacked two plain-clothes police officers who wanted to question him about a stolen car. A blank cartridge was fired into the face of one of the policemen. After the attack Everett fled to Australia, which the

Great Train Robbery fugitive Ronnie Biggs had made a fashionable hiding-place for British criminals, but he was traced in Sydney and arrested by Scotland Yard detectives. Later Everett was also tried, along with Foreman, for the murder of 'Ginger' Marks but was acquitted because of unsatisfactory evidence of identification. Mason, meanwhile, was cleared in 1976 of conspiracy in a £8 million raid on the Bank of America in Mayfair, which took place after an electrician hiding in a false ceiling above the bank vault watched through a miniature telescope as bank staff used the safe and noted down the combination.

The detectives sent out to Spain gathered a great deal of information about the likely whereabouts of the Security Express haul, but the proximity of the Brink's-Mat van to Horsley's garage was soon deemed to be nothing more than a mere coincidence. There were considerable doubts about the likelihood of certain members of the two teams ever agreeing to work together, and the sums of money the Marbella group were spending, although substantial, did not reflect a £26 million haul. Once again the whereabouts of the Brink's-Mat gold was anyone's guess.

9. A self-made man

Although the Security Express investigation took precedence over the Brink's-Mat inquiry for much of 1984, largely as a result of the information coming in from Spain, the Heathrow job was far from forgotten. Senior officers at Scotland Yard knew that, despite having hit the jackpot, the kind of men still at large who were experienced enough to have carried out the raid would be unlikely to retire. They could only guess at the new crimes the £26 million was financing: business frauds, drug-smuggling or perhaps even more daring and sophisticated raids that would be expensive to set up.

In June that year new steps were taken in what was fast to develop into a labyrinthine hunt for the gold – or the cash proceeds from its sale. Once again police had made full use of the criminal intelligence gathered during Operation Kate two years earlier and by now had drawn up a shortlist of men who they thought might have assisted Robinson and McAvoy in the robbery. There were also several other men whom they suspected of helping to dispose of the gold.

Now a letter from Scotland Yard's Fraud Squad was secretly sent to police on the Channel Island of Jersey, naming more than a dozen men who, it was alleged, were 'known to have been involved in the robbery [and] have also visited the island

and opened accounts or deposited monies in existing accounts at a number of banks'. Could they help in tracing the money?

Two of the names were those of men from north London, one of them an associate of the Knight brothers, but the rest of the list were mostly well-known 'faces' from Kent and south-east London. The names of Robinson, McAvoy and White, by then in prison awaiting trial, were included, since the police were anxious to establish whether they held any Jersey bank accounts. A Kent man, whose gardens were repeatedly dug up in the hunt for the gold and who later survived a shooting in a saloon bar, was also on the list, together with a south London video-shop proprietor living in Kent.

Other suspects included three members of a Turkish Cypriot family, some of whom are believed to specialize in armed robbery and to be major heroin suppliers. Another name was that of a former window-cleaner from Rotherhithe, who had gone on to share a house in Kent with the divorced wife of a well-known East End armed robber. The house, in Hever Avenue, West Kingsdown, Kent, had been built some years earlier by another man named on the list: a businessman and property dealer suspected of having disposed of some of the Brink's-Mat gold. Several months later he was to be responsible for putting the Brink's-Mat raid firmly back in the public eye. His name was Kenneth Noye.

West Kingsdown is a quiet, unprepossessing village in the Kent countryside about 25 miles south of London. It once straddled the main thoroughfare between London and the port of Folkestone, but, since the arrival of a near-by motorway, its only claim to fame has been its close proximity to the Brands Hatch motor-racing circuit. But, despite its lack of character, the village has in recent years attracted an influx of people from south-east London who have enough money to move out to the country but are reluctant to sever all connections with their roots. One such man was Noye.

A stocky, powerfully built man with a boxer's broken nose – the reminder of a childhood accident – Noye had grown up in a working-class family in Bexleyheath, a suburb of south-east London. His father was a Post Office manager and his mother a manageress at a greyhound-racing track; he had one sister, some years younger, a teacher who had married a legal executive.

At 15 Noye left the local comprehensive school with a string of O-levels to his name and attended a college of printing to study commercial art. But even at that early age he was busy looking for the main chance. To provide for himself, he worked both a paper round and an early-morning milk round as well as working as an assistant at a London department store on Saturdays, selling programmes several nights a week at the dog track where his mother worked and sometimes selling newspapers in the Strand too. The fact that he had held so many jobs at once as a teenager was later to become a proud boast.

The college course led to an apprenticeship as a Fleet Street printer, traditionally a job opportunity strictly controlled by qualified printers who, because printing is one of the most lucrative blue-collar occupations in the country, are anxious to keep such openings for members of their own families.

Once his apprenticeship was completed Noye worked nights in Fleet Street, but, despite the traditionally high wages, the pay was not enough for the man the newspapers were later to dub the 'crooked Midas', so he took a daytime job too, driving a tipper-truck. The aim was to make enough money to buy a plot of land on which to build a home for the childhood sweetheart he was to marry, Brenda, a former secretary in barristers' chambers. After a six-year courtship, by which time Noye was 23, they married and moved into Hever Avenue.

By now Noye had made enough money to buy his own lorry and, leaving the print, he set up his own haulage company in a battered caravan behind a garage in West Kingsdown. As the years passed, his haulage fleet grew to a dozen or so trucks, and he began to diversify, setting up a series of building companies and engaging in a number of property deals, including one that netted him £300,000, which was invested in a mobile-homes business in America. Always ready to do a deal, he also dealt in watches and jewellery as a sideline.

By the late 1970s Noye had made enough money to be able to move out of Hever Avenue. So a mile away, in 20 acres of grounds, he had constructed a six-bedroom mansion, inaptly named Hollywood Cottage, complete with a mock-Tudor façade and a large indoor swimming pool. The house, which contravened a number of planning regulations, was built on the site of a bungalow that had burned down in mysterious circumstances.

By 1984, when he was 36, Noye was regarded as a shrewd and highly successful businessman. Cautious with his wealth, he enjoyed one night out a week with the boys, when he would drink Bacardi and lemonade. For, despite a glamorous blonde girlfriend, whom he would secretly meet in a £50,000 flat that he had bought in Bexleyheath and had furnished almost exclusively from Harrods, Noye was ostensibly a happy family man, living quietly with Brenda and their two sons, Kevin, 12, and Brett, 9.

His few hobbies included squash (in 1983 a local squash club was bought by Brenda Noye for £110,000) and shooting, which had led him to purchase several guns and join a marksmen's club. His apparent respectability was bolstered by his membership of a Freemasons' lodge in west London, which he joined after an introduction from his friend Micky Lawson, the man who, in the weeks after the Brink's-Mat raid, had purchased the large gold smelter. It is a lodge where many members are dealers in bullion and other precious metals, and Noye is thought to have eased his way in with substantial donations to several Jewish charities.

Membership of the lodge was a natural step for as assiduous a collector of contacts as Noye, who boasted a circle of acquaintances that crossed all social divides and included several Kent magistrates. In the mid-1970s, for a reward of several thousand pounds, he had tipped off police officers about a lorry-load of merchandise, stolen from Liverpool docks, that the thieves were trying to sell on to him, so he numbered a few friends among the police too.

*

But Noye's role as a successful, respectable member of the community did not ring entirely true. With his south London accent, jewel-encrusted Rolex watch, which he claimed to change every year, gold bracelets, diamond signet ring with a stone just a little too large and suits cut just a little too sharp, he had never been able to get the image quite right. Despite working hard to escape the tedium of the anonymous south London suburbs where he grew up, Noye failed, once he had broken out, to ditch the streetwise credentials that had brought him through. People meeting him for the first time soon sensed a wheeler-dealer prepared to cut corners to make money. It was an impression enhanced by his tough manner – he was a man who, some neighbours were to say later, could have a frightening presence. One who had ventured to complain to the police about Noye's three dogs straying into his garden had been accosted by the angry haulier, who accused him of being a 'nark' and threatened to 'bury' him.

And even if he was not averse to picking up a little reward money on his way to respectability, Noye had also acquired a sizeable criminal record of his own. As a teenager he had been sent to Borstal for receiving stolen cars. That was followed, when he was in his twenties, by convictions for shoplifting, assaulting policemen, failing to have a licence for his shotgun and several charges of receiving stolen property. More recently he had also had a conviction for smuggling in a pistol from the United States after a visit to Miami. The list was hardly long enough to merit his inclusion on a register of all-time major criminals, but it did indicate a fairly entrenched disregard for the law.

Scotland Yard's interest in him was fuelled both by the knowledge that he was a friend of Lawson, who lived in Hextable, less than 10 miles away from Noye's mansion, and by gold dealings that Noye had carried out two weeks before the Fraud Squad wrote to the Jersey police. Indeed, it was these dealings that are thought to have led to the Fraud Squad request. For on 22 May 1984 Noye had flown to Jersey clutching a suitcase containing £50,000 in £50 notes. Turning up unannounced at the Charterhouse Japhet (Jersey) Ltd bank in

St Helier, he said he wanted to purchase gold worth about £100,000, which worked out at eleven 1-kilo bars. A surprised bank official told him that he couldn't just walk in off the street and buy gold; references would have to be taken up with his bank, and he would also have to open an account at Charterhouse Japhet. This he arranged to do, in his own and his wife's name. He was also told that a cash deposit was needed before negotiations could begin, and he agreed to deposit the £50,000 in the company's account at the Midland Bank, adding that, once back in England, he would arrange for the transfer of the outstanding £47,322.50 from his own bank account.

Further purchases, possibly 1 kilo a month, would follow. It was, he explained, an investment for his son. Staff were even more surprised when he added that, once the formalities were completed, he would personally pick up the gold. Their warnings about the security problems that would create were quickly dismissed. Staff later remembered that Noye also made a point of asking whether the serial numbers on the bars would be shown on the receipts and was told they would not.

Eight days later Noye returned to the island, travelling under the name of K. Swan, and collected the bullion. This time he claimed that the gold was to minimize his possible tax liabilities in England. Once again he ignored warnings about removing the gold from the bank's safekeeping. He was anxious, he said, to eliminate any connection between the bank and himself. He then asked if they had something he could take the bars away in, and a plastic shopping-bag was provided, which met with his approval. No one, he said, would suspect that it contained gold. Then, picking up the considerable weight in one hand, he walked out.

But Noye's wish to keep his connection with the bank secret was by then a forlorn hope. Staff at Charterhouse Japhet were already suspicious of him, as was DCI Charles Quinn, the Glasgow-born head of the Jersey police CID.

Earlier that morning Quinn had received a call, from 'Criminal Intelligence sources in the United Kingdom', tipping him off that Noye was to arrive on a flight from Gatwick and asking that he be put under surveillance.

Special Branch officers at Jersey Airport spotted Noye as soon as he left the plane, and CID officers watched as he went to collect the gold. When he emerged twenty-five minutes later he was followed on foot to the Trustee Savings Bank. There Noye hired a safe-deposit box, where he stored the gold after obtaining a form that allowed his wife access to the box. When he left the bank, detectives continued to follow him through St Helier but eventually lost him.

An hour later, however, Noye arrived at the airport to catch a flight home. He had just walked through the airport security screen when he was stopped by a Special Branch officer and was asked to fill out an embarkation form. Noye, visibly nervous, entered his correct name and address but couldn't, or wouldn't, produce any documents to prove his identity. He did, however, present his ticket, which carried the name of K. Swan, explaining that it had been bought for him by a friend who worked for the airline and was able to buy cheap tickets. When asked what he had been doing in Jersey, Noye became evasive, simply replying, 'Business,' and refused to specify where he had been.

Noye never returned to Jersey to pick up the gold he had deposited. Had he done so, the authorities would have known immediately. For after his visit to the Trustee Savings Bank his safe-deposit card there was marked in large letters CARE: DO NOT ALERT THE CUSTOMER, with a warning that if either Noye or his wife appeared at the counter, senior officials were to be told. They in turn were instructed to avoid acting suspiciously but to delay the customer for five to ten minutes while they contacted DCI Quinn, at his home if necessary.

Despite the Fraud Squad's letter, Noye's activities in Jersey were not, in themselves, deemed sufficiently interesting for any further police action to be taken. It was some months before detectives realized their mistake. For, they later claimed, Noye had obtained something he considered far more valuable than the gold locked away in the safe-deposit box: he had receipts showing that he had legitimately purchased eleven bullion bars. Those receipts could be produced to explain away any stolen or smuggled gold he was found in possession of – provided it was eleven bars or less. In short, it could have been an elaborate cover for future criminal transactions.

For some months the self-made millionaire was able to go about his business without attracting any further attention, but later in the year his name again came to the fore in connection with Brink's-Mat. A detective inspector in C11, who had extensive knowledge of the south-east London criminal fraternity, received intelligence that Noye seemed to be moving gold, and lots of it. He also seemed to have acquired a new acquaintance who warranted further investigation.

That acquaintance was Brian Reader, who, despite having only one criminal conviction for handling stolen property, was generally regarded as one of the best, and most ambitious, burglars in London.

Reader, aged 47, had secretly re-entered Britain earlier that year after spending several years on the run in Spain with his wife, Lynn. His exile had been prompted in 1982 by a burglary charge that he faced at the Old Bailey. While on bail he fled with his wife, but the couple were forced to return to Britain when Lynn's mother fell ill.

Reader had met the Noyes five years before at a wedding and now lived some 15 miles from them in a house owned by an old schoolfriend (then a publican) in Winn Road, Grove Park, another suburb of south-east London, close to the A 20, which continues through to West Kingsdown.

Although Reader was a wanted man, police were later to insist that they did not know that he was back in Britain when they began checking on his activities. They claim they did not, at that stage, know the identity of the man whom they suspected, with Noye, of being a conduit through which the Brink's-Mat gold was reaching the open market. Whether that is true is impossible to say. Scotland Yard is always reluctant to confirm that wanted men are sometimes allowed to continue operating even when their identities are known, so that it can check on their accomplices.

One thing is certain, however. By December suspicions about Noye and his new friend were so strong that it was decided both would be targeted in a full-scale Flying Squad investigation.

10. The middle-men at work

To mount an effective surveillance operation against the two new Brink's-Mat suspects Scotland Yard realized that the inquiry team needed reinforcement. By now it was down to just twenty officers, and the retirement of Commander Cater was imminent. A new detective would have to be drafted in to take charge and build up the squad.

The man chosen to head the investigation was Acting Detective Chief Superintendent Brian Boyce, a former member of the anti-terrorist squad, who had long before dismissed the prospect of advancement to the top policy-making ranks of the police force. The son of a West End barrow boy, Boyce had just one ambition on entering the police service: to become a top detective at Scotland Yard. Having achieved that aim (he was with Cater when the Kray twins were eventually arrested), he had no desire to swap the nitty-gritty of detective work out on the streets for the cosier confines of high office with its bureaucracy and the shadow of Whitehall administration.

Boyce's air of determined independence – he is an accomplished jazz musician, a mountaineer of considerable prowess and a man with a lasting interest in comparative religion, coupled with a professionalism born of sheer love of the work – made him an officer capable of inspiring considerable loyalty among Scotland Yard's elite detective force.

Boyce had spent his National Service twenty-six years earlier in Cyprus, where he gained some experience of military intelligence while tracking down EOKA. There he had learned the value of surveillance and constant intelligence-gathering – lessons that he was to bring to bear on the Brink's-Mat case.

By early January 1985, after a number of discreet inquiries had been made among London gold dealers, Boyce decided that the time had come to put both Noye and Reader under surveillance, an operation in which initially only C8 officers were used.

On Tuesday, 8 January 1985, detectives moved into position and had only a short time to wait for developments. At 9.05 a.m. Reader, in a green Cavalier car, was seen to leave Noye's address and drive back to his own home. Twenty minutes later he left and was shadowed by four unmarked Flying Squad cars to Cowcross Street in central London, close to Hatton Garden. Parking outside Farringdon Underground and mainline railway station, he went to a phone booth in the ticket hall to make a call. A detective who, seconds later, sidled into the booth next to him was close enough to observe the number Reader dialled. It was that of a near-by shop. After waiting a short while the 'target' walked out to the street, looked up and down, then returned and dialled the number again. The same thing happened again before Reader left the station and went into a café on the opposite side of the road.

Two detectives who followed saw him sitting at a table in a booth with two other men. One of them, they were later to learn, was 24-year-old Thomas Adams, an asphalter by trade. The other was a well-known figure around Hatton Garden, a gold dealer named Christopher Weyman, who ran a business called Lustretone Ltd in Greville Street.

Reader was writing on a piece of paper, which he showed to the two men; then the three of them left the café and walked across the road to Reader's car. Adams climbed in and brought out an unusually heavy, oblong parcel about 1 foot long. The parcel was placed in the boot of a near-by white Mercedes sports car, in which Adams and Weyman then drove away.

That same morning other detectives, who had been keeping Hollywood Cottage under observation, saw a Granada belonging to Michael Lawson driven up to the house by a man aged about 20. It drove away soon afterwards and when next seen was outside Noye's former home in Hever Avenue.

Early that Tuesday afternoon police outside Hollywood Cottage saw Noye and another man leave in a blue Range Rover. They followed them towards London and, after 12 miles, watched as the Range Rover turned left off the A20 Sidcup bypass into the secluded car park of the Beaverwood Club, a night-club built in Spanish *hacienda*-style and set back from the road behind a screen of trees. Noye stayed there for five minutes before driving off. (It later became apparent that this was a secret rendezvous spot used by Noye and Reader, and police now believe that he was there that afternoon to meet Reader, returning from London).

For the C8 detectives it had been a productive day's work. While it couldn't be said that they had conclusive proof of criminal activity, there was enough there to indicate they were on the right tracks. Noye was linked with the man living in Hever Avenue, as well as with Lawson, and Reader seemed to be up to something that required him to meet a gold dealer.

The prospect of a breakthrough in the Brink's-Mat case was important enough for Boyce next day to call in C11, but although he was well-versed in the branch's surveillance expertise, he knew there would be particular difficulties with the Noye/Reader operation, especially in the extensive grounds of Hollywood Cottage. One priority was to find officers who could remain outside for long periods of time, no matter what the weather conditions.

That Wednesday he asked for, and got, the C11 elite, men from the Specialist Surveillance Unit for whom the usual C11 course was just basic training. They were a handpicked group, no more than eight in total, whose instructors in reconnaissance and close-target surveillance included experts from the Special Air Service (SAS).

Four years before, when he had been a member of the anti-terrorist squad, Boyce had been asked to help set up the surveillance team and to draw on lessons he had learned while watching the Royal Ulster Constabulary (RUC) establish a similar squad (known as E4 A) to target terrorists. The resulting C11 team was trained along the same lines as the RUC: the course included hiding beneath floorboards, in a gap just 18 inches high, for three days at a time and spending a similar length of time dug into a hole in the ground in open countryside.

That day a team of C11 officers, including members of the specialist unit, joined with men from C8 to embark on the most intense surveillance operation Scotland Yard could mount. As Noye lived in Kent, approval had to be obtained for the operation from the Kent police force, but there was a problem. When the Metropolitan Police had arrested Noye in 1977 for receiving stolen goods, they had done so without the knowledge of the local force, as they knew that Noye had 'friends' there. This time it was too big an operation to keep quiet. The Kent constabulary had to be told, but only officers at the highest level were put in the picture.

The first priority for the surveillance team working in Kent was to establish a command centre, which the C11 team group duly did in a ground-floor room of the Stacklands Retreat House, a convalescent home for Anglican clergymen opposite Noye's home on School Lane, a quiet country road. The retreat was set back several hundred yards from the lane, but a hide fashioned from branches was carefully constructed in bushes under an oak tree at its gates, where round-the-clock observation could be kept on Hollywood Cottage. Further along, still in the grounds of the retreat, a video camera disguised as a bird box was installed in a tree directly opposite the gates to Noye's home. On the road outside Reader's house a variety of vehicles were used to maintain observation.

As the arrangements were being made, Lawson's car was again seen at Hollywood Cottage. Police were later to learn that it went on to visit Greville Street – a traffic warden there gave it a parking ticket.

But it was a meeting between Noye and Reader, watched by one of C11's woman detective constables, Myrna Yates, aged 36, that was to bring real results. Shortly before midday the detectives followed Reader as he drove from his home to the Crest Hotel, Bexley. Noye was already waiting in his Range Rover in the road outside the hotel, and as the Cavalier approached, he did a U-turn and drove off towards London. Reader immediately followed. A little further on the two vehicles turned into a side road and parked. Yates left her car and, remaining hidden, watched as Noye handed Reader a black briefcase.

The next day proved the most fruitful yet for the surveillance teams. Their observations were to enable Boyce to add an important link to the chain along which he believed the gold was being passed. Noye and Reader met at lunchtime in the car park of the Beaverwood Club, and a quarter of an hour later police followed Reader to the Royal National Hotel in Bedford Way, Bloomsbury, central London. Walking into the lobby, Yates saw Reader sitting at a table talking to Weyman and Adams. About ten minutes later the men left the hotel, Weyman and Adams driving off in the white Mercedes seen outside Farringdon station two days earlier.

The Mercedes was tailed, via north London, to Paddington railway station. There detectives saw that Adams was carrying a brown briefcase, which appeared to be very heavy. Both men seemed agitated. Two telephone calls were made, then first-class tickets were bought and the men boarded a train for Swindon, 80 miles west of London. Unbeknown to them, some of the other passengers were surveillance officers. Once at their destination, Weyman made several more telephone calls, then a long wait ensued. Eventually the two men shook hands and waved to each other as though they were parting company. One moved off and was followed at a distance by the other – a ploy, the watching detectives believed, to try to establish if anyone was following.

Further down the road the two men met up again and made

for a fish-and-chip bar in a street opposite the station. There they had another long wait until eventually a black Jaguar XJS pulled up. Inside were Garth Chappell, the 42-year-old managing director of Scadlynn Ltd, a bullion company based in North Street, Bedminster, a run-down area of Bristol, and Terence Patch, a Bristol businessman who occasionally worked for the company. Adams and Weyman wasted no time in placing the briefcase in the boot of the Jaguar, and it sped off, with detectives following, back to Scadlynn.

Chappell had come a long way since starting out in Bristol at the age of 22 by setting up a company for clearing builders' rubble. He had progressed to selling second-hand cars and car spares, then in 1976 he went into partnership with a former market trader, John Palmer, a man said to be of gypsy stock who had difficulty with reading and writing but possessed fully the entrepreneurial flair of a Romany. The two men embarked on a number of ventures, including the sale of furniture and flooring and estate agency.

Chappell's real graduation had come in the late 1970s, when he realized that the principles of car dealing could be applied to gold and jewellery, and in 1980 he and Palmer formed Scadlynn Ltd. It was not an immediate success, and as Chappell struggled to make the company pay, he grew careless. In 1982 he was fined £550 by magistrates for three weights-and-measures offences, and later the same year he received a suspended nine-month prison sentence for conspiracy to defraud. Then in 1983 he was fined £4,500, plus costs amounting to £9,750, for three false VAT returns. He also invested in a number of houses in Bristol, which he converted into bedsits, a process for which he failed to obtain planning permission.

By 1985 the company was still badly overdrawn at the bank. But its accounts showed that since the middle of 1984 there had been a sudden escalation in business involving gold worth more than £9 million. And there was certainly no denying the considerable wealth that Chappell had started to enjoy, which included Stonewalls, a luxury home complete with swimming pool in the picturesque Somerset village of Litton, in the Mendip Hills, where he lived with his wife, Joan, and two sons.

Palmer, aged 34, had resigned from Scadlynn in March 1984 to concentrate on the three jewellery shops that he owned in Bath, Bristol and Cardiff but still remained closely involved with the company. With his blonde ex-hairdresser wife Marnie, their two daughters, one aged 7 and the other 6 months, and two Rottweilers (small but immensely powerful dogs often used as guard dogs), he lived in a style equal to that of Chappell in the converted coach house of a remote Georgian country mansion called Battlefields, built by the famous Bath architect John Wood the Younger, near the village of Lansdown, outside Bath.

The man in the Jaguar with Chappell, Patch, was a 41-year-old demolition expert, building contractor and general dealer who owned scrap-metal and heating engineering businesses. He also had a major stake in a local country club. He was a relative newcomer to Scadlynn, in which he was considering buying a half-stake. He lived with his wife Diane and their two teenage sons at a luxury detached bungalow called Bali-Hi in Bishopsworth, Bristol, guarded by two Alsatians; his wife was able to indulge her hobby of horse riding. At the quiet village of Chew Magna, 4 miles out of Bristol, he also had a hideaway country cottage where he would spend evenings with a former beauty queen who had once reached the finals of the Miss United Kingdom contest.

Back in London, the Mercedes at Paddington station had been kept under observation throughout the afternoon, and at about 6.30 p.m. Adams and Weyman returned, one of them clutching another briefcase. From the station they were followed to Russell Square, where Weyman was seen to hand the briefcase to Reader.

On the Friday Reader made yet another visit to the car park of the Beaverwood Club, after making a phone call from a public call box. He stayed there just eight minutes.

There then followed a period during which nothing seemed

to happen, but six days later Reader made an evening visit to Hollywood Cottage before driving up to Cowcross Street, where once again he was met by the white Mercedes. All that a woman detective walking past Reader's car managed to establish was that Reader and a man leaning into the front passenger window were looking at some papers; she couldn't hear what was being said. Eventually the man at the window returned to the Mercedes and drove off. Police lost the sports car almost immediately when they tried to follow.

There was another wait – this time of five days – before the watching detectives had anything new to report. Once again, it was Reader visiting Cowcross Street, where he met Adams in the café they had used before. Twenty-five minutes later a taxi pulled up. Weyman and a man wearing a brown sheepskin jacket got out, both carrying boxes. Adams came out of the café and opened the boot of his sports car, where the boxes were left. The group adjourned to the café for half an hour, then the boxes were transferred to the boot of Reader's car. Reader followed by detectives, made immediately for Hollywood Cottage.

He was back in the Cowcross Street café the following day, talking to an acquaintance, a jeweller who also claimed to be an antiques dealer and had long been suspected by police of being a fence for stolen goods. While they were talking the white Mercedes drew up; when the driver (Weyman this time) entered Reader produced a green Marks and Spencer's carrier bag from his pocket and placed it on the table between them, keeping his hand resting on the package. In turn Weyman produced an envelope that he handed to Reader, who then let the package go.

Once again Reader drove straight to Noye's house and from there went back home, but within quarter of an hour he was travelling back to London, making once again for the Royal National Hotel. There he joined the jeweller whom he had met earlier that day, and they sat looking out of the window until the white Mercedes arrived.

When it pulled up Weyman got out, and Reader and the jeweller left the hotel. The three walked across to Reader's Cavalier, and Adams, who had left the sports car to join them, was handed from the Cavalier a large package wrapped in brown paper, which he promptly placed in his own car before driving off.

He headed for the M4, where an hour and a half later he took the Swindon turn-off, Junction 15, and 200 yards further on pulled into the car park of the Plough, a small country pub. He parked directly behind the Jaguar last seen outside Scadlynn Ltd. A little later a detective who walked past saw the boots of both vehicles open and a group of men clustered around the Mercedes. Two men then lifted an object out of the boot and transferred it to the Jaguar. It was heavy. Surveillance officers were sure it must be gold.

The Jaguar then left the car park, heading westwards, once again with police in pursuit. It was a futile exercise. The car turned off the motorway at an exit for Bath and was soon lost among the country lanes close to where John Palmer lived. Next morning detectives discovered it parked outside Scadlynn.

On the Thursday evening Reader again visited the Royal National Hotel. Larkins joined him, then Adams and Weyman appeared, the latter carrying a large brown leather briefcase with fold-over flaps. Later that night Reader was seen taking the case to Noye's house.

By the Friday, nearly three weeks after the start of the surveillance operation, Boyce believed that the transactions, whatever they were, had gone on long enough. It was now time to act.

That afternoon he presided over a briefing, in a south London police station, of the twenty or so officers who had been engaged in the operation, and warrants were obtained from a London magistrate for raids on thirty-six addresses in Kent, London and the Bristol area.

Boyce knew that he faced a considerable logistical problem. He believed that all or part of the £26 million of gold was at Hollywood Cottage, but he couldn't be absolutely certain. Some of the transactions involving Reader had been confusing.

While he had been seen to hand over heavy packages, on one occasion boxes had been placed in the boot of his car, which he had then driven to Noye's home. Was it possible that Reader, as well as acting as the conduit between Noye and Scadlynn, was also a conduit to Noye from some other source, delivering the gold to Hollywood Cottage for some kind of processing before handing it on further down the chain?

Having decided that the time was right to move in, the police faced an acute dilemma. Was there a chance that if the Flying Squad postponed some of the raids, those people they left alone might think they had escaped detection and unwittingly lead police at a later date to more of the Brink's-Mat bullion?

Boyce believed that three options were open to him. He could pounce at West Kingsdown and then decide what to do about London and Bristol; he could intercept the gold at Scadlynn and then decide if he wanted to follow up with further raids in London and Kent; or he could move in while the gold was actually in transit and decide then which raids to carry out.

It would be the movements of Reader and Noye, he decided, that would determine which of the three options he chose. Officers from the special surveillance unit would continue their observation of Hollywood Cottage to provide the most detailed information possible on movements there, and teams of C8 officers would cover other areas. One would be placed on standby at the retreat, to remain in contact with the C11 post; a second C8 team would be posted close to Reader's home; a third would be in place in central London; and a fourth would take up positions in the M4 area, west of London. A smaller fifth unit was kept mobile, ready to give back-up where it was needed.

Boyce set a time limit for the operation of seventy-two hours. At some stage during that period they would have to move in, otherwise the operation would be aborted. One reason for this was purely routine: in common with every other senior officer at Scotland Yard, Boyce had the daily frustration of balancing the necessity of police work against its cost in overtime payments, and this was an operation that was not only manpower-intensive but stretched over a weekend as well. There was a more important reason for the time limit. Seventy-two hours was the maximum length of time a surveillance officer could be expected to stay hidden out in the open and remain competent. Although it was not envisaged that any C11 officer would face such a stint, Boyce wanted to be ready for any eventuality.

Another problem facing Boyce was the question of the firearms at Noye's house – and after careful consideration he came to the firm conclusion that none of his men would be armed. Guns can be issued to most sections of the British police only when senior officers conclude that without them there would be a serious danger to police officers or members of the public. The detective could see no evidence that anyone's life would be jeopardized. Noye's shotguns, he felt, were not kept for nefarious purposes but were part of the country-squire image that the millionaire liked to promote. And while Boyce was willing to concede that the Brink's-Mat robbers were violent men, he was satisfied that in this instance they were dealing not with the robbers but with middlemen.

His reluctance to issue arms was also based partly on the outcry there had been two years earlier when Stephen Waldorf, a film editor, was shot five times and seriously wounded in a London street when mistaken for a violent criminal. A C11 policeman was subsequently accused of attempting to murder Waldorf. Although the officer was later acquitted, the incident had led to a massive reappraisal of the circumstances in which British police should be armed and to greater awareness of the stress that can be induced by arming an officer who would not usually carry a gun. At the time Boyce had been serving with C11 as the superintendent in charge of operations and had been party to authorizing the arming of the officer.

A third factor was Boyce's distrust of Kent police. If an armed officer of one force enters the area of another, the Chief Constable of the second force has to be informed immediately and must provide armed officers from among his own men as back-up. Boyce could only guess at the number of Kent policemen who would need to be told of the raid. How could he be sure Noye would not be tipped off?

For his part the police chief, although in charge of the planning of the operation, was unable to get too closely involved in its execution. At the time he was still formally part of the anti-terrorist squad, where he had been handling three major cases. One involved a gang that had kidnapped Umaro Dikko, the former Nigerian president, from his London home and another an IRA active-service unit that had bombed Harrods. The third case, that of two Britons, Godfrey Shiner and Anthony Gill, who had been picked up in Egypt for allegedly plotting the murder of an exiled former Libyan prime minister on behalf of the Gadaffi regime, had several weeks before taken Boyce to Cairo, where the two men were still being held.

The detective, aware there could have been developments in any one of these cases at any time, decided that his part would have to be such that he could withdraw and return to Scotland Yard at a moment's notice. Instead his deputy, DCI Ken John, was placed in charge of coordinating the operation from Scotland Yard.

At the Friday afternoon briefing one Flying Squad officer was appointed local controller of the observation team outside Noye's address and another placed in a similar role outside Reader's home. They each had full authority to execute a search warrant on the premises for which they were responsible if they felt it necessary. Boyce was to be told as soon as possible afterwards.

And members of the specialist surveillance team were warned that they might be called upon to enter the grounds of Hollywood Cottage before the search party arrived. For Boyce was unsure whether the gold was hidden in the house itself or somewhere in the grounds. He was aware that the area had been used during the Second World War as part of the wartime headquarters of the Special Operations Executive, the organization set up in 1940 to assist resistance groups in Nazi-occupied Europe, and he believed that, in common with a school next-door to Hollywood Cottage, there were a number of concrete bunkers in the garden where the gold might be hidden.

In addition, given the fact that the gates to Noye's drive were generally kept locked, opening by remote control once callers had been identified over a closed-circuit television system, he was concerned at the amount of warning the occupants of the house would have about a raid. He wanted to insure against people either fleeing or hiding incriminating evidence in the grounds while police were still trying to get in.

His request to the C11 specialists struck them as nothing out of the ordinary. It was the kind of work they had been trained for. But it was a strategy that was to go horribly wrong.

11. 'He's done me. He's stabbed me'

The hide was cold and dark. It was 6.15 in the evening, and the January night was already bitter. For some time the only sound had been the hum of traffic from the motorway a mile away across the fields. The order over the radio to move in was greeted by the surveillance officer with relief and not a little excitement. There was snow on the ground, and despite his rubber wetsuit, camouflage clothing and two balaclavas he welcomed the chance to move.

Leaving his makeshift observation post hidden behind a screen of bushes, he crept stealthily across the quiet country lane until he reached a low wall. There he was joined by another officer, who had been hiding behind bushes directly opposite the entrance of Noye's home where, spreadeagled on the freezing ground, he had ensured that in the darkness the number plates of any car visiting Hollywood Cottage were fully noted.

Beyond the wall the two officers could see, by the light of a string of mock-Victorian lamps, more than a hundred yards of sweeping driveway, with a small copse and shrubbery to one side and an open lawn to the other, dotted with newly planted saplings. At the top of the drive were the lights of Hollywood Cottage. In seconds, without a word being spoken, the two men were over and crouching low, waiting to see if they had been spotted. Then a minute later, satisfied that all was clear, they began their laborious approach towards the house, leap-frogging forward, one of them advancing while the other held back as look-out to warn if discovery seemed imminent.

Hugging close to a perimeter fence, they made for the copse and shrubbery in front of a large barn, known as the apple store, that would give them enough cover to watch events at the house undetected.

Ten minutes later their colleagues at the retreat received the first indication that the surveillance operation was going wrong. Just two words crackled over the air from the grounds of Hollywood Cottage: 'Dogs – hostile.' The men had been discovered by two, maybe three, Rottweilers – the breed of guard dog used by the Bristol gold dealer John Palmer.

The message was the start of a chain of events that would result in the death of one of C11's top undercovers from ten stab wounds within the hour, lead to the trial of Kenneth Noye and Brian Reader for murder at the Number One Court of the Old Bailey, and push the Brink's-Mat gold-bullion case back on to the front page of every national newspaper.

It was the Saturday after Boyce's briefing, and surveillance officers had been on duty in the hide outside Hollywood Cottage since first light. The two on day-time duty, DC Russell Sinton and DC Stephen Matthews, had had a long wait before there was anything to report, and then all that occurred was an innocent-looking domestic drama.

During the morning Brenda Noye was preparing to take the two children to stay with her mother, but there was a hold-up when the Ford Granada she intended to use would not start. She called her husband, who thought that one of the battery terminals in the car needed cleaning. Kenneth Noye later claimed that he took a knife from the kitchen, then, on discovering that the terminals looked all right, started the car instead with jump leads from a Range Rover parked alongside. Brenda Noye and the two children drove off in the Range Rover; Noye left moments later in the Granada, having tossed the knife into the footwell on the passenger side of the car. It was an unremarkable episode but one that, at the Old Bailey nearly a year later, would form an important part of Noye's defence against murder.

At Reader's home there was no movement until, at 1.10 p.m., he was seen to drive off in his green Cavalier in the direction of Hollywood Cottage, with two Flying Squad officers, DS Anthony Yeoman and DC Bruce Finlayson close behind in a covert surveillance vehicle. The police were elated when, 4 miles down the A 20, the Cavalier turned off into the car park of the Beaverwood Club. A new gold transaction seemed to be in the offing. But there was a snag: Noye was nowhere to be seen.

Four minutes later Reader left the car park and there followed a half-hour drive that was to test Yeoman's surveillance-driving training to the hilt. To kill time while waiting for Noye and to avoid attracting attention in the car park, Reader drove up and down the A 20 to the Ruxley Corner roundabout 2 miles away, where he turned and doubled back on his tracks. Even the most unconcerned driver covering such a route would notice if another car were to follow too closely, and Reader, the detectives knew, was a man who would check if he was being followed. Eventually, for fear of alerting Reader to the fact that his movements were being monitored, Yeoman pulled back to such an extent that he lost him.

In fact, Reader had turned up at the Beaverwood Club too late. The previous evening he had arranged to meet Noye outside the club at 1.00 p.m. Noye, despite problems with the car, had been there on time. He had waited some twenty minutes, even joining the AA at a nearby kiosk, before deciding that Reader wasn't going to show up.

Reader was next seen by police at 2.25 that afternoon, outside the gates of Hollywood Cottage. The C11 officers in the hide watched as he found that the gates were locked and that no one was in and drove away again. Noye, meanwhile, had taken a woman friend out for a drink and had gone on with her to another friend's house before returning home.

The next appearance of Reader at Hollywood Cottage, at 6.12 that evening, by which time Noye and his wife had returned home, was the trigger police had been waiting for. They were convinced that Noye and Reader had missed an important rendezvous earlier that day. 'I felt a search was needed then and there, as this might be a rare opportunity to strike at Hollywood Cottage when an exchange was taking place,' acting DI Robert Suckling, the detective who had interviewed Tony White and was now the local controller for Hollywood Cottage, was to explain later. Parked 2 miles away in a C8 vehicle outside the Brands Hatch motor-racing track, he ordered the surveillance team into the cottage grounds at 6.15 p.m., three minutes after Reader arrived at the cottage.

In the hide by this time were two C11 officers who had worked together for five years, often in conditions of extreme danger: DC John Fordham and DC Neil Murphy. They had gone to the hide shortly after 5.00 p.m. to relieve Sinton and Matthews and were resigned to the fact that they might be there all night.

Of the two men Fordham, a strong family man with three children, from Romford in Essex, was the most experienced. Sometimes called 'Gentleman John' by his friends for his old-fashioned courtesy, he had been in C11 for nine years, turning down chances of promotion to remain at the 'sharp end' of police work. It was his first day on the operation, and he was pleased to have the opportunity of working with Boyce again. The two had been together in Northern Ireland and had a mutual regard for each other.

Fordham had been a late entrant to the police force, joining while in his late twenties after a variety of occupations, including those of merchant seaman and New Zealand prison officer. He had also travelled extensively throughout Europe and Asia by van. Once in the force, his professionalism, sense of responsibility and quiet self-confidence born of his earlier experiences soon singled him out as an above-average officer and, unusually for the Metropolitan Police, he became a detective without having to sit the customary formal examination.

It was to be a trust he lived up to. During the course of his career he won four commendations for bravery, and by the time he was put on to the Brink's-Mat inquiry he had a reputation for being, in the words of a senior Scotland Yard officer, 'one of the most experienced and best-trained surveillance officers in the country'.

Neil Murphy, a bachelor, was Fordham's back-up man. Murphy came from a close-knit mining family in a County Durham pit village and had joined the Metropolitan Police nine years earlier following a short career as a regular soldier. In 1980 he had been recommended for a posting to C11 and had proved to be a natural. A keen sportsman in the more solitary pursuits of skiing and windsurfing, he had the right degree of fitness and self-sufficiency for the job. He had something else too – an actor's eye. Even when off-duty he would constantly study the mannerisms of people in an effort to improve his powers of disguise.

His dedication had so impressed John Fordham, the instructor who had introduced him to the ways of C11, that after his apprenticeship they had continued working together, and the teacher–pupil relationship developed over the years into one of friendship, although Fordham was still the senior partner.

Once inside the grounds of Hollywood Cottage, the two officers were to communicate with police by the two radios each carried. Their experience had taught them that the tiny body-set radios that surveillance officers usually wear were inadequate for transmission in rural areas, where they could expect to spend much of the time either lying on the ground or crouching down. The proximity of the aerial to the ground tended to interfere with transmissions, particularly when they were sending messages, so, as an experiment, each had a large set for sending messages and the much smaller body-set radio ear-piece for receiving. Their point of contact at the command post was DS Robert Gurr, a crusty veteran of C11 with whom they generally worked.

A golden rule for such operations was that once the detectives had moved forward to take up their close-surveillance positions, their subsequent actions would be left entirely up to them. A third party who was not physically with them would not have enough information to give valid instructions. They were effectively their own 'controlling officers'.

On previous operations both Fordham and Murphy had, in C11 parlance, been 'compromised' by guard dogs and, knowing there were three Rottweilers at the cottage, they had sought guidance on how best to deal with them. Metropolitan Police dog-training experts had told Fordham that the only sure way of pacifying a dog was to knock it out, which was obviously not an option open to them. As a poor second-best, yeast tablets were suggested as a means of keeping them quiet. Fordham, who before going on duty that day is said to have been unusually withdrawn and preoccupied, had procured a bottle of the pills, the contents of which he divided with Murphy before going over the wall.

Fordham was also equipped with a pair of light-intensifying night-sight binoculars, a webbing scarf, gloves, two balaclavas, a woollen helmet, a camouflage hood, a peaked, camouflage-coloured forage cap and a green webbing harness to keep the larger radio set in position while crawling through the undergrowth. Behind him in the hide, hanging from a tree, he left another tool of his trade, a leather harness for supporting the head during long periods of observation. Murphy was similarly equipped.

Despite their surveillance training, the arrival of the Rottweiler dogs, barking and running forward as though to attack, took the two officers totally by surprise. They had just reached the cover of the shrubbery and copse surrounding a derelict garage some 60 yards from the front of the cottage, with Fordham in front on one knee beside a tree waiting for Murphy to move forward, when out of the darkness the dogs appeared.

Murphy, who afterwards could not be certain whether there were two or three animals in the initial attack, was later to admit candidly: 'I was terrified of them.' His hand flew to his pocket, and he tried feeding the yeast tablets to the dogs but to no avail. The Rottweilers weren't interested. Instead they continued barking, loudly enough, Murphy realized, to alert the occupants of Hollywood Cottage.

It was Murphy's radio message, 'Dogs – hostile', that was picked up by police in the retreat. After gesturing to Fordham, Murphy began to withdraw – a decision that was later to cause him months of anguished soul-searching. For he presumed that Fordham would guess what he planned to do and follow suit – an assumption that proved wrong.

At the Old Bailey nearly a year later Murphy was to deny that his withdrawal was caused by sheer terror of the dogs. The first maxim a C11 officer is taught is 'Blow out rather than show out'. And if his presence is discovered, he should still attempt to withdraw. The final resort, if that fails, is to identify himself as a police officer. In the case of hostile dogs that couldn't be pacified, withdrawal was the only option. 'It was obvious to me that because of the noise the dogs were making the occupants of the house would come out, so I moved away,' he said. At 6.26 p.m. he transmitted, 'Neil out towards fence,' and, walking through the shrubbery, made for the end of a wooden fence that separated Noye's land from another house in School Lane. Once at the boundary, Murphy walked down to the end furthest from Hollywood Cottage and, using a tree for support, climbed up to balance on top while he took stock of the situation. He was already aware, following a radio message from Fordham at 6.27, 'Somebody out, half-way down drive, calling dogs', that somebody had left the cottage to investigate the cause of the barking. Looking down to where he had last seen the Rottweilers, Murphy spotted a figure with a torch obviously searching in the shrubbery.

Surprised that Fordham hadn't followed him, surprised that he heard nothing from him over the radio and surprised that the dogs hadn't pursued him to the fence, Murphy decided to attract the attention of the dogs and the figure with the torch by kicking on the fence and shouting, 'Keep those dogs quiet!' He hoped to be mistaken for an irate neighbour and that the dogs would either be called off or come down to the fence to investigate the new intrusion, giving Fordham a chance to escape.

The figure with the torch, claimed Murphy later, appeared to move towards him, so he dropped into the garden on the other side of the fence.

*

Only one man now knows the true course of the events that followed. That man is Kenneth Noye, who freely admits that on discovering Fordham in the shrubbery, he stabbed him ten times, 'terrified for my life'. After his arrest Noye refused to tell police officers what had occurred, but he gave a full account to the jury at the murder trial.

Noye admitted in court that earlier that day he had intended to meet Reader at the Beaverwood Club. Although he and his wife planned to go out for dinner that night, he half expected Reader to show up before they left. When Reader did appear, he was shown into the kitchen to admire photographs, taken earlier that month, of the cottage covered in snow. A cup of tea was made, then Noye took Reader into his study to discuss business.

He was 'having a go' at Reader because of the missed rendezvous when he heard the dogs outside begin to bark. Concerned that they might be disturbing two elderly ladies who lived in a cottage adjacent to the front of his grounds, he opened the study door and shouted to his wife to go and call them in. Brenda Noye appeared at the door of the room to tell him that the dogs were down by the barn. She added, 'I'm not going down there. It's too dark.'

Taking his leather jacket from behind his chair, Noye went to the front door. 'You'll need a torch,' his wife said, but he remembered there was one in the Granada, which by then was in the garage. It was lying in the passenger footwell – beside the kitchen knife he had earlier used to try to scrape the battery terminals.

Stepping out into the night, he went to the garage, retrieved the torch and, noticing the knife, picked it up to return it to the kitchen once he had got the dogs. 'If Brenda had found it, she would start complaining again about using a kitchen knife in the car,' he explained.

Then, holding both items in his left hand, he went down the drive calling to the older of the dogs, Sam, which he knew to be out with one of the puppies, Cleo. The other puppy, Cassie, was in the kitchen, having been out all day.

Reaching the area of the apple store, he saw the dogs on a pile of sand barking into the shrubbery, and he swung the flashlight beam in the same direction. 'I shone my torch around the area to make sure there definitely wasn't anyone around because in the summer I caught some glue-sniffers there,' he said, although moments earlier in the witness box he had stated that he hadn't been anticipating an intruder because it was early in the evening.

Noye then moved into the wooded area. 'I was looking mainly on the floor. I thought there may be an animal that might be trapped. It's happened before, so I was looking in front of me.' A noise to his left attracted his attention, and he swung the beam in that direction, denying that he was conscious of anyone kicking the fence or shouting, 'Keep those dogs quiet!' Instantly the beam fell on a masked figure 4 or 5 feet away. 'I just froze with horror,' Noye recalled. 'All I saw when I flashed my torch on this masked man was just the two eyeholes and the mask. I thought that was my lot. I thought I was going to be a dead man. As far as I was concerned, that was it.'

An instant later, according to Noye, the figure had struck him a strong blow across his face with what he thought (although in retrospect he couldn't be sure) was a weapon. 'A masked man usually relates with a gun,' he said.

The blow 'woke me up. Made me so I could move again. Immediately the blow came across my face I put my hand up. I dropped the torch, obviously, and put my left hand up to his face and grabbed his face or head. I shouted out, "Brenda, help!" and started striking with all my strength, as fast as I could, into the masked man. I didn't have to think about using all my might. I thought I was a dead man.

'When he came straight at me I struck into the front of him, all of five times. As far as I was concerned, I was fighting for my life. I had struck the man in front, but it didn't seem to have any effect. He was overwhelmingly on top of me. He just looked grotesque, big.

'I am totally amazed at the amount of wounds the man had – I just didn't think it was having any effect. He was just totally overwhelming me . . . I suspect in a way I was bringing him towards me because I had hold of him. He looked like a giant. I didn't really relate to the masked man as a human being – I stabbed him in a panic.' In the tussle both men fell to the ground. 'I don't think I fell under his weight . . . It might have been his weight or me losing my footholding. Over we went. He came down on top of me and, as he came down on top of me, I struck him again,' said Noye. 'This was my only chance to get away because I was having no effect on that person. I took it. I got up and started running up the drive, looking over my shoulder to make sure he wasn't coming after me. When I looked, I saw the man running towards the front of the wall. My dogs were with him.'

Back at the cottage, before hearing the shout for help, Brenda Noye had been waiting by the front door to call the Rottweilers once her husband had located them. The dogs, claimed the Noyes, were untrained and would respond more quickly to her than to her husband.

On hearing his shout, her reaction was immediate. She went upstairs and took a shotgun from one of the half-dozen in the bedroom cupboard, then grabbed four cartridges out of the bedside cabinet. Loading the gun as she ran, Brenda Noye, in a track suit and slippers, and Reader, headed off down the drive in the direction of the shout. Half-way down they saw Noye approaching, his face covered in blood. 'There's a masked man down there,' shouted Noye, and he grabbed the gun, which was now in Reader's possession. Later he could not remember at what point he dropped the knife, but he was adamant that once he had left the shrubbery he never used it again on the intruder.

Running to the copse, with his wife and Reader close on his heels, he picked up the torch and then made towards the gate, where Brenda Noye could see the dogs and the figure of a man lying slumped on the ground. 'Who are you? Who are you?' Noye shouted as he approached the dying policeman.

In the quiet intensity of the Number One Court at the Old Bailey Noye had no difficulty in rationalizing his decision to go after the camouflage-suited man again, a figure that only moments earlier had put him in terror of his life. 'I didn't want him to get away in case he came back another time, when I wasn't there, to sort Brenda and the children out,' he said. He was also worried that the hooded man might have had an accomplice.

Noye could not believe the experience he had just been through. The struggle in the shrubbery had left him overwhelmed and shocked. Now, as he approached Fordham, who was still wearing his balaclava hood, he spotted the policeman's night-sight binoculars. The explanation that leapt to mind was that he was dealing with a rapist.

'Who are you? Take that mask off!' he shouted several times, pointing his shotgun at the prone figure. There was no response. 'If you don't take that mask off and tell me who you are, I'll blow your head off,' he threatened.

Then, according to Noye's account, Fordham gave a reply that he must have hoped presented a chance, albeit slim, of hiding the real reason for his presence in the garden and perhaps preventing the operation from ending in failure. 'SAS,' he groaned, taking off his hood. To the next question – what was he doing there? – he managed to force out the words 'On manoeuvres'.

'Show us your ID then,' Noye ordered. There was no reply. But by now, Noye told the jury, he realized from the pallor of the man's face that he was badly injured.

For a man apparently shocked and overwhelmed, Noye thought fast. There was obviously going to be an inquiry and he wanted to make sure that his version of events was believed. On leaving the shrubbery, he had realized that he was bleeding from cuts to his eye and his nose. The injuries, he maintained, were caused by the blow that Fordham struck him at the outset of the struggle. He wanted photographic evidence both of those injuries and of the mask and the suit that Fordham was wearing. 'I was terrified of the mask disappearing,' he explained.

His wife was dispatched to the house to call an ambulance and collect a camera and flash gun to take the necessary pictures. She left, followed by Reader.

Noye stood there for a moment or two, looking down at Fordham, then the policeman moved, pulling open his jacket, and Noye could see better the wounds he had inflicted. 'I knelt down to him because I could see now the man was in a very bad way,' said Noye. 'I said, "What on earth are you doing here?" but he didn't answer. He didn't say anything. His head was down and I put my arm under him to put it in a better position. Then a car drove in.'

The C11 officers in their base at the retreat had taken immediate action following Murphy's warning, 'Dogs – hostile'. DC Stinton and DC Matthews, who were about to go off duty, were sent back down to the edge of the retreat's ground to see if they could devise a means of drawing the dogs away from the two policemen. Even so, Acting DCI Suckling, who had by now left Brands Hatch and was close to the junction of the A 20 with School Lane, saw no reason at that time to take any action.

It wasn't until a message at 6.37 from Murphy, warning him 'Man compromising John. Stick/shotgun', that he ordered all units to converge on Hollywood Cottage. Murphy had taken five minutes, after dropping over the fence when he believed he saw the torch move towards him, to make his way out on to School Lane.

At first he could see nothing, but as he walked back along the lane towards the wall at the front of the cottage grounds, he heard shouting and a woman screaming. Moving into some bushes beside the entrance to the retreat, virtually on top of the hide where he and Fordham had been earlier, he looked into the grounds and could see two men and a woman. Both of the men were shouting and looking down at the ground, one of them holding what he took to be either a shotgun or a stick.

At some stage during the shouting, Murphy claimed, he saw the man who was not holding the shotgun step forward and make a kicking motion. Although he was unable to see Fordham's or Reader's feet because of the wall, he said later, 'It was obvious to me at the time that he kicked John.' It was that kick, which Noyes and Reader denied was ever delivered, that was among the factors leading to Reader's appearance beside Kenneth Noye when both were charged with murder.

Murphy remained in his hiding place, transmitting back to the retreat everything he could see and hear. In doing so he was following classic C11 training. He was there in a surveillance role, not an operational one. Taxed by the defence at the murder trial as to why he did nothing when he saw the plight his colleague was in, he said, 'It didn't occur to me. I knew that control would be organizing for other officers to go in, far better-equipped than I was.'

Looking at the scene from a position in the retreat's grounds further along School Lane, DCs Matthews and Sinton also took no action. They had been delayed at the retreat because Matthews had already partially changed and had to put his surveillance kit back on. By the time they reached their vantage point it was too late to try to draw the dogs away. Their surveillance training to the fore, they did nothing, realizing that better-equipped officers were at hand, ready to go in. They were able, however, to corroborate much of Murphy's evidence about what he saw and heard from his position in the bushes.

The first men into the grounds were Flying Squad DCs David Manning and John Childs. They had been in an unmarked police car in the retreat's drive, moving slowly forward, when the order came. When the words 'All units AM' (a C11 code) came over the radio, they tore out into School Lane. Luck was on their side. The gates to Hollywood Cottage had been left open after Reader's arrival, and they swept into the drive.

Once again Noye's account and that of police officers about what transpired at the scene differ markedly.

According to Manning, a stocky 38-year-old Welshman, a former professional footballer who had been in the force twenty years, they entered the grounds to see Fordham lying on his back, with the dogs pulling and tugging at his clothes. Noye was still standing over the C11 officer, pointing his shotgun at him. Childs, 39, the driver, radioed to all Flying Squad units on their way to the cottage to stand by – which meant they were not to enter the grounds at that point – and Manning, quickly followed by Childs, got out. Holding up his warrant card, Manning shouted, 'I am a police officer,' and Noye moved towards him, pointing the shotgun and shouting, 'Fuck off or I will do you as well.'

'Put the gun down and get those dogs away from the officer,'

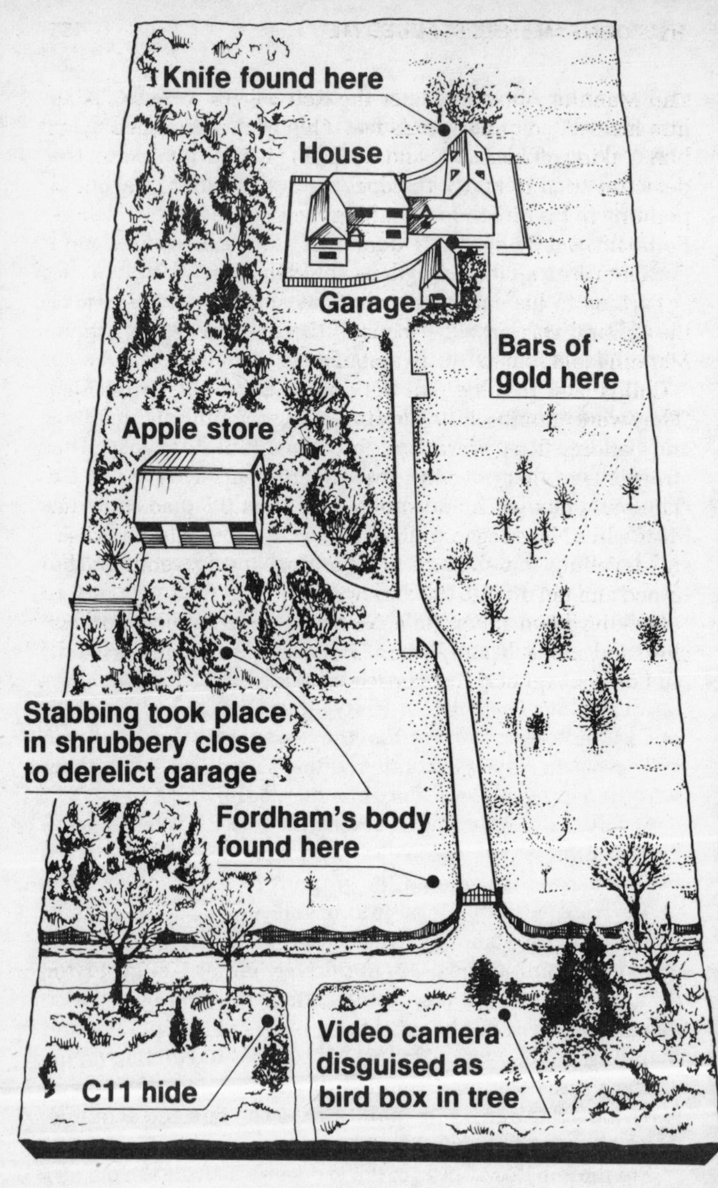
Knife found here
House
Garage
Bars of gold here
Apple store
Stabbing took place in shrubbery close to derelict garage
Fordham's body found here
C11 hide
Video camera disguised as bird box in tree

said Manning; moments later the Rottweilers were attacking him instead, snapping at his feet. One of them jumped up at him. Taking off his jacket and wrapping it around his arm, the detective tried to knock the dogs away. Ignoring the shotgun pointing in his direction, Manning then walked over to where Fordham was lying. 'He's done me. He's stabbed me,' said Fordham with all the strength he could muster.

Turning to his colleague, who was standing at the rear of the car and was now the focus of the Rottweilers' attention, Manning told him to call an ambulance.

Childs later recalled that the dogs were 'totally terrifying'. 'They were jumping, biting my trousers, crowding me, snarling and barking. They were very ferocious.' But he managed to struggle past them back to the driver's seat, from where he called an ambulance and ordered all Flying Squad units in. Meanwhile Noye began walking backwards towards the house, still levelling the shotgun at Manning, until eventually he turned and ran off into the darkness.

Looking down at Fordham, Manning could see blood on his chest and stomach, and he immediately started giving first aid, but Fordham quickly lost consciousness.

12. 'I didn't know he was a policeman'

Later Noye was to recount in vivid detail the moments when he first discovered that the man whom he had killed was a police officer. In an account that differed markedly from that of DC Manning, Noye told the jury at his Old Bailey murder trial: 'I was kneeling down to Mr Fordham. The car went past, then he [Manning] saw us and immediately backed down. I didn't think they were police officers – I thought they were the man's friends. I left Mr Fordham and ran straight across to the car. The windows were wound down, and I put the shotgun at the passenger. I said, "Who are you?" and he said, "Police." I said, "Get out and show us your ID." He got out, put his hand in his back pocket and got out his warrant card and showed it. I then immediately broke the gun. He said to me, "What's happened?", looking at my face. I said, "What's happened? Look at me and look at that – that's what's happened."'

'Then Mr Manning said, "He's a police officer."

'The SAS man! I said, "What are you on about – 'He's a police officer'? Look at him: he's masked up!" I just couldn't believe it. By now there were three dogs. Cassie had come out. They weren't getting in the way, jumping up or anything. He said, "Get those dogs out of the way." I said, "I can't get the dogs out of the way. They haven't got their collars on and they don't pay any attention to me anyway." He said, "Go and get the leads," which I then went off to get.

'It was only a minute or so later before I returned. I bumped into my wife coming down the drive. She had the camera, flash gun and mobile phone. I took the camera off her. I took the flash gun and put it in my pocket. And I took the portable telephone from her because she said she wasn't able to phone the ambulance as the lines were unobtainable. Round that time of the night you sometimes had to wait thirty seconds to get a dialling tone. I sent her to go and get the dogs' leads.

'I went back to the driver and said, "My wife hasn't been able to phone the ambulance," and he said he had done it. Mr Childs said, "Whose radio phone is that?", looking at my mobile phone. I think he thought it was the masked man's.

'Mr Manning said, "Where are the dog leads?" I said, "I've sent my wife." He got a bit agitated because the dogs were getting in the way. Although they were not harming anyone he was obviously anxious to help his colleague. He said, "You go and get them."'

Noye added that at no stage had his dogs troubled Fordham or any other officer. They were not kept as guard dogs but were totally untrained and kept as family pets. 'These dogs, all they done that night – and this is 100 per cent – all they did was bark.'

'My dogs are not ferocious,' he added under cross-examination. 'I looked the word up in the dictionary. It means savage, fierce and cruel. My dogs are exactly the opposite – loving and affectionate.' In fact, said Noye, he had planned to have the dogs trained later that year.

However, he claimed that on Manning's orders he ran up to the house and placed the gun in a broken position on a wall beside the front door. Then: 'A car pulled up and two men jumped out with baseball bats. I ran. I thought I was going to get a beating.' Noye demonstrated the size of the bats, which he thought were about 3 feet long.

The two men he saw jump from the car were DS Yeoman and DC Finlayson, who had earlier that day followed Reader from his home to the Beaverwood Club and later trailed him to

Hollywood Cottage. When Reader had arrived at Noye's house they stationed themselves in the car park of the Portobello Inn, a pub some quarter of a mile away, opposite the junction of School Lane and the A 20.

Brenda Noye confirmed her husband's account that the detectives at the scene were armed with 'big sticks, baseball-type', but both officers categorically denied in court that they were carrying the longer truncheons, although such weapons are part of the equipment that the Flying Squad had access to, and Yeoman agreed that he 'very frequently' used them.

In court Yeoman described what happened as they arrived at the front door. 'I noticed Noye running from his main doorway across in front of the building. It was no more than a jog. I recall that he was carrying a camera – I believe, over his right shoulder. Before he disappeared from view I shouted to him, "Come here, you!" But then he disappeared momentarily, then subsequently reappeared. He didn't respond immediately to the command. He ran out of sight between the garage and the swimming pool for a matter of seconds. Under the circumstances I thought that was an inordinately long period of time.

'When he reappeared he started to walk back towards the front door. DC Finlayson grabbed his left arm and said, "Police." Noye's response to that was, "I know."

'He seemed agitated and nervous. I said to him, "What on earth happened?" and then Noye said, "I took the knife from him and did him. Old Bill or no, he had no fucking business being here." I then cautioned him. He didn't make any reply and we started to walk towards the front door.'

Meanwhile Suckling, who had driven up, saw Brenda Noye standing at the front of the house. 'You're being arrested,' he said approaching her.

'Why?' she asked.

'A policeman has been very badly hurt here tonight. You're being arrested in connection with that.'

'He shouldn't have come here,' she replied.

Yeoman continued: 'The door was locked and we had to send for the keys. I vaguely remember them being retrieved from Mrs Noye, who at that time was sat in the back of a police car. On the wall I saw a shotgun. It was loaded but it was broken.

'Once inside, the first thing I said was, "Where's the knife?" Noye said, "Down there," and with that he pointed towards the area of the gate. DC Finlayson said, "What kind of knife was it?" and he said, "A penknife." Finlayson said, "Don't be silly."

'At that point Noye shrugged his shoulders and said, "It was a kitchen knife. I got it before I went out."

'I was then joined by another officer, Sergeant Robinson. He said, "Did you stab him?" Noye said, "Yeah. I did him before he took the knife from me." Sergeant Robinson cautioned him again. Again he made no reply. Then Robinson said, "Where's the other man?" The response to that was: "He left about half an hour ago." We then decided to conduct a search of the ground floor to establish whether in fact Reader was still in the building and subsequently we landed up in the study.

'We still didn't know at that stage who Reader was. Sergeant Robinson said, "Who is he?" Noye said, "What's that got to do with it? Mind your own fucking business." Sergeant Robinson said, "Who do the vehicles outside belong to?" Noye said, "They are mine." Sergeant Robinson said, "How about the Cavalier?" The reply to that was: "That's mine."

'I was very distressed. It was at this point that I said to him, "Do you realize that the police officer you stabbed is dying?" He said, "He shouldn't have been on my property. I hope he fucking dies."

'I lunged at him and pushed him hard against the wall. I said to him, "What sort of animal are you that could wish anybody dead?" The reason I lost my temper was because I couldn't believe how callously he treated life. I finally lost control.'

Yeoman added that he was separated from Noye by Robinson, who told the prisoner, 'Just calm down and be quiet. Be under no illusion that you are under arrest for a very serious assault.' Noye was then handcuffed, and shortly afterwards Yeoman left the house.

Noye disputed this version of events. He denied ever saying,

'I took the knife from him and did him. Old Bill or no, he had no fucking business being here.' Said Noye, 'I don't call police officers "Old Bill"; I call them cozzers.' He denied ever saying that the weapon used had been a penknife, and he denied saying that he had taken the kitchen knife out with him. He also adamantly denied saying that he hoped the man he had attacked would die. 'I would not want anyone dead. Not a person. I wouldn't even want an animal dead.' He added that when Yeoman lunged at him he was already handcuffed to a police officer and claimed the attack came when he said a kitchen knife was used. 'He was very annoyed, I expect because it was his colleague. I don't know.'

While Noye and his wife were under arrest at the house, police officers at the bottom of the drive were making frantic attempts to save the life of their dying colleague. 'Let me go,' he groaned, but he was given cardiac massage, his mouth was forced open and he was given the kiss of life. Shortly after 7 p.m. an ambulance arrived, and DC Fordham, his pulse barely discernible, was placed in the back for the journey to Queen Mary's Hospital, Sidcup. Murphy and another C11 officer, DI Roland Heming, who had been in charge at the hide opposite Hollywood Cottage, went with him.

As the ambulance set off, Murphy assisted ambulanceman Bryan Moore by holding an oxygen mask over Fordham's face while Moore checked for signs of life. The pulse had stopped. Cutting through the five layers of clothing the policeman was wearing, Moore applied cardiac massage but to no avail.

Twelve minutes later they were at the hospital, where Fordham was seen by the surgeon on duty, Graham Ponting, who found ten stab wounds on the body. He could detect no sign of a pulse, although tests showed that there was still electrical activity in the heart. A blood transfusion into Fordham's ankle was set up and an operation carried out. Several attempts were made to get the heart going again, using direct injections of drugs and electric shocks, but at 8.20 p.m. Fordham was pronounced dead.

Pathologist Dr Rufus Crompton, who examined the body the following morning, found that the stab wounds were all consistent with blows from a single-edged blade about 1 centimetre wide and 7 centimetres long. Five of the wounds were on the front of the body; three were on the back; one was in the armpit; and one was on the head.

The two wounds that were fatal both penetrated Fordham's heart. One, delivered with the force of a punch, had severed the fifth rib to enter the left ventricle, and the other, 2 centimetres below, had just nicked the right ventricle. In both cases the knife had been plunged in to a depth of 7 centimetres, and a small bruise beside the cutting edge of each wound suggested that the knife had been pushed in to the hilt. The two fatal blows, together with another wound to the front of the body and two to the back, one of which had entered the spleen, formed a horizontal group, all struck at practically the same angle, probably very rapidly. The close proximity of the five wounds, and their similarities, suggested that after the first one all had been inflicted while Fordham was immobile. They were consistent with a right-handed assailant, face to face with the policeman, who had delivered the blows to the front and had then reached behind to stab Fordham in the back.

Those wounds, together with the strong likelihood that Fordham had received them while immobile, were the key reason why Reader was included in the murder charge. Although this was never stated in court, the suggestion always implicit in the prosecution case was that Reader had held Fordham while Noye did the stabbing. Giving weight to this scenario was the fact that Fordham had sustained no defence wounds, commonly found on victims of knife attacks because a person being attacked receives cuts to his hands or arms as he tries to fend off the blade.

Three other wounds seemed to have been inflicted by a knife held like a dagger, providing Fordham was still on his feet when he sustained them. Noye was to deny in court ever holding the knife in such a fashion. The first, a vertical wound on the right of the chest, pierced the chest wall but missed any organs. The second, further over towards the left, pierced a lung. The third, in Fordham's back, behind his left shoulder, went into muscle. The wound in the left armpit was a flesh injury, while a cut on the right ear was contiguous with a sliced scalp wound behind the ear.

When the torso was dissected a bruise to the chest, not visible to the eye, was also revealed; if it was not due to cardiac massage (and Crompton thought that unlikely), it was consistent with a blow from a light object, a fall, a punch or a kick.

There was no bruise to any of Fordham's knuckles, which might have been expected had he delivered the blow that, Noye maintained, precipitated the struggle, although Crompton said he would not have expected to find a bruise had Fordham been wearing gloves, and the policeman certainly had a pair with him that night.

Although Fordham's body was found by the front gates, no attempt was made at the trial of Noye and Reader to suggest that the stabbing was done anywhere other than in the shrubbery. Despite the extent of Fordham's injuries, Crompton believed that the policeman would have been able to cover the 220 feet from the shrubbery to the front of the grounds, where his colleagues eventually found him, although he would have been losing a lot of blood and the effort would have hastened his eventual collapse. Fordham's escape attempt would have been possible, according to Crompton, because in the case of a knife going into the left side of the heart, it can enter thick muscle, and the pump action of the heart effectively seals the wound. It is not uncommon for someone with such an injury to remain conscious for some minutes afterwards. People with wounds on the right side of the heart, where the wall is much thinner, generally stay conscious for a matter of seconds. In Fordham's case, however, the wound to the right side was very small.

After the stabbing Reader had fled from the scene, leaving his car behind. Making his way out of the area through private gardens, he eventually reached the A20 leading back to London. But for a man at the centre of a gold bullion distribution chain he chose an unusual way to make good his escape: he tried to hitch a lift.

By now, Kent Constabulary had been alerted to what had

happened and, because the killing had taken place in their area, they took control of the inquiry, despatching a squad of detectives to West Kingsdown to help in the search for Reader. It was 7.40 p.m. when DS Barry McAllister, travelling in the London direction as he hunted for Reader, spotted him standing beside the road on the outskirts of West Kingsdown, just past a pub called the Gamecock. McAllister had already been given a description of the man missing from Hollywood Cottage and recognized him immediately.

He stopped his unmarked police car some 20 or 30 yards further on and watched in the rear-view mirror as the fugitive ran up. DC Paul Gladstone, in the passenger seat, wound down the window.

'Is there any chance of a lift to London?' asked Reader, drawing up. 'Yes, get in,' said Gladstone, and he got out to allow Reader to climb into the back.

As the car pulled off Gladstone revealed that he and McAllister were policemen and asked Reader where he had come from. 'The pub,' said Reader, indicating the Gamecock.

'Where were you before that?' he was asked.

'What's all this about?' replied Reader.

'We're looking for a man in connection with a serious incident tonight. Where did you come from before the Gamecock?'

Reader made no reply but instead went to put his right hand into his pocket. Gladstone, who believed that he might be armed, asked to see what he was holding. Reader showed him a few coins, then was ordered to place his hands on top of the back of the front passenger seat. He was handcuffed and driven back to the car park of the Portobello Inn, where other Kent CID men were waiting. There he was told that he was being arrested on suspicion of assaulting a police officer earlier that evening. 'What?' said Reader, and he was told a second time. 'You must be joking!' he exclaimed.

Even if Reader had escaped the attention of the two Kent detectives, it was unlikely that he would have got far. For travelling into West Kingsdown from the London direction, as he stood by the road thumbing a lift, were Flying Squad DSs Alan Branch and John Redgrave, also in an unmarked car.

Redgrave recognized Reader from surveillance duties he had carried out on 8 January outside Farringdon Street station, while Branch recognized him from the station and Russell Square two days later. Both detectives leapt from the vehicle to arrest him, but by that time Reader was already running up to the Kent police car.

Noye, his wife and Reader were all taken that night to Swanley police station. 'Hands on your knees and don't speak,' Noye was ordered as he climbed into the police car.

From the outset, according to police, it was clear that Noye, the respectable business entrepreneur, was rather more familiar with the uncompromising, aggressive approach of more experienced members of the criminal fraternity towards police matters than was quite usual. He harboured deep suspicions that evidence would be invented against him and statements concocted, and he was not slow in demanding his legal rights. Throughout, one of his main concerns was that the matter should remain the province of Kent police. It was to be a constant refrain over the next two days. His reasoning was never made clear but undoubtedly reflected the suspicion with which professional criminals regard Scotland Yard, particularly the Flying Squad.

Another major concern was to ensure that the police took adequate note of the injuries to his face. They would be crucial in paving the way for a plea of self-defence.

One of the first policemen to see him in custody was the station sergeant, David Columbine. He asked Noye if he knew why he was being held. Noye said he didn't. 'You're here for the attempted murder or murder of a police officer,' said Columbine.

'Is that all?' the prisoner allegedly replied. He was searched, and nearly £850 was found on him.

At 11.30 that evening police went to Noye's cell (the 'female' cell at the small station) to ask for his clothing for forensic examination. PC Fred Bird was unsure of the identity of the prisoner, for up until then Noye had refused to reveal his name.

'You are not having my clothing until I have seen my brief,' Noye said, using the London slang word for his solicitor. 'I want this photographed,' he added, pointing to his eye and nose and the mud on his clothing.

'If I do, will you allow me to take your clothing?' asked Bird.

'Yes.'

Noye was escorted to a first-floor room where the photographs were taken. Then, on returning to his cell, Noye said, 'All right, you can have my clothes.' As they were being taken from him he asked, 'Will I be moved to London?'

'No. The offence happened in Kent. You will be dealt with here,' he was told.

Bird was not lying. At that stage the killing was a Kent police inquiry. The Metropolitan Police did not formally take over until 2.00 p.m. the following Monday, after a top-level meeting at Scotland Yard between Brian Worth, the Yard's Deputy Assistant Commissioner in charge of serious crime operations, Anthony Coe, Kent police's Assistant Chief Constable in charge of operations, and Detective Chief Superintendent Duncan Gibbins, head of Kent CID.

In Britain, which does not have a national police force, only a series of local county forces, police-force boundaries are closely guarded. A confidential Home Office memorandum in 1982, however, set out the circumstances in which serious crime investigations can be coordinated across boundaries. In this instance the handover, when it occurred, took place only as a result of further developments at Hollywood Cottage that established a direct link with the Brink's-Mat robbery already being handled by the Yard.

When Scotland Yard did take the inquiry over, it was placed in the hands of Commander Philip Corbett from C11. Running such an operation is usually outside that department's remit, but it was one of their officers who had been killed. Corbett had also received the relevant training in running an inter-force inquiry, and, after all, the investigation into Noye had been initiated largely by intelligence provided by C11. It made little odds, however, as C11 allowed the on-the-ground investigation to be handled by Boyce and his officers in C8.

'I didn't know he was a police officer. All I saw was a chap in camouflage gear and a balaclava mask. I wouldn't have stabbed him if I knew he was a police officer,' continued Noye.

'I can't discuss this with you. Can I have your name?' asked Bird, but Noye still refused to divulge it.

Bird said he was being silly and told him he could well be facing a murder charge.

The sombre warning seemed to work, for the next moment Noye stuck out his hand and said, 'My name is Kenny Noye.' He again repeated that he hadn't known Fordham was a policeman.

Later that night Noye was transferred from Swanley to Dartford police station. 'Well, is he alive or dead?' the prisoner is said to have asked as he sat in the back of the police car.

'No comment,' replied one of the police officers with him.

'What's the unofficial answer?' persisted Noye, but his escort would not be drawn.

It was his facial injuries that were uppermost in his mind when, in the early hours of Sunday morning, he was examined by police surgeon Dr Eugene Ganz. His attitude by then was 'commanding'. 'He literally ordered me to make a note of his injuries,' said Ganz later. They included a black left eye, which was also slightly cut, and a cut nostril. Both wounds Ganz described as trivial, adding that Noye's face was slightly smeared with blood. Noye also complained of pain in the abdominal area and the back, saying he had been kicked, but there was no bruising. There was also swelling on the back of his right hand. When the doctor noticed scratches on his left hand he refused to allow it to be examined, saying, 'That's nothing.'

At Swanley police station Reader also refused to identify himself. He was searched, and his pockets were emptied. When asked to sign a form listing what had been taken, he at first refused, then appeared to do so but instead wrote down the name and address of a firm of solicitors. His identity still a mystery, he was told that his clothing would be taken for forensic analysis, but after his shoes, a scarf, a handkerchief and a blue zip-up cardigan were removed he refused to part with anything else until alternative clothing was provided. Eventually a boiler suit was produced, and his trousers and shirt were removed.

Noye's first formal interview took place at lunchtime on the Sunday. He was seen by DCI Peter Humphrey, a Kent policeman, and – as was to be the case at a number of the interviews involving Noye, his wife and Reader – another detective who made a note of all the questions and answers.

Throughout the first interview, which lasted seven minutes, Noye refused to answer questions unless his solicitor was present. 'I was promised my solicitor when I got to Swanley last night. Now it's Sunday, one o'clock, and I still haven't seen him,' he complained.

The policeman was unmoved. 'Has anyone told you that the man you stabbed last night has died?' he asked.

'No reply unless my solicitor is present,' replied Noye.

At the end of the interview a statement was drawn up of what had been said. Noye requested that the letters 'p.m.' be inserted after the time 'one o'clock' and that a line be drawn from the end of the last word on each line to the edge of the page to prevent anything being inserted later.

That afternoon his request for a solicitor was granted. His legal representative of some twelve years' standing, Raymond Burrough, was ushered into the cell to see him. Burrough had reacted with amazement when told of the incident the previous night at Hollywood Cottage. The Kenny Noye he knew was 'a jovial sort of fellow – gregarious'. Burrough later told the Old Bailey jury, 'I know he abhors violence because he has expressed that to me in the past in relation to the fear that he has – and lots of us in rural areas have it – as to his wife and children when he wasn't home. I have never seen him lose his temper on any occasion or show the slightest signs of violence at all.'

The Kenny Noye who greeted him that afternoon was 'very agitated and very distressed'. Briefly the prisoner outlined what had happened. But as he told how he had surprised a masked man in the bushes and an instant later received a blow to his face, Burrough cut him short. The cell door had been kept open a foot or two by officers guarding Noye, and two of them remained outside within hearing distance. 'I didn't think it was conducive in that cell to take further instructions from him because of the atmosphere at that police station. There was much coming and going of officers. One could almost cut the atmosphere with a knife,' Burrough explained.

He added that Noye was 'terrified'. 'He put it to me that it was either the man or him. He was very remorseful at the death of this man and very frustrated at the same time at the manner in which it had occurred, that it had led to both the man's death and his arrest. There was a deep sense of frustration that he was in the position that he found himself when he had only gone into the garden to see what caused the dogs to bark. His main concern was the hood aspect of the dress of the victim. He seemed convinced in his own mind that the hood would be spirited away. He was also extremely worried about the detention of his wife.'

Nicholas Purnell, QC, the prosecuting counsel, cross-examined Burrough, pointing out that, as he hadn't recorded the interview, he was relying on memory. 'Yes,' replied the solicitor, 'but it's burned into my mind. He said he saw the eyes, and it was instantly followed by the blow.'

Reader too had been taken from Swanley to Dartford police station and was in a cell next to Noye. At 3.15 that afternoon he was seen by Detective Superintendent David Tully of the Kent police force. He immediately expressed concern about his wife, who was a diabetic and due to go into hospital the next day for treatment to her pancreas. 'Where's my wife?' he demanded. He was told that she had been arrested and was at Gravesend police station. 'I want you to know, Mr Tully, that she is a very sick woman and needs medical attention. She is due to go into hospital tomorrow for treatment,' said the prisoner.

Tully said that after the interview he would go to Gravesend to ensure she was all right. 'Thank you,' said Reader. 'She needs special food, like boiled fish, otherwise she gets ill.'

'At some stage you will be interviewed about the incident at Mr Noye's home on Saturday evening. You understand that you have been detained in connection with that incident?' asked Tully.

'It's a very serious matter. I know a police officer has been murdered, and I was told I was responsible. I want you to know, Mr Tully, that I do not know anything about it and I did not have anything to do with it,' said Reader.

Reader then said he would not answer any questions without his solicitor being present, and gave the name of his legal representative, Stanley Beller of Beller Jarvis, based in Oxford Street, central London.

'You must understand,' said Tully. 'A large amount of money was found at your house when your wife was arrested, and she, as well as you, will be asked to account for the possession of that money.'

'That money is mine. It's nothing to do with my wife,' said Reader.

Hollywood Cottage and its grounds and Reader's neat, pebble-dashed home on a suburban estate, distinguished from its neighbours only by the ornate, white, Spanish-style wooden shutters, had indeed been searched. At Reader's house, which police (who by now included armed officers) raided within an hour of Fordham's being taken to hospital, a black briefcase was found in the bedroom containing bundles of £50 notes, nearly £66,000 worth, all with the prefix A 24. A further £3,000 were found in the kitchen, and a lump of silver-coloured metal was discovered, which Lynda Reader said her husband had given her. Maps, Spanish hotel brochures, papers with numbers on them, correspondence and photographs were also taken away for examination, as were three note books and a diary. An Access card and an international driver's licence were also seized, both in the name of the jeweller whom Reader had been seen meeting earlier that month. In an interview given to a London magazine later Lynn Reader claimed, 'There were about ten of them. They were like a crowd of cowboys.

One was drunk as a sack. They were screaming at me, "Has your husband got a green Cavalier?" I just screamed back at them, "What's all this about?" Then they got a message on their radio that a green Cavalier was approaching, and one of them stood with a gun pointing at the front door.'

In the case of Hollywood Cottage and its grounds the searches were to go on for six weeks and included an aerial reconnaissance by a helicopter equipped with an infra-red device capable of pinpointing metal buried underground or hidden in buildings. In the days immediately after the killing the grounds were thoroughly checked by a line of policeman moving slowly forward, shoulder to shoulder.

The initial haul inside Hollywood Cottage was encouraging. Quantities of copper coins of a kind used in the re-smelting of gold were found in several rooms, and a child's pad containing a picture of a gold bar was found in a kitchen drawer. There was also a 1985 edition of the *Guinness Book of Records* with a circle drawn around the entry of Brink's-Mat as the largest British robbery. A small kitchen knife was found in a dish-washer in the kitchen.

Outside a police dog in woods behind Hollywood Cottage located a flick knife, and a similar weapon was found in the door pocket of Noye's Granada. And at the back of the house, close to the corner of the swimming pool, a Maidstone police constable, Arthur Cannadine, found the knife that police have always believed was used to carry out the stabbing. White-handled, it was a kitchen knife thrust blade-down into the ground at the foot of a tree. The knife and the soil around it were taken away for forensic examination, but no trace of blood was found. Both Noye and his wife believe that the knife was left there by one of their children, who sometimes used to sleep out in a tent in that part of the garden. Noye claimed in court that he had no knowledge about what happened to the knife that he used to carry out the stabbing.

A camouflage hat worn by Fordham was also discovered close to the shrubbery where he had hidden, while inside the sbrubbery police found his peaked camouflage cap.

It wasn't until 4.20 that Sunday afternoon, however, that a

1. Unit 7: the Brink's-Mat warehouse on the Heathrow International Trading Estate the morning after the raid.

2. Brink's-Mat side entrance: the door through which the robbers entered.

3. Flying Squad Commander Frank Cater, at a press conference, holding a package similar to those containing the Brink's-Mat gold.

4. Tony Black: the security guard who let the robbers in.

5. Tony White walking free from the Old Bailey.

6. The Bully: Micky McAvoy, sentenced to twenty-five years' imprisonment for his role in the Brink's-Mat robbery.

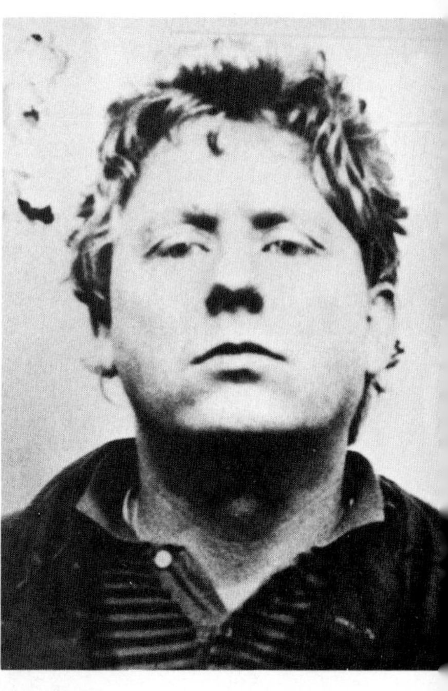

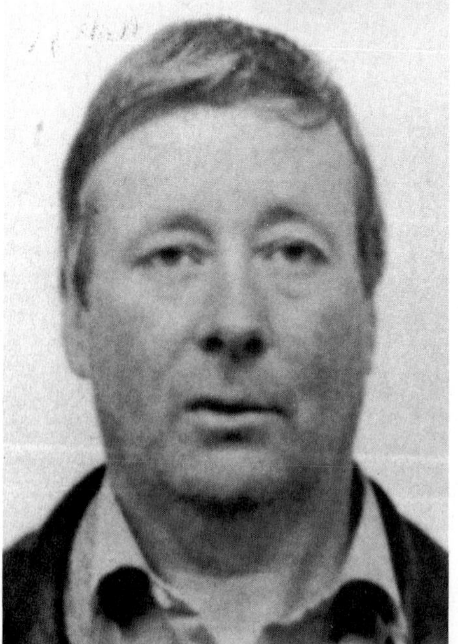

7. The Boss: Brian Robinson, also known in south London as the Colonel. Sentenced to twenty-five years' imprisonment for his role in the robbery.

8. Hollywood Cottage: Noye's mansion in the Kent countryside.

9. The two faces of Kenneth Noye. The successful and . . .

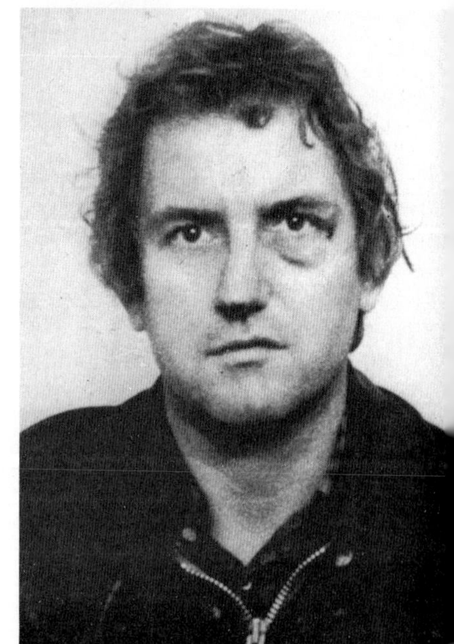

10. . . . the stolen bullion fence the night after stabbing DC John Fordham to death.

. 'Gentleman' John
›rdham: one of
otland Yard's top
ıdercover police
ficers.

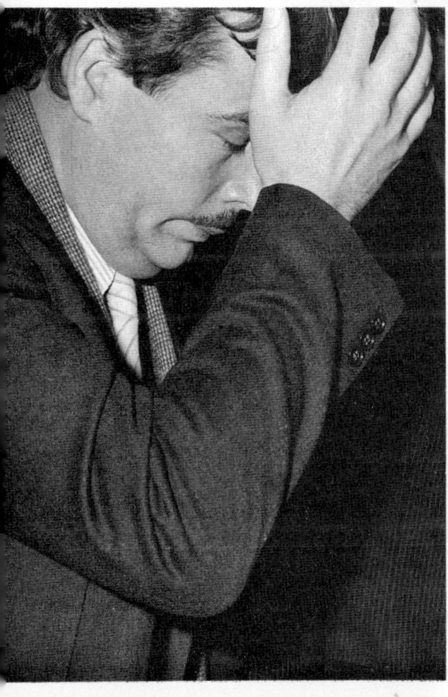

12. DC Neil Murphy after Noye's and Reader's acquittals for murder.

13. How Fordham would have looked caught in the beam of Noye's torch. This picture, a reconstruction, was taken by the defence and shown to the jury at the Noye/Reader murder trial.

14. Detective Chief Superintendent Brian Boyce, who took over the hunt for the bullion gang.

15. Deputy Assistant Commissioner Brian Worth before his retirement from the Metropolitan Police. He set up the Specialist Operations task force to tackle organized crime.

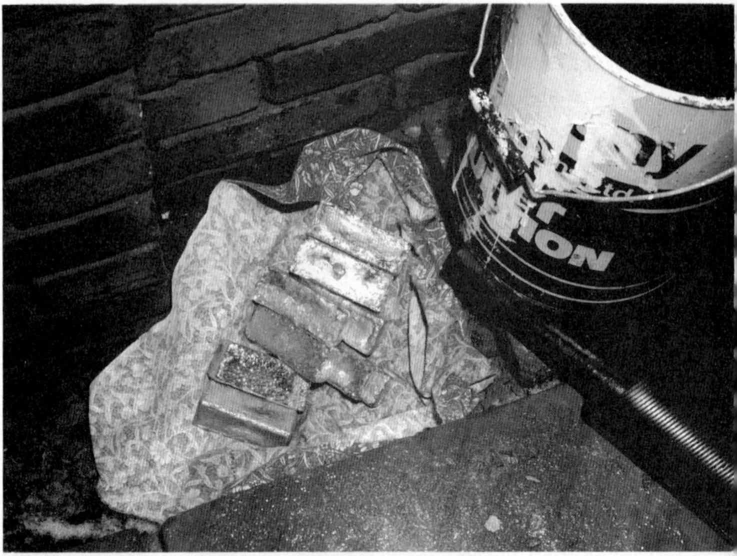

16. Some of the eleven bars of gold hidden beside Noye's garage.

17. Brian Reader: jailed for conspiring to handle some of the Brink's-Mat bullion.

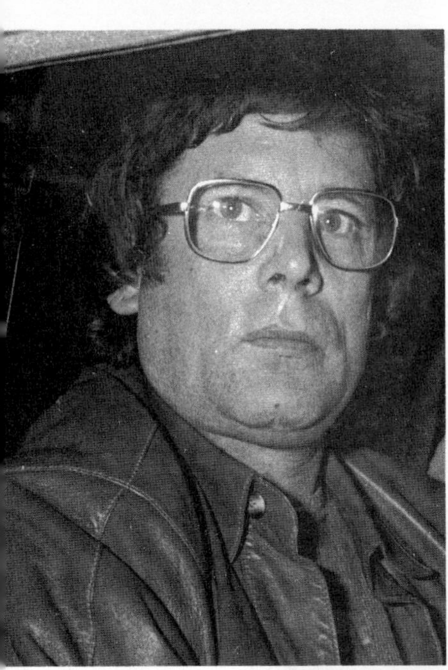

18. Garth Chappell: the Bristol gold dealer who made millions from the Brink's-Mat bullion.

19. Terence Patch: the Bristol businessman cleared in the Brink's-Mat trial.

20. Matteo 'Matty' Constantinou: well known for years as a top-class fence for stolen property.

21. Scadlynn Ltd: it made so much money under Chappell that cash was just dumped on the floor in sacks.

2. John Palmer and his ife Marnie soak up the ın in Tenerife. Back in ritain police were onducting an ıch-by-inch search of ıeir home for the gold.

3. The smelter behind ohn Palmer's home – idden from view by ushes and a horsebox.

24. John Fleming returns to London after losing his battle against deportation in the USA.

25. Scott Errico, alleged hit man for a Florida-based drugs gang, after his extradition from Britain to the United States to face trial for three contract killings.

26. Detective Superintendent Tony Lundy at a press conference in Miami.

27. Patrick Diamond (left) entering the court in the Isle of Man.

Gravesend police sergeant, Peter Holloway, who was searching the ground beside the garage, found the evidence that the Flying Squad really needed to link Noye and Reader to the Brink's-Mat bullion case. It was that discovery that enabled Scotland Yard formally to take over the investigation into Fordham's killing. Lying in a shallow gully beside the garage wall, and hidden from view by a tin of paint covered by a rubber mat, was a red-and-white piece of material. Inside the cloth were eleven gold bars, amounting to some 13 kilogrammes, at that time worth £100,000. The bars, roughly cast, were all of a similar size, 3 inches long, 1 inch high and 1 inch wide. (The gold was later produced in court, exhibited in a lentil soup box. The judge insisted on handling a bar, saying it was the first time he had ever seen one. The bar was then handed to the jury for its inspection.)

Material matching that in which the gold was wrapped was later discovered in Noye's Granada, and operating instructions for the model of furnace bought by Lawson thirteen months before were found in the apple store.

Close examination and forensic tests over the next few days were also to reveal globular fragments of gold, which would have been produced in a smelting process, on the Granada's boot mat. Similar globules were found on the boot mat of Reader's Cavalier, the rear mat and rear floor area of a Ford pick-up truck found near the apple store, on a leather apron and two gloves inside the store, on the front mat of a Cadillac parked nearby and on a pair of gloves found in Noye's Range Rover.

Other gold particles produced by a mechanical process such as drilling or machining also turned up in the back of a Ford Transit at Noye's house, in the back of the pick-up truck, on a pair of driving gloves taken from the Granada and on a pair of gloves taken from Noye at Swanley police station. More telltale globules and particles were discovered in the briefcase at Reader's home.

Searches at Hollywood Cottage over the next few days also revealed a safe hidden in the floor of one room. It contained a large quantity of jewellery and £2,500 in new £50 notes with the same prefix as those at Reader's house. The wood panelling in all the rooms was removed and a number of secret compartments discovered. One, hidden at the back of a built-in bedroom cupboard, contained antique Meissen porcelain worth about £3,000, which had been stolen two years earlier from the home of Lord Darnley.

Secret compartments were also found under a corridor leading to the swimming pool and in an alcove above the pool. Paving-stones from the patio were torn up and tiles removed from the swimming pool, but there were no more gold bars to be found. Another £50,000 in £50 notes with the prefix A24, divided into £12,500 bundles, were, however, found wrapped in a bright-orange blanket at the edge of woods behind the houses where Noye's parents and his sister and her husband lived in West Kingsdown. Mrs Rosemary Ford saw the bundle poking out from beneath her back-garden fence and, on picking it up, found a Marks and Spencer's carrier bag full of money. Thinking at first that it was a practical joke, she took it to another neighbour to inspect and, on realizing it was the real thing, so great was her anxiety to get it out of the house that she took it straight round to the police at Hollywood Cottage.

On the Monday after the killing, when the inquiry had been taken over by the Metropolitan Police, Noye and Reader were interviewed by detectives from the Flying Squad. Senior officers decided that at that stage none of the detainees should have access to a solicitor. Boyce strongly believed that police inquiries could be jeopardized by the appearance of a third party. Again Noye and the police differ widely over what was said.

The interview that took place after lunch was conducted by DI Anthony Brightwell, acting DCI Suckling and DC Michael Charman, with Noye standing for much of the time by the cell door, shouting out intermittently that he did not want to be interviewed by Flying Squad detectives and that he wanted his solicitor present.

According to the officers, the interview began with a formal question-and-answer session, a contemporaneous note being taken by Charman. Throughout that session to each question

Noye simply said, 'No reply.' Noye was asked to sign the note but instead requested that a line be drawn from the last letter on each line to the edge of the page. The police then continued questioning him, without the note being taken, in the hope that he would speak more freely.

Brightwell told the subsequent murder trial that he reminded Noye of the decision of senior officers not to allow access to a solicitor and went on: 'Mr Noye, you have got to face facts: you have killed a man. You have already admitted that to several officers. At some time you are going to have to give some explanation.'

Noye replied, 'You have got to believe one thing – I didn't know he was a policeman.'

Suckling said, 'Then tell us about it.'

Standing up, Noye replied, 'I don't want to talk to you about it. It's nothing to do with you. It's a Kent inquiry. I want to talk to someone from Kent. I have said I am not answering any questions unless my solicitor is present.'

Told that they were the only three officers who would be seeing him and that no solicitor would be allowed at that stage, Noye retorted, 'I've got nothing to gain by telling you. I will give my story to the judge and jury.'

'Why won't you give an explanation?' asked Suckling. 'As I see it, the truth of the matter can't be any worse . . . You being a cold-blooded killer who has killed a policeman to protect stolen property and a wanted man is the way it looks. The truth can't be any worse than that, so what harm is there in telling us?'

'You say I'm a cold-blooded killer. You weren't there, so how would you know?' countered Noye.

Noye then asked if they knew the dead officer, his children, what sort of man he was and where he lived. He was told that John Fordham was known to them all, that he was married and had three children, a girl aged 12, and two boys who were older.

Noye said, 'You must hate me. I have killed one of your mates and there is no way out for me. All you want to do is make sure I go to prison for the rest of my life.'

Brightwell told the court, 'I explained that we were interested in the truth of what happened leading up to the death of DC Fordham. Any feelings that we might have about DC Fordham in no way affected our actions. He said again that he knew we must hate him. We would be completely against him, and whatever he told us would be twisted to show him in a bad light.

'I said all we were interested in was the facts. DC Charman said to Noye that it must be the worst time of his life and any normal human being faced with such a terrible dilemma would be only too anxious to put his story if he wished to be believed. Noye then said he couldn't kill an animal and was not a cold-blooded killer.

'Suckling pointed out that he had already admitted killing DC Fordham, which didn't fit in with his claim that he couldn't kill anything. Noye then asked me how long I thought he'd receive in terms of imprisonment. I told him I was not in a position to give any indication about time of imprisonment. That depended on the court. In the circumstances it would be impossible to gauge, as no explanation was forthcoming in respect of the killing.

'Noye then said to me, "You can't tell me I would get less than thirty years, whatever I say."

'I said, "You have been talking for some time now and, apart from saying that you are not a cold-blooded killer, you have not said anything at all about what happened on Saturday evening. It is obvious to me that you want to talk to us to get this off your chest, and it is also apparent that you will not be drawn on specifics, which makes me think you have something to hide. Why do you insist on evading the issues?'

Noye then recounted a story of having found two men on his land trying to enter his barn to steal a car. The incident had taken place some time before. He said he'd gone out with the dogs and a shotgun and told them to go elsewhere if they wanted to steal a car. He had not injured them in any way, although he could have done. He added that he had often been alerted by his dogs to people moving around in the grounds and he was aware that, living in such a place, he might become a target for someone coming to kill or rob him, but he had never injured any trespasser.

Brightwell said, 'What was so different here then? You killed John Fordham. Why?'

'You know how he was dressed. What would you have done?' replied Noye. 'I have a wife and family. You see someone dressed like that – what do you do? It's you or him. Your brain doesn't work right. Your governors are going to be in a lot of trouble letting a man like that come in like that on his own. If he had a badge saying he was police, it wouldn't have happened.'

'He wasn't on his own,' said Suckling. 'There was another policeman with him who ran away, which was what John probably tried to do. That's what he was trained to do.'

Charman was scornful: 'You say you were frightened for your wife and family,' he told Noye. 'You saw one man on your land, and you and the other man Reader, who was seen to go to your house on numerous occasions, went out to him with three dogs, a knife and a shotgun. That man was trying to get away: why did you have to kill? It certainly wasn't to protect your children because they weren't even at the house, were they? Who was there?'

Noye said, 'Just my wife.'

Charman said, 'We know Reader was there. Was it just you, your wife and Reader?'

Noye said, 'Yes.'

'You are still not telling us what did happen,' pressed Suckling. 'Whatever way you look at this, we still have you, your wife, Reader and the dead police officer on your land and no account from you. You seem to be implying that you did it in self-defence, but that doesn't fit in with the fact that there were three of you and three dogs and that John Fordham was on his own, as you believed.'

Noye's only reply was: 'What would you do if you found someone on your land?'

Brightwell told him, 'I would call the police.'

'Oh, yeah,' replied Noye.

'So why didn't you?' he was asked.

'Put your head on my shoulders,' he replied. 'The way he was dressed, I didn't know who he was.'

'That was all the more reason to call the police, to find out what he was doing on your land,' Charman told him. 'The truth is that you were probably seen by John doing something with the gear we found on your property. You were with Reader and killed John Fordham to protect your own interests. The difference between us is that I don't have stolen property on my land, therefore I can call the police.'

Noye's reply was constantly to repeat the sentence 'Put your head on my shoulders.' He added that his wife was not responsible for the killing. He then asked the detectives who was in charge of the inquiry.

Brightwell said, 'DCS Boyce.'

Noye said, 'Who's in charge of him?'

He was told, 'Commander Cater is the head of the Flying Squad.'

'So if I wanted to speak to anybody, Cater is the best man,' said Noye, but he was told that Cater was due to retire in the following few days.

'Whatever you have to say we will pass to Mr Boyce,' said Brightwell.

'No, I've nothing else to say,' replied Noye.

According to Brightwell, Noye went on to inquire about his dogs, apparently fearful that they had been put down. He added that the dogs had not touched the dead police officer. 'I can tell you that they didn't touch him.' Noye said. 'He stood still. He obviously knew he should. They wouldn't touch him if he stood still. He knew that. He just stood there. They had him there for over five minutes.'

'Where did they have him for over five minutes?' asked Brightwell.

Noye didn't reply.

'By the old brick shed, wasn't it?' persisted the detective, referring to the derelict garage in the shrubbery.

'I don't want to answer that,' said Noye.

'That was where his hat was found,' said Brightwell.

'I don't want to answer any more of your questions.'

'That was where Detective Constable Fordham was stabbed, I believe.'

There was no reply.

'That was where it happened, wasn't it?'

'All I can say is that he was on my land. If he hadn't been, I wouldn't have killed him.'

Noye's defence counsel, John Mathew, QC, who had previously defended Tony White at the robbery trial, questioned the fact that the interviews had been carried out by officers who all knew John Fordham, and in the witness box Noye denied emphatically most of the remarks he was alleged to have made. He insisted that, during the part of the interview that was conducted when a contemporaneous note was being taken, his replies to the questions had been, 'No reply unless my solicitor is present.' He also denied saying at any stage during the interview that he stood watching for five or ten minutes while the dogs kept Fordham surrounded.

He told the court, 'I didn't know the man was there for five minutes. He could have been there twenty minutes for all I knew. I can't imagine he had been there five to ten minutes. It's preposterous.' He added, 'They could see that I had a black eye and cuts on my face. Not once did they ask how I got my injuries, how I felt, what my feelings were. They didn't mention the mask. I just sat there and let them give me their opinions about what had happened. At one stage Suckling told me my life had been destroyed and I would end up in the gutter. They weren't really questions but impressions. I was shouting to get out of the cell, but they wouldn't let me out, and the police officers outside weren't taking any notice.'

Asked by Purnell why he was so concerned to find out who was leading the inquiry, Noye replied, 'I wanted to get rid of all those officers to stop them questioning me and giving me opinions about what happened.'

That evening there occurred in the cells at Dartford what the prosecution at the Old Bailey was to term a 'piece of pantomime'. Shortly after 7.00 p.m. Kent police sergeant John Laker was standing in the corridor outside the cells when he heard Noye call out, 'Have you got a solicitor, Brian?'

Reader replied, 'Yes.'

Noye then said, 'Don't tell them anything, Brian.'

Reader, in the adjoining cell, assured him, 'No, I haven't.'

Noye continued, 'No, don't tell them anything. They don't know about the other geezer.'

Reader replied, 'I don't know anything.'

Noye persisted, 'No, well, don't say anything. They don't know about the other geezer yet.'

That exchange, police were sure, was an effort to confuse their inquiries.

Later that night the three officers returned to Noye's cell for another interview. On that occasion, according to their statements later, Noye was told again that the attack on Fordham looked like the cold-blooded killing of a police officer to protect a wanted man and stolen property. Noye replied that he had not known that Reader was wanted and at that moment the stolen property was unimportant to him; his only concern was the death of a policeman.

Charman told him, 'The truth of the matter is that you went out with Reader, three dogs, a knife and a shotgun and cornered John Fordham for five minutes or so while you decided between you what the best way to deal with him would be. I suspect that he was stabbed by you while Reader held him because I don't think that anyone would have stood there to be stabbed nine times, and I think John gave you that black eye in a desperate attempt to escape a man who was frenziedly stabbing him to death.'

'I didn't know he was a policeman, and I didn't take the gun out with me,' said Noye. 'I saw him in the grounds. The dogs had him. He just stood there. You didn't see the way he was dressed. He just stood there for five to ten minutes, then I saw him stagger off and fall near the gate. That's why I had the gun – in case he had some others with him.'

'You cold-bloodedly murdered him after having him cornered for a long time, and I suspect that you and Reader were going to dispose of John Fordham's body, probably by burying it somewhere on your land,' said Suckling.

'The gun wasn't for him. It was in case he had mates. I was with him for five minutes before the others got there.'

'When you discovered John was a policeman you told Reader to leg it. You knew he was a policeman because you had undone his clothing and found his radio,' said Brightwell.

'I didn't know he was one,' insisted Noye.

'Then why did you kill him?' persisted Suckling.

'Whoever he was, he was on my land. It wouldn't have happened if he hadn't been on my land,' was the weary reply.

'Could it be,' suggested Suckling, 'that you thought he was a rival villain who knew you were dealing with the Brink's-Mat gold, or saw you and Reader with it and was trying to get the gold from you by one way or another? You obviously realize that the stolen gear we've been talking about is the gold beside your garage, the gold you were caught with. You could see your whole lifestyle falling apart, so you killed a man, policeman or not, to protect your stolen property and your wealth. We've seen from our observations that you've been concerned in the disposal of a large quantity of gold. We only started those observations because our inquiries indicated that you were disposing of the £26 million worth of gold from the Brink's-Mat robbery. That's what you were trying to protect.'

'You won't find £26 million worth of gold at my house,' said Noye.

Brightwell interrupted. 'Mr Noye, I believe that you are in a position to assist us greatly in relation to the theft of that gold bullion. You are now aware that it was because of this that police were present at your premises on Saturday night. What can you tell me about the gold bullion of the Brink's-Mat robbery?'

Noye looked him in the eyes and smiled. 'You could ask me a thousand questions, and I could give you a thousand answers. The gold is nothing to what I have done. I am not interested in telling you about the gold. My only worry is the murder. If I tell you about the gold now, I'm only adding to it. It won't make any difference to what you charge me with, will it?'

Brightwell sensed that the prisoner was trying to strike a bargain. 'I hope you're not insulting my integrity by suggesting that you could use the Brink's-Mat gold as a bargaining point in this matter,' he said.

'Who knows what would have happened if only that policeman was alive,' was the intriguing reply.

The interview was at an end. Noye was asked whether he wanted to see Detective Chief Superintendent Boyce and replied, 'I'll leave that to you.' He was also asked if he wanted to make a written statement but was alleged to have replied, 'No, because whatever I say you will make it work against me. I don't trust you. I have seen some deals written up. You give me one of those, and I'll be able to interpret it in four different ways. I will tell my story to the judge and jury.'

13. 'I'm not a hard bitch . . .'

Flying Squad detectives also saw Reader that day, questioning him during the afternoon in his cell after he had refused to go to an interview room. The questioning was carried out by DI John Walsh, who had led the search party at Reader's home. According to his account, Reader at first would not respond, so, deciding to let the prisoner reflect a little longer, Walsh made as though to leave the cell.

The tactic worked, for immediately Reader began to talk, once again expressing concern for his wife's health; he was anxious to find out whether she had been allowed to see a doctor. 'She hasn't eaten since Monday, and the doctor said that if she doesn't look after herself, she could die,' he warned Walsh.

Walsh replied that Reader didn't seem to be showing much concern for the policeman who had died.

'That's not true. I am concerned,' protested Reader. He paused, then added, 'I never assaulted or hurt anyone.'

'Then I don't understand why you won't answer my questions,' rejoined Walsh. The only response was a plea from Reader that he be allowed to see his solicitor.

'Let's not play cat and mouse,' said Walsh, adding that there was no chance of his seeing a solicitor while the inquiries were continuing. He then asked what had occurred at Hollywood Cottage.

'When my solicitor is here I will tell you everything I saw, but I'll just say that I didn't assault anyone,' said Reader.

'I can't understand why you're prepared only to tell me partially about this,' said Walsh.

'Because you'll just add it to that when you go out,' said Reader, nodding in the direction of Flying Squad DS Russell Jones, who was making a contemporaneous note.

'The officer I saw last night said you were straight down here, but I've been nicked before – well, you know that – and verballed. Do you know what I mean?' (His admission that he had been arrested before was omitted from the evidence presented at the Old Bailey for obvious reasons.)

'I understand what you are saying,' replied Walsh.

'How do I know the same won't happen here?' asked Reader.

Walsh was quick to try to set the prisoner's mind at rest. 'Listen to me,' he ordered. 'Let me make two things clear to you. We are very upset at the death of our colleague; it is not going to help his memory if we start verballing people. We intend to get to the truth of the events of Saturday night. Nobody is going to be threatened or verballed, but our thorough investigations and minute examinations are going to reveal exactly what happened on Saturday. We are merely giving you the chance to tell us your side of things.'

Once again Reader said that he would talk only with his solicitor present, but Walsh refused to give up and continued to ask him about the killing of Fordham.

'I wasn't involved in assaulting that person,' said Reader.

After a few more minutes of questioning, during which the only positive reply Reader gave was that Fordham had been wearing camouflage dress, Walsh and Jones left the cell.

Four hours later they picked up where they had left off, this time dispensing with the contemporaneous note after Reader had made it clear that he would refuse to answer any questions if they started writing.

This time he was at first a little more forthcoming. 'I told you I am not violent. I saw things, heard things and did things, but I am not prepared to say what until my solicitor is present.'

'Did you have a knife with you on Saturday?' asked Walsh.

'I never carry a knife,' said Reader. 'I have never carried a knife in my life.'

'Did you have a knife at all on Saturday?' pressed Walsh.

'No comment.'

'That's an odd reply,' said Walsh. 'You say you never carry a knife and happily explain that, yet you are keeping open your option about Saturday. Do I take it that you did handle a knife on Saturday?'

'No comment.'

'We know exactly what you and your associates have been up to over the past months. Are you prepared to talk about that?' persisted Walsh.

'When my solicitor is present,' came back the stock reply.

'I don't understand why you're prepared to admit you were present at Noye's on Saturday when the police officer was killed, yet refuse to give any details of your actions,' said Walsh.

Reader thought for a minute. 'Look, I think I can trust you two. You seem all right, but I don't know. A policeman has been killed, and you might not want a pint of blood – you may be after two gallons,' he said.

'If we didn't want to get to the truth of what happened and just wanted vengeance, do you think we would be trying to persuade you to write and sign our questions and answers or make a written statement?' said Walsh. 'We are determined to bring those responsible for the officer's death to court, but equally I assure you that I would not offend John's memory by trying to implicate people who were not involved.'

'I think you are all right, but I have got to be careful. I could tell you everything now and then later regret it,' said the prisoner.

'I don't know how you can be surprised at anything later if you sign and agree everything now,' said Walsh.

'I'd rather be advised by my solicitor, who I know. I don't know you two,' said Reader. He then voiced another misgiving.

'I keep thinking about that job forty years ago, Bentley and . . . ,' he said.

'Craig,' prompted Walsh.

'That's right. Look what happened there,' said Reader, clearly appalled at the details he was calling to mind. He was referring to the murder, in 1952, of a policeman on the roof of a Croydon warehouse by a youth named Christopher Craig, who was armed with a pistol. Craig was only 16 and too young to hang – at that time the mandatory sentence in Britain for murder. However, his accomplice, Derek Bentley, a retarded 19-year-old with a history of epilepsy, was old enough to face the gallows and did so, even though he had taken no part in the shooting.

The case had been a *cause célèbre* in Britain – even the jury had recommended that Bentley be shown mercy – and paved the way for the abolition of the death sentence thirteen years later.

'How many people were present on Saturday at the Noyes'?' Walsh now asked.

'No comment,' said the prisoner.

Reader was then shown a black-handled knife and was asked if he had ever seen it before. The answer was, 'No comment.'

'Tell me one thing, if you're prepared to. Are you frightened of any people with whom you are involved, or is your sole concern our integrity?' asked Walsh.

There was a long pause. 'You are the only people I am frightened of. I think you might want blood,' was the eventual reply.

Walsh then tried a surprise tactic to show Reader just how much they already knew. Several of the bars of gold discovered at Hollywood Cottage were produced and shown to the prisoner. 'Do you want to tell me about this?' Walsh asked quietly.

Reader smiled. 'I will tell you all about that when my solicitor is present,' he promised, but then he became suspicious. 'What's in your briefcase?' he asked, suddenly fearful that the interview was being recorded.

Only books and papers, he was assured.

*

Detectives at Dartford police station were having almost as frustrating a time trying to find out from Brenda Noye exactly what had happened. She too had been seen by the solicitor, Burrough, when the killing was still a Kent police inquiry, but after the investigation was taken over by Scotland Yard she had been denied further visits.

Flying Squad D S Kenneth O'Rourke first saw her at lunch-time on the Monday. 'Do you know why you are here?' he asked.

'Yes,' she replied. 'A man was killed.'

'Yes, we know that, but how?'

'I don't know anything.'

'You must know something. There were three people there, and you were one of them.'

'I don't know about anyone else. I was in the house and didn't see anything.'

'There was a green Cavalier outside your house. The driver of that was a visitor. Who was that?'

'I don't know anything about a Cavalier or any visitor. I don't know what a Cavalier looks like.'

By this time, O'Rourke was to tell the jury at the murder trial, 'She had the sniffles. That's about as far as I would call it.'

He continued his questioning: 'It's a light-green saloon car.'

'I have never seen a light-green saloon car at my house.'

'Don't be silly,' said O'Rourke. 'It was there when the police arrived, on your drive.'

'I didn't see it,' she replied. 'Anyway I know that I don't have to say anything to you. My solicitor told me.'

'That's correct,' said O'Rourke. 'Is there any reason why you shouldn't answer the questions?'

'No reason.'

'Does the name Brian Reader mean anything to you?'

'No, I have never heard that name.'

'Before the incident, not long before, you, your husband and Reader were seen near the boot of the Cavalier together. What have you got to say about that?' said O'Rourke. (His claim was, in fact, incorrect.)

'I was in the house.'

'And you never saw anything regarding that incident where the man was murdered?'

'I told you, no.'

'You were heard to scream by the officers near by.'

'I don't want to answer.'

'You were seen to run from the area where it happened back to the house.'

'I went to get on the phone.'

O'Rourke seized the opening. 'So you were out there. You did leave the house.'

There was no reply.

O'Rourke tried to press home the advantage. 'You were a witness to a murder. Do you want to sit there and say nothing about it?'

Again no reply.

'The man was stabbed nine times. Did you stab him?'

'No.'

'There were only two other people there. Which one did?'

'I love my husband,' she replied.

'Are you saying that he did it but you won't say so?' asked O'Rourke.

No reply.

O'Rourke continued, 'The green Cavalier has been seen at your house, with Reader driving, almost daily. This is the culmination of a year's work. We haven't just stumbled on you.'

'I realize that,' replied Mrs Noye.

'I'm sure you know more than you are saying. We'll continue this interview later,' said the detective. He then gave her a chance to check and sign the contemporaneous note that had been made, but she refused.

Some four hours later she faced another interview with the same officer.

'I can't help you,' she began.

'Can't or won't?' asked O'Rourke, and he told her that the police believed that her husband had carried out the killing.

'Look, I can't help you,' she repeated, then added, 'My husband couldn't do such a thing.'

'Are you saying it was the other man, Reader?' queried O'Rourke.

'I don't know his second name.'

'You won't know this,' said O'Rourke, 'but we have found a large quantity of gold on your premises. Is that the reason your husband went to the extremes he did?'

'You will have to ask him if he did it, why he did it,' she said.

'You did know he was dealing in stolen gold?'

'Why should I know?'

'He's your husband. You were seen at the boot of the green Cavalier that night. You live with him. You must have known. Why not tell us from the beginning what happened?'

'I can't, I just can't,' said Mrs Noye, adding, 'I'm not a hard bitch like you think. My stomach is knotted up. My life is destroyed.'

Once again, at the end of the interview, she refused to check or sign the notes that were taken.

14. Communication breakdown

Police moved in on the other suspects in the bullion chain the following morning with a series of thirteen coordinated raids in London and the Bristol area. At dawn nearly fifty officers, some with dogs, sealed off the village of Litton, where Garth Chappell lived. Shortly before 8 a.m., as the Scadlynn boss was preparing to take one of his sons to school, his wife looked out of the window and saw a group of cars outside the house. Seconds later the door bell rang and a squad of eight detectives burst in.

'There was a terrible, terrible fuss. A film producer could not have been more dramatic. They were angry because a policeman had been killed,' said Chappell later.

'One second it was all peace and quiet, the next thing there were sirens everywhere. It was real *Sweeney* stuff,' said a stunned neighbour.

The detectives immediately demanded to know if there was gold on the premises. Chappell revealed there was, upstairs in the bedroom and, when marched up to find it, pointed to a black briefcase lying beside the bed. The case contained nearly £15,000, including £12,500 in £50 notes.

'Can you tell me what you are doing in possession of this large amount of cash?' asked DI James McGoohan from Scotland Yard.

'I'm a businessman. I always carry a large amount of cash. I don't have to answer your questions,' replied Chappell.

A plastic bag was then pulled out of the case; it contained a £5 Queen Victoria coin and a mounted krugerrand. Five other packages of krugerrands were also found, each containing twelve of the coins.

'Can you tell me about these?' asked McGoohan.

'I deal in them. So what?' said Chappell.

'What do you mean, you deal in them?'

'I'm a businessman. I do deals of half a million pounds a day. That's all I am saying,' replied Chappell.

The rest of the house was searched, and the police took possession of a large amount of correspondence, then Chappell was led outside to his Jaguar, where a pickaxe handle was discovered in the boot. 'It's for my protection,' he explained. 'We got robbed not so long ago.' A knife in its sheath was also found in the glove compartment. That, said Chappell, was also for his protection. 'I've taken legal advice on this,' he added. 'It's not an offensive weapon. It's not over 9 inches long, so you can't do anything.'

Told he would be taken in for questioning, he replied, 'Do as you want,' and, turning back to his wife, he explained, 'They are taking me back to London. Don't worry. I might see you in a day or two; if not, you won't see me for a long time.'

Terence Patch was lying in bed in his luxurious bungalow when the police arrived. He was immediately arrested. After a search of the house, during which six £50 notes were found, together with an accounts book, in his handwriting, that described some of Scadlynn's gold dealings in mid-December the previous year, he was taken outside to a blue Jaguar – the one seen by police at Swindon railway station earlier that month. Patch explained that it belonged to Chappell but that he had borrowed it to use the car telephone, as the one in the house had been disconnected. A pickaxe handle similar to the one found in Chappell's other Jaguar was found on the back window shelf. Once again the explanation was that it was for protection.

In Patch's garage police found five crucibles, four metal trays and two pieces of heavy metal.

'Why are these here?' he was asked.

'I brought them from the office to clean them. You can't clean them when they're hot, so I brought them here to cool down.'

'I don't really understand that,' said Flying Squad DS Michael Ruffles. 'Surely it would have been better to let them cool down before moving them?' Patch made no reply and, a little later, was taken to London for further questioning.

Later that day his girlfriend, Julie Marcus, was taken by police to the cottage in Chew Magna that she and Patch used, although 'neither of us ever lived there or stayed overnight.' Police later claimed that, on the front of a telephone dialling-code book, they found written the number of the shop in London that Reader had been seen dialling while under surveillance at Farringdon station.

Scadlynn Ltd was also raided that morning, and invoice books, papers, telephone books, bank paying-in books, petty cash accounts and even a picture of an island scene were removed from the offices for further examination. Among the paperwork Weyman's telephone number was discovered. The safes were also inspected and silver trophies and gold watches removed.

The biggest police operation, however, was mounted at Palmer's home, the coach house at Battlefields. At dawn about thirty police officers quietly staked out the building, many of them armed. Then, shortly before 7 a.m., C11 officers drove past to see if anybody was stirring. Satisfied that the time was right to move in, police cut the electricity supply to the house to give them the advantage of added surprise.

Local farmer Fred Cullimore and his 12-year-old son George, on their way past the building in a Land Rover to pick up a friend, drove straight into the operation. George spotted what he thought was a police van hidden in a lane, then, moments later, his father was forced to brake sharply as a police car slewed across the road in front of them, blocking the entrance to Battlefields.

'We were stopped right opposite the entrance of the coach house,' Fred Cullimore told us. 'Suddenly I heard a thundering sound. I couldn't tell what it was at first. I looked in my wing mirror and saw a small army of men, dressed in black, running down the drive. The noise was from the heavy boots that they were wearing. Their arms were stretched out, and they had pistols in their hands pointing at the coach house. Only two weren't armed, one of whom was carrying an axe, the other a sledge-hammer.

'Two officers came round and said quickly to put off the lights and engine. At the time I was not frightened, and my son was enjoying it, saying it was like television. They were not local lads – they were too professional. They were S A S-type chaps. It was wonderful to see them working. There were about two dozen of them, but no one said a word.'

At the front door a police sergeant shouted, 'Open up: police,' followed by, 'Open the door: armed police.'

At the second shout a man whom the police officer could see in the hallway holding a telephone dropped it and ran upstairs. Then the two policemen with the axe and sledge-hammer moved in to break open the door. 'Quicker,' Fred Cullimore heard, as the blows fell. After a moment or two the door gave, then two downstairs windows were smashed, and four armed officers rushed in, followed by Flying Squad detectives.

Quickly establishing that the ground floor was empty, they cautiously made their way upstairs – a manoeuvre that police firearms officers particularly dislike. A foolproof method of climbing a staircase while guarding against attack from above has yet to be devised.

At the top of the stairs, to the right, was a locked door. 'We are armed police. Open the door!' shouted the sergeant, banging the panels loudly. Muffled shouts could be heard from inside. Several more demands that the door be opened were ignored, forcing police to break the lock. Inside armed police officers found three men, John Thomas, Lee Groves and James Harvey, and, in an adjoining bathroom, a girl, Carole Howe. Of the

Palmer family there was no trace. John Palmer, his wife and their two children had left the day before Fordham's death for a three-week package holiday in the Canary Islands.

The men were spreadeagled on the floor and searched. Howe, the Palmers' 25-year-old groom, who had agreed to look after the house and the family's two Rottweiler guard dogs, which were locked in the stable block, was taken downstairs to the kitchen.

'Are you okay now?' asked a detective.

'Yes,' she replied. 'I thought you were robbers.'

It was an understandable mistake. Earlier that morning Harvey, Palmer's 30-year-old partner in a building company, and Groves, an 18-year-old assistant employed at Palmer's Bath shop, had been smelting some of the Brink's-Mat bullion in a furnace hidden in a small wood behind the coach house. The shed, with three vents (one for emitting smoke, another for allowing the gases to escape and a third to increase the supply of oxygen) was surrounded on three sides by bushes, with a horse-box parked in front to conceal it from view.

The two men had already produced three ingots there the previous Sunday and, at 6 a.m., had started smelting again. The bullion, four or five packages of it, had been collected from Chappell the previous night.

After smelting two ingots, Harvey and Groves were driving back up the private road to the coach house when they noticed two men in a car ahead of them. 'I thought they were villains,' explained Harvey later.

As they reached the coach house, the car, which was, in fact, an unmarked police car, drove off. Ordering Groves into the house with the gold, Harvey, with an Alsatian dog and a shotgun, went off in his pick-up truck to investigate. Groves, by now well and truly frightened, hid the two gold bars under a cushion on the settee and then discovered that Carole Howe's boyfriend, John Thomas, who was also staying there, had noticed the car too and taken its number.

Before they could decide what to do, Harvey had returned from his recce. A few moments later the doorbell rang. Still unaware that it was police officers outside, Harvey told Groves to phone the police. Thomas, meanwhile, pressed a panic button connected to the local police station, then they all fled upstairs to hide.

'But the officers at the front were in full uniform,' a perplexed detective said later to Thomas, the 33-year-old green-keeper at a local golf course.

'All I saw was the guns,' he replied.

'I understand you have been smelting this morning. Is that right?' a detective asked Groves.

'Yes.'

'What were you smelting?'

'I don't wish to say.'

'Why not?'

'I don't want to.'

'Where were you going with Harvey?'

'I'm not prepared to say.'

Groves was then told to show police the smelter. It was still hot from the morning's work.

Back at the house, the police began searching the premises. The two gold bars, still warm, were found on the settee, a shotgun and rifle were removed from the master bedroom, and another shotgun taken from a tack-room by the kitchen. Papers, correspondence, diaries, cheque-book stubs, a red wallet containing three £50 notes and three bags of copper coins found in Palmer's garage were taken away.

In the back of Harvey's pick-up truck police also found a shotgun and a crucible with two large ingot moulds still hot enough to have caused condensation to form over the windows.

Groves and Harvey were taken away for questioning, but police were later satisfied that they had no knowledge that the bullion they were smelting was stolen. Detectives then began interviewing the neighbours in the nearby mansion, which had been converted into flats. They were told by one that she had been woken on a number of mornings in recent months at about 5 a.m. by 'a noise I can only explain as a boiler, like a roaring noise'. It had been the smelter in action.

That evening a truck with a crane arrived to remove the

smelter for forensic analysis, and the next day earthmovers were brought into the grounds and large sections of grass were excavated. An area around the pool was dug up with pneumatic drills, and the floorboards inside the coach house were removed, but it was all to no avail. There was no more gold to be found.

That day the police were also busy in London, but the three-day delay since Fordham's death – caused, police claim, by the intensive inquiries into his killing – enabled Weyman and the jeweller seen meeting Reader to go into hiding.

At the time that Palmer's house was being raided detectives arrived at Adams's front door in Islington. A detective knocked once, but there was no reply, then Adams was seen peering out of a ground-floor window. 'We are police officers and have a search warrant. Please open the door,' shouted the detective. There was no reply, but moments later a policeman watching the back of the house suddenly saw the suspect walk along a wall and jump down into a neighbouring garden. Dashing after him, police found him hiding beneath a clump of bushes.

'Why did you run away?' asked DC Anthony Davis.

'You've got to take the chance and run, haven't you?' Adams allegedly replied.

'What have you got to run from, though?'

'I knew you were coming eventually,' was the answer.

'What have you got to hide?'

Adams smiled, but made no reply.

His flat was searched. Detectives even checked the contents of his dustbin, and at the bottom of a bedroom wardrobe they found a 4½-inch-long gold bar, together with nearly 200 assorted rings, six watch chains, seven krugerrands and a quantity of gold sovereigns. A set of scales and more rings were found elsewhere in the flat.

'How do you account for all the jewellery I've found, in particular the gold bar?' asked Davis.

'If you'd done your homework, you'd know all about me,' replied Adams.

He was asked whether he or his wife had the use of a car and said they didn't, but he was then shown a set of car keys that had been found in the basement. Police took them outside and inserted them into the lock of a BMW parked near by. They fitted, and behind the driver's seat a black briefcase was found.

Indoors, Adams was asked: 'Is the BMW yours?'

'What BMW?' he replied.

'The keys are the keys for a BMW. It is your car.'

'No, I know nothing about it.'

Papers and correspondence were then removed, a soil sample was taken from a trench in a disused coal cellar to see if it showed any traces of gold, and Adams was taken into custody.

That day police also arrested the man who had played a key part in helping Scadlynn to organize its end of the gold chain by providing it with a cover story to explain where it had obtained the gold.

Elderly London jeweller Matteo Constantinou, of Italian parentage, was a man long known to the Metropolitan Police and HM Customs as a top fence. In the 1950s he had been imprisoned twice for receiving stolen property – brandy and ham on one occasion and £25,000 worth of glucose used in the confectionery trade on another. In the mid-1960s he had been found not guilty of receiving stolen diamonds, rubies and gold dollars, but in 1974 he had been convicted of smuggling imitation gold coins into Britain. A one-time street trader believed to have links with organized crime, he now lived in a large house in Whetstone, north London, and ran his own business, the International Precious Metals Company, in Greville Street.

Until Fordham's death police had not known of Constantinou's involvement in the chain – he had not entered the picture once during their surveillance operation. But he had aroused considerable suspicions in another quarter – among officers of HM Customs and Excise Investigation Division, who, as it transpired, had also been conducting an investigation into Scadlynn.

*

One of the strangest and least understandable twists to the Brink's-Mat story – one that may shed a different light on the reason why police waited three days before moving against the rest of the chain – was this apparently complete breakdown of communications between Scotland Yard and the London-based HM Customs and Excise Investigation Division. For late in 1984 customs investigators told two senior Scotland Yard officers that they were keeping Scadlynn under surveillance, warning that they believed the company was dealing in smuggled gold – or, possibly, some of the Brink's-Mat bullion. The Yard appeared to show no interest, however, so customs officers continued investigating on their own account.

The customs investigation had started when the Investigation Division received a tip that a man called Roger Feltham, using the name Peter James and giving a false address, was endeavouring to sell 110 krugerrands across the counter in the City of London. That in itself was not illegal, but the false VAT number he gave was, and that meant that in all probability the krugerrands, worth about £285 each, had been smuggled in and Feltham was banking on pocketing the extra 15 per cent that a VAT London dealer would have to pay.

Feltham was tailed by customs investigators from the dealer's shop, and it quickly became apparent that he was wary of being followed. Buying a ticket at a Tube station, he went down on to the platform, threw a cursory glance at the people standing there, then doubled back to the ticket barrier, a favourite dodge of criminals anxious to establish if they are being tailed. Several trains passed before he returned to the platform, checked if there were any faces he recognized, then boarded the next train.

But he hadn't thrown off the customs officers on his tail. He was shadowed to Farringdon station, where he collected a car from a near-by car park, and was followed as he drove to the Plough public house outside Swindon, where a blue Jaguar was waiting – which was traced to Garth Chappell. Later that night he was followed to Patch's house.

Feltham was regarded as being too unimaginative to have constructed his cover story or to have thought himself of the precautions he had taken, but Chappell, customs officers knew, ran Scadlynn, a company that had proved highly uncooperative in the past in declaring VAT and letting VAT inspectors in to check its books. It was also one whose name had cropped up in connection with a number of fraud cases, and although it had not been the subject of any particular inquiry, customs officers already had considerable suspicions about its affairs. Feltham's behaviour warranted a much closer look at the company.

An initial check of Scadlynn's records in the national VAT computer at Southend revealed a surprising picture. Since summer 1984 the company's fortunes had undergone a remarkable change. Millions of pounds' worth of gold had started going from Scadlynn to an assay office in Sheffield, where its purity was officially calculated, then on to gold dealers on the open market. Scadlynn claimed that this was scrap gold made up from jewellery that the company had bought, but the amounts were too large for that to be a credible explanation. In addition, the gold was being moved in a very suspicious manner; Feltham sometimes visited Patch's house as early as 4 a.m. to collect consignments. Another suspicious factor was that the ingots they were sending up were so badly smelted that the assay office could not determine their true gold content without re-smelting them. They later likened the bars sent by Scadlynn to a badly mixed cake in which all the currants (the gold) ended up on one side, and few appeared elsewhere in the mix.

The suspicions of the customs officers increased after several apparently routine visits to Scadlynn to inspect its VAT accounts, which revealed the names of the dealers to whom they were selling on. One such visit had taken place just ten days before Fordham's death. Chappell, when asked to produce his accounts, told a customs officer: 'I am a dealer. I don't understand books. Books are all Chinese to me.' Two days later the customs officer had returned to tell him that he owed nearly £80,000 in outstanding VAT payments.

Checks with Scadlynn's customers, particularly a company in Leeds, showed that the prices that Scadlynn was obtaining were only marginally above what the company claimed the gold had cost it. Somewhere along the line, the business just did not make sense. The only logical explanation was that Scadlynn's paperwork was false. But the company had all the documentation it needed to show that it was buying the gold legitimately from one Mr Matteo Constantinou.

Scadlynn, the customs team under senior investigator Jim McGregor decided, had to be handling fine gold – or bullion, to give it its other name. Krugerrands couldn't account for the volume involved, and anyway the price of coins included a 4 per cent premium, which made it less profitable to smelt them down for sale as ordinary gold.

If it was bullion, the odds were that it was either smuggled or stolen – but which?

The team working on Operation Law Degree (so named because the initials of the three towns involved, London, Leeds and Bristol, also denote a degree in law, Ll.B.) began by checking whether anybody connected with Scadlynn had import/export business interests. That might show how the smuggling racket, if it existed, worked.

The investigators learned that an associate of former Scadlynn director John Palmer was a man called John Groves (the father of Lee Groves, arrested in the police raid on Battlefields), whom Bristol police and customs officers had suspected for some time of being a smuggler. Nothing more specific was forthcoming, but checks into his affairs revealed his involvement in a company called James White Cars, which specialized in importing vehicles from the Channel Islands.

One factor struck the investigators immediately: the cars that the company chose were hardly valuable enough to warrant the trouble and expense of bringing them in for resale, particularly as the company's representatives were apparently eating up whatever small profits might have accrued by regularly flying out to the islands to choose the models they wanted.

The customs team also learned that Groves had come to the attention of the Jersey authorities the previous year, when he arrived on the island in a Rolls-Royce that had previously belonged to Palmer. Although the export of currency was legal, £20,000 had been found concealed in the car, half of which, Groves said, he had borrowed from Palmer. (The money, it subsequently transpired, was used to buy krugerrands.)

Further checks into the company also revealed that James White was an alias – the man behind it was James Harvey (later arrested at Battlefields), a known associate of both Chappell and Palmer.

Were the vehicles being used to bring the gold in? Or, more unlikely, was it hidden on Groves, Harvey and their accomplices when they re-entered Britain?

Both men were placed under surveillance, and in January 1985 Groves and a woman friend flew out to Jersey and bought a Mini car for £150.

It quickly became apparent that this was a krugerrand-smuggling trip. A number of the coins were hidden in the Mini's petrol tank, but while driving around the island Groves was questioned at such length by a local policeman, who knew nothing of the customs operation, that he panicked.

He believed that he and the car were being watched, and any attempt to remove the petrol tank so he could transfer the krugerrands to a better hiding place would be spotted. The solution was to summon Harvey to the island to buy a second car. Both vehicles would then be taken to the neighbouring island of Guernsey, where the krugerrands could be swapped between the two petrol tanks.

The plan went without a hitch – or so the two smugglers thought. Harvey duly flew over and bought an Audi, which he took to Guernsey by ferry. Groves's woman friend followed suit with the Mini, while Groves made the trip by air. Then, in a remote spot on the north of the island, against a snow-clad landscape, the petrol tank was removed from the Mini, and the krugerrands were retrieved and inserted into the petrol tank of the Audi. The car was then sent off on a ferry to the mainland as unaccompanied freight.

On 17 January the vehicle arrived at Weymouth docks, where it stayed for six days while Harvey and Groves, who had flown back, waited to see if it attracted any suspicious interest.

Eventually, satisfied that the coast was clear, Harvey collected the car on 23 January.

But he was still taking no chances. Half a mile behind him as he drove to Bristol was an accomplice in another car, who was tailing him to ensure that he wasn't being followed. Unbeknown to him, however, customs officers had already checked the vehicle over and even had photographs of the krugerrands, which would have netted the gang £4,000 profit. They had been taken out of the petrol tank and then replaced.

(Later Groves and Harvey were both arrested. Groves admitted to conspiring to smuggle krugerrands worth £489,000 into Britain and was sent to prison for a year, six months of it suspended. Harvey, who pleaded guilty to the same charge, was sentenced to six months, half of it suspended. The court heard that sixteen trips in all were made, and customs duty totalling £73,400 had been evaded.)

It was now clear to customs investigators how the krugerrands were being brought into the country, but they were no closer to discovering the supply of the bullion.

Their inquiries, had, however, led them to establish a secret observation post in an office opposite Scadlynn. They had discovered Palmer's furnace, and they knew that the company claimed to be acquiring gold quite legally from Matteo Constantinou, who was due to receive a visit in the very near future. His VAT record, when it was checked, had given no hint of where he was supposedly obtaining such large quantities of the precious metal.

Today both police and customs prefer to throw a diplomatic veil over the breakdown in communications. Boyce, when asked by us why no action was taken over the information given by customs officials in late 1984, replied: 'I certainly had no knowledge of it whatsoever. I took that inquiry over days, or a week, before the Noye operation began, and I had no knowledge of the customs operation, and no one mentioned it to me.'

It was not until after Fordham's killing that customs officers became aware that the police raids on the gold chain were taking place. When the two inquiries did finally merge, customs officers had to provide police with much of the information about the Bristol end of the operation – even, in some instances, which addresses to raid. One customs investigator has confirmed: 'They made contact with us before the Bristol addresses were turned over. We told them where to go. They made use of our knowledge of the West Country scene. They were not well informed about the places and people.'

It could all have been a straightforward administrative mistake, but in some quarters of the customs service suspicion still lingers that inter-agency rivalry overshadowed the more important matter of criminal investigation. For the intense competition between customs investigators and Scotland Yard detectives is today common knowledge.

For their part, the customs investigators tend to be wary about the honesty of some detectives, having encountered corrupt officers in both pornography and drugs inquiries. It is also true that the customs service is likely to attract recruits who are educationally of a higher calibre, although new graduate-intake schemes are ensuring that the make-up of the Metropolitan Police is steadily improving in that respect. With the Customs Investigation Division just 600 strong nationally, management and supervision are obviously far easier than among the massed ranks of London's detectives.

But perhaps the most fundamental difference between the two services, particularly in relation to the Flying Squad and the Customs Investigation Division, is the very different nature of the work for which they are respectively employed. Customs investigators, particularly when it comes to VAT offences (which every officer will spend at least part of his time in the service investigating), start from a position in which no crime is immediately apparent. They have to set out to prove that one has been committed, which means lengthy investigations and, at the end of the day, evidence that must be virtually unassailable. To assist them in this task they have more powers than the police, in the sense that they can require those registered for VAT to submit documents and furnish explanations. They also have the 'writ of assistance', which has to be renewed only at the end of a monarch's reign, that entitles them to search premises without a warrant while hunting for smuggled goods.

In other aspects of their work, notably combating drug smugglers, the evidence will often be found in the possession of the person arrested, which means that less additional evidence is required to secure a conviction. The courier will often point to other people higher up in the chain and will sometimes be prepared to give evidence against them in order to serve his own interests. The Flying Squad, however, reacts to crimes that are all too apparent, committed by criminals with a lot to lose. The maximum penalty for VAT offences today is seven years. The maximum penalty for armed robbery is life imprisonment. The result is that even if an armed robber confesses when in police custody, he will still, more often than not, plead not guilty in court in the hope of securing an acquittal. In the process, attempts are often made to discredit police officers in an effort to sway the jury.

Detectives are used to taking 'verballing' allegations, and accusations of fabricated evidence, on the chin, but this does in some cases produce deeply cynical officers who are prepared to cut corners to get convictions, certain in the knowledge that even if they follow the letter of the law, the claims of injustice are not going to be any less. It is this blunt – some would say bitterly realistic – approach that customs officers dislike and view with suspicion.

Adding to the rivalry between the two services is the almost tangible impression that the police can give that they don't much like anyone, no matter who, interfering in the business of law enforcement. Consequently they have gained a reputation (once again, particularly where the Flying Squad is concerned) for taking as few people as possible into their confidence. Some critics among criminal defence lawyers put this down to a Flying Squad desire to keep the glory for themselves while preventing anyone from examining their methods too closely. Others describe it as a self-protective attitude that is wholly understandable, given the nature of their work. Whatever the explanation, some customs officers today believe that Scotland Yard's failure to involve them in the Noye inquiry at an earlier stage was not an oversight but a conscious decision.

It is clear, however, that on the death of John Fordham all

rivalries were forgotten, at least for the time being, in the desire to bring as many people as possible to justice for the crime he had been investigating.

Instead of a visit from customs officers, Constantinou was surprised, at 6.30 that Tuesday morning, by members of the Flying Squad who, after removing cheque books and paying-in books for examination, escorted him to Greville Street, where the offices of International Precious Metals were searched. There an account book was found, and Constantinou was asked by DC Anthony Purdie: 'Does this book contain your current business transactions?'

'Yes.'

'I've had a brief look, but it seems that you have not done any selling or buying since October 1984.'

'Yes, that's right,' said Constantinou.

'Are you really telling me that you have done no business whatsoever since October 1984?' asked the detective.

'I haven't done any business much at all,' was the reply.

He was arrested and taken in for questioning.

15. Charged with murder

In his police cell that Tuesday, Noye for the first time did not face an endless round of interviews. He was seen twice by Boyce, on the first occasion being shown three knives and asked if he recognized them. 'No reply unless my solicitor is present,' was his only response.

Two and a half hours later Burrough was present and told the detective: 'My client does not to wish to say anything at this stage.' Noye was asked if he would provide blood, saliva and hair samples for forensic analysis. Burrough intervened. 'Permission is not given and will not be given until we have taken counsel's opinion on it.'

Noye was also seen for a short time by Suckling. 'How's my house?' Noye asked.

'What do you mean?'

'I suppose you've wrecked it.'

The detective then mentioned that the police knew that there might be concrete bunkers dating back to the Second World War in the grounds.

'I can't find them,' said Noye. 'You'd be doing me a favour if your lot could. I've had a JCB in there, and I don't know where they are.'

'What did you want to find them for? Was it to hide gear in?' he was asked.

'No, I was going to open one up for the kids to play in.'

When police saw Reader he once again refused to go to the interview room, insisting that the questioning be carried out in his cell. 'I'm sorry about what has happened,' Reader told DI Walsh.

'Last Saturday is not the first time you have been to Noye's to collect gold, is it?' challenged the officer.

'What does he say?' asked Reader.

'That's not relevant. Unfortunately we can't separate the two incidents and offences. You and Noye were disturbed moving the gold. You were involved in transferring the proceeds from one of the largest robberies ever. You were caught in the act, and I put it to you that you and Noye decided you had to kill the officer.'

(The statement made by Walsh after the interview shows that the detective also claimed that during the transfer of the gold Noye and Reader had realized that Fordham was watching them – although this was not mentioned at the trial.)

'I didn't agree to kill him. That's not true,' said Reader.

'What did you decide?'

The reply was one that kept sending Walsh back to first base. 'I am not answering until my solicitor is present.'

The detective tried again. 'Did you at any stage touch the police officer?'

'I've told you, I didn't assault him,' insisted Reader.

'That was not my question. Did you touch him or hold him at any time?'

But Reader made no reply.

'Did you kick him?'

No reply.

'Look, Brian, you obviously want to say more because of the way your brain keeps ticking over between every question. I can tell that you're close to saying what happened. Why do you still keep holding back if you genuinely were not concerned in the attack?' coaxed Walsh.

'I am worried that you are going to do me with murder,' was the anxious reply.

'The charge that you face will depend upon the facts,' he was told.

'I want to speak to my solicitor,' Reader demanded.

Walsh pretended not to have heard. 'Where was the officer when you first saw him?' he pressed.

'No comment.'

'Where were you when the events leading up to his death first began?'

Reader at first made no reply, then said, 'Look, I was in the house.'

'Where were Mr and Mrs Noye?'

'We were all in the house.'

'What happened?'

'The dogs started barking.'

'Did you go out?'

'Not at first.'

'What does that mean?'

'I . . .' His voice trailed off.

'Did someone else go out?'

'You know what happened,' replied Reader.

'I know some of what happened,' said Walsh. 'One of the men went out of the house. Was it you?'

'No.'

'So it was Noye?'

'You know it was.'

'Did you go to follow him?'

'No comment.'

'Why did he go out?'

'You know.'

'You joined Noye in the garden, didn't you?'

'I didn't join him.'

'What does that mean?'

'I went out, but I didn't join him.'

'Did you see the officer at that stage?'

'No comment.'

'What went through your mind when you realized that the police officer had seen you?'

'I don't know. Things just happened.'

'What things happened?'

'No comment.'

'Where was Mrs Noye at this time?'

'What does she say?'

'That doesn't concern you,' said Walsh, and then he changed tack. 'I am interested in anything you and Noye said to each other in the garden.'

'No comment.'

'Did Noye tell you that he was going to assault the officer?'

'No comment.'

'That's an odd answer, isn't it?' pressed Walsh. 'If it's "no", surely that can't cause you problems?'

Reader's response was to demand again to be allowed to see his solicitor, saying that if he did so, he would answer the questions.

Walsh carried on regardless. 'You have told how the officer was dressed. How do you know?'

'What do you mean?'

'Where did you first see him?'

There was no reply.

'Did you see him before he was up near the gates, lying on the ground?'

'I haven't said that I saw that.'

'I know, but other people have. Police – and now, more importantly, someone connected with the house – also says that you were with Mr and Mrs Noye, standing by the officer when he was there on the ground,' said Walsh, referring to an answer given by Brenda Noye earlier.

'No comment.'

'I've just told you, other people are starting to be more explicit than you. Your time to make up your mind is nearly here, isn't it?'

There was a long pause, then Reader gave slightly. 'Yes, all right, I went to see what had happened, but I never stabbed him.'

'Did you know at that stage that he had been stabbed?'

'I will tell you what I know when I have seen my solicitor.'

'Did you have a knife?'

'I told you, I never carry a knife.'

'Did you see or touch one?'

No reply.

'Did you have a gun? A shotgun?'

'I never had a gun.'

'Did you see anyone else with a gun?'

No reply.

'Did you take any action to help the officer?'

'No.'

'Why not?'

'I couldn't, could I? I just ran off.'

'Did you ask anyone else to help him?'

No reply.

'But you didn't just run off, did you? You moved the gold, didn't you?'

'I will tell you about that when my solicitor is present.'

'Why did you run off and not take your car?'

'I knew what had happened. I couldn't drive out, could I?'

Walsh then brought up the question of the money and property found in Reader's house at Winn Road. Referring to Reader's wife, he said, 'She has been asked about a briefcase full of money found in your house.'

'That's mine,' protested Reader.

'So she says. Where does it come from?'

'I'll tell you that when I have seen my solicitor.'

'Your wife says you have taken large sums of money home before recently. What's that all about?'

'Look, it's nothing to do with her. She never even knew how much was there.'

'She says the same, but she does say she knew it was not honest money.'

'I'll tell you about that when I have seen my solicitor.'

'We also found £3,000 in your kitchen. Whose is that?' asked Walsh, and once again Reader took responsibility, saying he had borrowed it. He was also questioned about the lump of silver-coloured metal his wife claimed he had given her.

'That's just a bit of jewellery from a bad assay. I've had it a while. It's only got a small gold content. It's only worth about £40,' he said.

'Is it the residue of a smelt?'

'Yes.'

'Where is the smelter being used for the gold you've been dealing in?' asked Walsh hopefully.

Reader laughed. 'I don't know where it is.'

'Whose man are you – Noye's or the other end?' persisted Walsh.

'No comment.'

'How long have you known Noye?'

There was no reply, and the interview was brought to an end. Later Reader was twice visited by Boyce. On the first occasion the prisoner was told that he would be charged with murder and was shown three knives, which he said he did not recognize. He did, however, agree to provide hair, saliva and blood samples for forensic examination. On the second occasion he was seen while his solicitor was present. He was asked if he was prepared to answer any questions. The reply surprised no one. 'I don't wish to say anything.'

Meanwhile Brenda Noye had been moved to Gravesend police station, where she was seen shortly before 8 o'clock that morning by O'Rourke. It was to prove a slightly more productive meeting than the earlier ones.

According to O'Rourke, he began on a sympathetic note: 'I appreciate that these are not surroundings that you are used to, but we have to get to the bottom of this. A policeman has been murdered. A quantity of gold has been recovered from your house – maybe as much as £60,000–£70,000. After speaking to you yesterday, I think you want to tell us but you are frightened of something or someone.'

Playing on her fears appeared to fail. 'I'm not frightened of anyone,' she said. 'I didn't see anything. I was out after. It had all happened by then.'

'All what?' asked O'Rourke.

Her defences wavered. 'Whatever happened to him. I didn't take any part. The dogs were making a lot of noise, so Kenny went to see. He was out for a few minutes and the dogs were still barking, so Brian went out and a bit later Kenny came running in and got his shotgun. I knew then that something was wrong. I went down the drive and could see Ken and Brian standing over something. I got closer and could see it was a man. He didn't move.'

'Did you know he had been stabbed?' asked O'Rourke.

'No, I didn't see any knife.'

'Did you think he might be dead?'

'I didn't know what to think. I can remember becoming hysterical and shouting. I suppose I must have thought that. I was just shouting at the two of them. I can't remember what I said.'

A few more questions followed, then O'Rourke said, 'Let's talk about the gold. You did know they were shifting gold, didn't you?'

'Of course I did. You said yesterday, I am his wife.'

'Did you know it was stolen?'

'Obviously it must be.'

'Did you know from where?'

'No.'

O'Rourke enlightened her. 'I think it's from the bullion robbery at Heathrow over a year ago, when £26.5 million was stolen,' he said.

The explanation suprised her. 'I never gave it much thought,' she said.

'How much has been moved from your house?'

'I don't know.'

'Who brings it?'

'I don't know. We have loads of cars coming and going all day.'

'Does your husband bring it to the house?'

'I don't know. My husband is just doing a favour.'

'Who for?'

'I don't know, he doesn't tell me.'

'How long has it been going on?'

'I'm not around all the time.'

'When do you think it started?'

'Some time before Christmas.'

'How long?'

'I don't know.'

'Every day?'

'I don't know. I told you. I wasn't there all the time.'

'How much was your husband getting?'

'I don't know,' replied Mrs Noye, adding, 'I have already said more than I should have done. I'm not answering any more of your questions. My solicitor told me that I don't have to if I don't want to. I didn't really want to talk to you in the first place. I understand that you have a job to do, but I mean it this time.'

The interview was at an end. Once again, according to O'Rourke, she was offered the chance to sign the notes of the interview, and once again she refused.

Later, appearing at the Old Bailey as a defence witness for her husband, she was to deny every remark attributed to her in the interviews, with the exception of her admission that she had left the house, adding that no notes were taken while she was being questioned. 'It's nothing but lies,' she claimed. 'My solicitor advised me not to say anything unless he was present, and I didn't.'

After her visit from O'Rourke Brenda Noye was moved back to Dartford police station and, during the afternoon, was interviewed by Boyce. He told her that she was to be charged with murder and gave her five minutes to consult alone with Burrough. Re-entering the cell, Boyce asked if she was prepared to answer any questions.

Burrough told her, 'This is something you must decide. It must be your decision.'

'No, I don't wish to answer,' she replied. Asked whether she would provide blood, hair and saliva samples, she refused, saying she would seek counsel's advice.

Early that Tuesday evening the Noyes and Reader were charged with murder, the Noyes exclaiming, 'No!' when the charge was read out. 'I'm innocent of that charge,' said Reader.

Four months later the murder charge against Brenda Noye was dismissed at a committal hearing at Lambeth magistrates' court in south London because of insufficient evidence against her. The defence exercised its right to the hearing as an opportunity to discover what a number of prosecution witnesses were going to say about crucial issues in the case. The hearing was also an attempt by Brenda Noye and Reader to have the charges against them dismissed.

In her case it was successful. Magistrate George Bathurst-Norman said, 'The only evidence against her is her presence at the time Fordham was on the ground. It's not surprising that she was at the scene. If someone comes into your premises, it is not surprising that you go to see who that person is.'

His remarks were a flavour of what was to come.

16. The £1-million bribe

'What we have to deal with now is the question of gold bullion found at your address and your involvement in the £26 million bullion robbery at Brink's-Mat.'

It was the Wednesday morning after Fordham's killing, and Noye was being interviewed again at Bromley police station by detectives Suckling and Charman.

The prisoner was less than impressed. 'I think that's the last thing I need worry about at the moment, don't you?' he said defiantly.

'Well, we are going to ask questions about it, as you know,' said Suckling.

By that time questions about the gold were the only ones that police could put to Noye. He had been charged with Fordham's murder – which meant that it was not permitted to interrogate him again about the killing.

The conditions under which a prisoner in England and Wales can be questioned while in custody are laid down by a legal convention, known as Judges' Rules, designed to ensure that confessions forthcoming during interviews with police are reliable. First introduced in 1912, the rules were updated in 1964 after approval by all the Queen's Bench judges; they are backed up by the Home Office, with the agreement of the judiciary. On the issue of questioning a prisoner about an offence with which he has already been charged, the rules are quite specific. It can be done only in 'exceptional circumstances', and a further caution must be administered. If it is found that the Rules have not been observed – if, say, a judge deems that the circumstances are not exceptional enough – anything the prisoner is alleged to have said can be ruled inadmissible as evidence.

As both Noye and Reader had already been interrogated about the killing, there was little point prolonging the questioning on that front and providing the defence with an opportunity to claim in court later that the police must have been very unsure of their facts to continue questioning after the charges had been made. The eleven bars of gold found at Hollywood Cottage, however, were a different matter. No one had yet been charged in connection with them, and police were now anxious to establish that they were part of the Brink's-Mat haul.

After Suckling's opening gambit the prisoner thought for a moment, then asked, 'Tell me, what happens when you go out of here?'

'What do you mean?'

'Do you write all this down?'

'Yes, we make notes on what's been said.'

'I can't say anything then, can I?'

'Why?'

The reply Noye gave showed just how familiar he was with the Brink's-Mat story. 'That Black's a dead man, isn't he?' he asked, referring to the gang's inside man at the Brink's-Mat warehouse. 'You lot wrote down what he had to say. Now everybody knows what he's done. He's a dead man when he comes out. You don't think I'm going to get myself killed because you've told people I've helped you.'

Charman interrupted him. 'Are you saying you've got things you can tell us about the gold if we don't write down what we say here?'

'The thing is,' continued Noye, 'what good is it going to do for me? I'm going away for a long time for what I've done. I don't see you can help me if I tell you anything. They won't cut my sentence. It won't make any difference at all.'

Charman could sense the prisoner feeling his way towards a deal. 'The things that have happened to you over the past few days can't be altered in any way, and it would be wrong if we suggested they could. We've arrested you with what I'm pretty sure is some of the Brink's-Mat gold. Our interest is to recover what's left of the £26 million worth which was stolen. You can help us, I'm convinced.'

Noye was scathing. 'I can help to get myself killed as well. You know what these situations involve. I'm a businessman. If I thought there was any way I could put things in my favour, I'd tell you as much as I know. But this is a pretty one-sided sort of deal, from what I can see.'

Noye was then told of the surveillance operation police had mounted on both him and Reader. The day when Reader was seen leaving Hollywood Cottage and driving up to Cowcross Street, where he exchanged something with two men (8 January) was referred to. 'That was gold from the Brink's-Mat robbery, wasn't it?' pressed Charman.

'If I tell you anything, I'm on my own. What guarantees have I got that you'll help me?' asked Noye.

Suckling avoided the question. 'On that day, I suppose, the gold must have gone down to Bristol, but – I will be honest with you – we didn't follow it, so I don't know. But we do know on other occasions the gold has ended up in Bristol, at a bullion dealer's called Scadlynn. It looks very much as if you are the organizer of this whole chain of events, leading up to the realization of the Brink's-Mat gold.'

'Like you said, there's other people involved. I can't take the blame for what they do,' said Noye.

'Yes, but you're evading the issue. I'm not talking about what they do. I'm saying it all starts with you,' said Suckling.

Noye was shocked. 'It doesn't start with me, no. I've never done a robbery in my life,' he said.

He was then asked how he had paid for Hollywood Cottage

and claimed it had been with money from an insurance claim on a boat and other money he had earned. Asked how long he had been helping to dispose of the gold bullion, he ingeniously replied, 'How long have you been watching me?'

He was told, 'Since 8 January,' but Suckling added, 'We know it goes back beyond that.'

'How?' asked Noye.

'Because of what people down in Bristol and Hatton Garden have said,' said Suckling, claiming that Constantinou had admitted to having been involved since the previous October.

'I don't know him. You haven't seen me with him, have you?' challenged Noye.

Charman answered, 'We'll accept that. Will *you* accept that not everybody is capable of disposing of or dealing in gold?'

'Yes, I'll accept that,' replied Noye.

'Will you accept that you have been to Jersey with others in a private plane and that you bought gold there?' continued the detective, incorrectly. (Noye had taken a chartered flight for the trip.)

Noye smiled. 'Yes. So what?'

Suckling told him that they believed the gold was bought to provide legitimate paperwork to cover the moving of stolen gold. He was also told that he had been watched at the Beaverwood Club handing gold over to Reader.

'Perhaps that was the gold I bought in Jersey,' he ventured.

'It wasn't,' replied Suckling. 'We know that gold is still in vaults in Jersey.'

Charman tried to drive home just how much the Flying Squad already knew about the gold run, saying, 'From what we've seen, the activity round you tends to indicate that you are the trusted middle-man who has got the contacts and the money to get what's necessary done.'

'I know what you want from me, but any business I do with you will get me done in,' was the dramatic reply.

'Aren't you exaggerating a bit?' asked Suckling.

'I know enough about the people involved to know that if I say what I know, and anything happens after that, they'll know it can only have come from me. If I do anything to get you back that gold which they think belongs to them, then that's me done.'

'Well, two of them can't bother you, surely; they are locked up for twenty-five years,' said Charman.

Noye then began to voice his suspicions about how the police had got on to him. He named a man who, detectives believed, had taken part in the original raid but whose involvement they had been unable to prove. 'He's probably given you my name because you gave him some help. He's made sure his share is all right. The only sort of deal I'll do is like my business – if it's all in writing and signed by the people concerned.'

With that Noye fell silent for a few moments, then told the detectives that he would be prepared to speak to Boyce.

'We will speak to Mr Boyce when we leave you,' promised Suckling. 'What can you tell us about Tony Black?' he added, picking up Noye's remark at the start of the interview.

'I can tell you he's as good as dead,' said Noye. 'I know all about false identities and all that, and I know that won't help him at all. They'll find him and they'll have him.'

'Who's going to have him, then?' asked Suckling.

'There's enough money from this to get anyone to do it. They don't need to get their hands dirty.'

'Do you know if anyone has been hired or propositioned to do it?'

'No, but they'll get that sorted out. It's easy enough.'

Noye was then asked about the instructions for the furnace found in the apple store and, once again, about where he got his money from.

'I'm a businessman. I told you what I am,' he insisted.

His attempt to preserve a vestige of respectability annoyed Charman. 'What you are, Mr Noye, is a man well acquainted with villains, armed robbers and the sort of men who come into large amounts of money, who will come to you to launder their cash. You're trusted to keep your mouth shut, and you share in the profits of crime by percentages, without having to put yourself up front.'

'I put myself up front the other night, didn't I?' said Noye bitterly.

Charman continued. 'It always goes wrong for these people at one time or another. Why protect them? I suspect that if they were in your position, they wouldn't hesitate to put your name forward. In fact, that's something to bear in mind for the future with this inquiry. A lot of people have been arrested.'

The appeal failed. 'Then they will have to watch themselves like Black, won't they?' said Noye coolly.

As the interview drew to a close Noye inquired again about Fordham's family, asking how they were.

'I think you can guess that as well as we can,' said Suckling.

'If that hadn't happened, I think we could be talking now,' said Noye.

'What do you mean? What could we be talking about?' asked Suckling.

'All I'd have to worry about would be the gold, and I think perhaps I might have got a deal and you might have got what you wanted.'

Three hours later Noye was again interviewed in his cell, this time by Boyce. It was an interview that, when recounted during Noye's Old Bailey murder trial, was to cause headlines in its own right. How it came about, of course, is a matter of fierce dispute between Noye and the police.

Boyce entered the cell with his deputy, DCI John. He explained that he wanted to ask questions about gold found outside Hollywood Cottage and cautioned Noye in the usual manner that anything he said could be used as evidence later.

Boyce told the Old Bailey jury what then transpired.

Noye said, 'Mr Boyce, can I speak to you alone?'

'Yes, if you prefer,' said the detective, and John left the cell.

Noye said, 'I want to speak to you off the record. I won't if you write anything down. Have you got a tape recorder going?'

Boyce replied that he hadn't, opening his briefcase and emptying his pockets to put the prisoner's mind at rest. 'I won't write anything down,' he promised.

Noye began by asking if the policeman thought he was a cold-blooded killer. Boyce said he didn't know, but there seemed to be nothing in his record to indicate that he was. Noye then asked what Boyce thought would happen and was told that would be up to the court.

'Yes, but what you say can make or break me,' replied Noye.

Boyce told him all he could do was to present the evidence. The rest would be for the court to decide. Noye then asked if he could 'talk' to him.

He began by saying that he was a very rich man, having done lots of deals, and that he wanted to give some money to Fordham's wife and family. Boyce said he understood. Noye then got on to matters closer to home. If he went to prison for a long time, his life and that of his family would be destroyed.

Noye asked Boyce whether he had any family and was told he had, then went on to inquire when the detective was due to retire. 'I said that I concluded some thirty years' service in four years' time,' Boyce told the court. 'He said to me that he would make sure I had a good retirement, that he would ensure that I had plenty of money after I left the police. He would put £1 million in a bank anywhere in the world that I instructed, where no one could trace it, if I would make sure that he would not go to prison. I told him he was wasting his time talking to me in that vein and refused the attempted bribe.'

The only kind of help he wanted, Boyce told Noye, was for the prisoner to reveal the whereabouts of the Brink's-Mat bullion.

'If I told you where it is, I am a dead man,' said Noye.

As Boyce was giving his evidence, the only other sound had been frantic scribbling at a packed press bench. Colin Adamson, a reporter from the evening paper the *London Standard*, knew that here was a story that guaranteed him the front-page splash in the late-afternoon edition. Within minutes he was filing his copy over the phone from the Old Bailey press room. By the end of the lunchtime adjournment, the presses were already rolling. 'I was offered £1m bribe,' screamed the headlines.

After lunch Boyce resumed his evidence. Information leading to the recovery of the gold was the only deal that interested him, he had told Noye, so the prisoner had better weigh up whether he was going to tell him or not. Noye replied that he would think about it but that Boyce should remember his offer. He was a man of his word.

Noye repeated that he wanted to compensate Fordham's widow and told Boyce again to think of his offer. Boyce said there was no question of his accepting. The only deal would be that if Noye revealed where the gold was, the Home Office, and the judge who heard his case, would be informed that he had cooperated.

Noye went on to state that his wife knew nothing of his criminal activities and should not have been charged with murder. He admitted stabbing Fordham but said his wife took no part. He added that there was no point in Boyce sending anybody else to interview him, as his solicitor had advised him not to sign anything.

At the end of the interview Noye had mentioned that there was no record of their conversation and, according to Boyce, looked shocked when told that interviews conducted on the basis that detectives wrote nothing down were, in fact, written up by the interviewing officers as soon as possible afterwards, and the note could be presented as evidence. (Noye had apparently already been told this at an earlier interview by Suckling.) However, the prisoner had soon rallied. 'You are on your own,' he said, and again offered the bribe.

After Noye's trial some detectives suggested that Boyce had used a clever deception to encourage Noye to trust him. During the search of Hollywood Cottage police had discovered that Noye was a member of the Freemasons. To gain his confidence, Boyce, on entering the cell, had shaken Noye's hand using one of the secret grips by which Freemasons the world over recognize one another. Membership of a Freemason lodge is supposed to be a secret affair, and members are forbidden to reveal what takes place at meetings. As a result, contacts and dealings between fellow Masons have a seal of confidentiality. The clear suggestion was that, believing he was talking to a brother Mason, Noye might say more than he would otherwise have done.

By the time Kenneth Noye came to give evidence at the Old

Bailey, he was denying almost the entire scenario outlined by the Flying Squad detective. He did admit that when Boyce arrived at his cell, he asked to talk to him alone – 'to get my view across that I wasn't a cold-blooded killer. I wasn't a murderer and I didn't know the man [Fordham] was a policeman.' He then claimed to have started by asking whether Boyce knew a detective chief superintendent in the Metropolitan Police called Ray Adams, who had investigated a case in which Noye had been involved some ten years earlier. (In 1987 Adams, who had spent much of his career working in south London, became commander at C11.)

Boyce replied, 'Yes, very well.'

Noye then said, 'I am a bit concerned that I have been charged with murder. I am not a violent man. I am not a killer, and I didn't know that man was an officer. I'm more concerned that my wife is charged with murder. She has never done anything wrong in her life. Do you honestly think, looking at me, that I am a cold-blooded killer?'

Boyce had admitted that it didn't appear to look like that.

'Well, you ask Ray Adams. He will tell you that I am not a violent man or a killer.'

Noye went on to ask about Fordham's family, as he was anxious they were being looked after financially.

Boyce then got up and said, 'You can help me and I can help you.'

'How can I help?' asked Noye.

'I want that gold back,' exclaimed Boyce.

Noye told the court, 'He wanted it bad, very bad. He said that basically he had been on very important cases and solved them.' One investigation had even taken him to Egypt; from the way Boyce spoke, Noye thought it had been a recent trip. (Boyce had indeed gone to Cairo some weeks earlier on the Shiner–Gill inquiry.)

Noye continued: 'He said he had done certain special jobs abroad in different places and he had solved them all. He said he had four years left to do and, if it took four years, he would solve this.

'He said he knew I was very wealthy. I said I didn't know

where the Brink's-Mat gold was, and he then started pacing the floor, wagging his finger, saying he knew I could help him and, "I could help you."

'He said that if he got the gold back he could walk up to Leon Brittan's right-hand man and get the charge reduced to manslaughter. [Brittan was then the Home Secretary.]

'I was sitting down at the time and I jumped up and said: "Manslaughter! I happen to be innocent. What would you do if a masked man attacked you like that on your own property? What would you do?"'

Boyce had turned on his heel and walked out.

Under cross-examination Boyce denied having said that he knew Ray Adams 'very well'. He told the court: 'I know him as a colleague.' Boyce added that it was Noye who had originally mentioned his trip to Egypt. 'He asked me if I was the officer that went to Egypt. He seemed to want to know something more about me than he already knew.'

Asked whether he had held out to Noye the offer of reducing the charge to manslaughter, Boyce replied, 'Under no circumstances did I say it. At no time would I have said that the charge could be reduced.' And he denied fabricating the remarks about the bribe with the explanation: 'I couldn't be mistaken about being offered a million pounds.'

Twice that day Reader was interviewed by Walsh about the gold, on the first occasion with his solicitor present in the cell at Orpington police station.

Walsh began by asking: 'You admitted you were at Noye's address. You would not say whether you touched him [Fordham]. You said that you saw certain things, heard certain things and did certain things. Do you now wish to tell me why you went to Noye's address last Saturday evening?'

Walsh decided to allow Reader to consult his solicitor in private, leaving the cell with the words: 'All right – do you trust us now?' Reader smiled but made no reply.

Five minutes later Walsh returned. The news from Reader was entirely expected. 'I do not wish to answer any of your questions on legal advice.' Walsh then let Reader read through the interview notes. The prisoner objected to the phrase that he had refused to say whether or not he had touched Fordham. Reader said that he had always denied touching, assaulting or causing any injury to the dead policeman.

In court Reader's defence counsel, Edward Lyons, QC, added that Reader had also objected to the phrase 'saw certain things, heard certain things'. What he in fact said, according to Lyons, was 'I have seen or heard part of certain things.' Not so, said Walsh. If that had been the case, Reader would have insisted on having it inserted when checking the notes.

The second interview took place in the early evening, with Reader saying that he would not reply to questions if anything was written down. Walsh's caustic observation was that this was so Reader could, at a later date, deny anything that was said.

'You know what you know and that's it,' said Reader dismissively.

'Brian, we want to find out the extent of your involvement. That could range from Mr Big to a relatively minor involvement,' said Walsh, anxious to get the proceedings on to a more even footing.

Reader was incredulous. 'Look, you know I'm not Mr Big. Don't talk silly. You know what I've done, and I'll have to answer for that.' And for the next few minutes he refused to answer any further questions.

The deadlock was broken by the arrival of Boyce at the cell door, saying that he would not object to bail for Lynn Reader when she appeared in court two days later. He left and Reader told Walsh, 'She doesn't know anything about it.'

'She's well trained, isn't she?' said Walsh, unimpressed.

'She's not well trained. I never involve her in what I'm up to,' snapped Reader.

'Let's go back to square one for a minute,' said Walsh. 'Do we still agree that you were conveying stolen gold for Noye to the Hatton Garden contacts?'

'That's it, and that's all I've ever done. I wish I could put the clock back,' said Reader.

'I cannot see how it can harm your case to specify how you became involved, when you became involved and how many times you've done the run. I'm not asking you,' Walsh added cautiously, 'to implicate or name other people if you don't want to, just to put on record your full involvement, particularly if it's relatively minor, as you claim.'

'Mr Walsh, I'd never name anyone,' was the emphatic reply. 'I got involved with a supergrass named Gervaise. He was a good friend of mine and he ruined my life by turning supergrass. I'd never have got involved in this if it hadn't been for him.'

Gervaise's claims had led to the burglary charges involving £1.25 million of gold, silver and watches that had caused Reader to flee the country. By the time he fled, however, Gervaise had turned into a 'hostile' witness for the prosecution, more intent on naming policemen who, he alleged, were also armed robbers than on informing on his old chums. Reader was tried for the burglary offences after the Fordham murder trial and acquitted, although he was jailed for two years and fined £2,000 for absconding.

'Okay, Brian, I respect your feelings over that, but it does not prevent you from putting on record exactly what your involvement has been,' said Walsh.

'You know my involvement. I just took the gold to town and that's it,' said Reader.

'Where did you collect it from?'

'I'm not saying any more.'

The following day, Thursday, Walsh and Jones were back again, and this time Reader was asked whether he knew Micky McAvoy and Brian Robinson, the convicted Brink's-Mat robbers. Reader said he didn't but was then asked: 'Does this gold come from the robbery they were arrested for?'

He looked puzzled. 'I can't understand you,' he said. 'Of course it does.'

When asked what form the gold was in that was found at Noye's house he became even more confused. 'What do you mean, what form is it in? It's pure gold, isn't it?'

'I don't know if it's pure gold. That's what I'm asking you,' said Walsh.

By this time Reader was frankly baffled. He thought hard for a few moments. 'All that gold is pure. I don't know what you mean.'

'Is the gold I showed you, and the gold you've already handed over, in the same shape as it was when it was stolen?' pressed Walsh.

'You know it's been smelted,' replied Reader.

'That's what I mean,' said Walsh. 'Now when it was smelted was anything added to reduce its gold content?'

'No, it's pure gold.'

'So the only purpose of smelting it was to change its appearance so it could not be identified. Really it was just melted. Is that what you're saying?'

'Well, that's what I thought,' said Reader.

Noye was also interviewed that day, this time by Suckling and Charman, who wanted the combination to the safe found buried in the floor of one of the rooms at Hollywood Cottage.

At first Noye refused to reveal it, saying he feared the police could use it to plant evidence. He wanted to talk to his solicitor before deciding what to do. All it contained, he added, was a diamond, some jewellery and some money. Once told, however, that unless the combination was forthcoming the safe would be forced, he revealed the figure sequence.

The two detectives then asked him about the secret compartments that had been discovered. 'Lots of big houses have secret compartments,' he replied.

*

On the Friday morning Suckling and Charman were back to talk about the Meissen china that had been discovered in one of the compartments. It matched other pieces recovered by police at Noye's former house in Hever Avenue.

He was also told that fifty brand-new £50 notes, in serial-number sequence, had been found in his safe. 'That's not much,' he replied. Asked where it came from, he said he couldn't remember. He was then told about the £50,000 that had been discovered behind his father's and sister's homes.

'What's that got to do with me?' he replied.

'The prefix of the number on the notes, all £50 notes, is the same as that on the notes in your safe – A 24. What's more, they are all new notes.'

'So what? It's not mine,' said Noye.

He was then told that the prefix also corresponded to that on £50 notes found at Reader's house and on people concerned with the gold runs down in Bristol.

Suckling gently turned the screw further. 'You must admit that the series of £50 notes, like our observations of you and the others, seem to link all of the people concerned in the disposal of the gold.'

'I want to see my solicitor,' said Noye. 'It's gone far enough.'

Reader also decided that day that he had been asked enough questions. In an interview that began shortly after 9.30 a.m., Walsh said casually: 'You've told us that you do not know where the gold is being smelted. Can you explain why our scientists tell me that there are traces of gold smelt on the wing of your Vauxhall?'

Reader was furious and shouted, 'That's it! I knew it. You're stitching me up.' (Later the only evidence of gold found in the car was traces on the boot mat.)

'Calm down, Brian,' said Walsh. 'We're not stitching anyone up. I gather you're saying you've been nowhere near a smelter. Could anyone else have done so, using your car?'

'No, that's it,' said Reader. 'You're stitching me up. I'm not saying any more.'

*

Ten minutes later he was charged with conspiracy to handle stolen bullion and conspiracy to handle stolen cash. He made no reply. Later that morning Kenneth Noye was charged with conspiracy to handle stolen bullion. His only reply was, 'No reply until I see my solicitor.' Brenda Noye was not charged with any bullion offence until the murder charge against her was dismissed at the committal hearing. Then she was re-arrested as she left the court and charged with conspiracy to handle stolen bullion.

17. The gold chain

By the time Noye and Reader were charged with the bullion offences, police knew rather more about how the Brink's-Mat gold had been disposed of, but they didn't have the full picture. That took some months to build up, but when the facts did emerge, there stood revealed an operation so simple in its execution that today those defendants who are behind bars must be wondering how they got away with it for so long.

For the story that detectives pieced together from interviews with Noye, Reader and others involved in the bullion chain, and from a massive trawl through Scadlynn's paperwork, was this: either Noye, or the unknown source from whom he was obtaining the Brink's-Mat gold, was resmelting the bullion to remove all identifying marks but leaving the content still essentially pure.

Noye then handed the gold over to Reader, who would take it into central London and pass it on to Adams and Weyman, the unsuspecting middle-men for the Bristol end of the operation. They in turn would transfer it on to Scadlynn, through Chappell and an unsuspecting Patch, who would pay for it in new £50 notes. The money involved would be conveyed, via Adams and Weyman, back to Reader, who would then pass it on to Noye.

Once in possession of the gold, Chappell would have it resmelted, mixing in copper and silver in a poor attempt to disguise its purity. Scadlynn would then sell it as 'scrap' gold on the open market. But it had to be sold quickly, as the income was needed to pay for the next consignment.

To disguise the operation, in the dying days of the summer of the previous year (1984) Scadlynn had placed advertisements in West Country newspapers, offering bargain prices for 'scrap' gold, copper, zinc and other precious metals. Leaflets were also circulated stating: 'Absolutely no one in this country can equal our prices. No amount too big, or too small.' Other dealers were taken aback by the generosity of the terms – but Scadlynn could well afford it. Its secret supply of Brink's-Mat bullion easily covered the amounts it had to pay out in order to look like a company legitimately thriving. And thrive it certainly did, with Chappell soon producing an average of a dozen bars of 'scrap' gold each week.

The scale of the racket was phenomenal, as could be seen from Scadlynn's bank accounts. Between September 1984 and January 1985 cash deposited in Scadlynn's account at Barclays' Bedminster branch by dealers buying the 'scrap' gold amounted to more than £10 million. Only months earlier the company had been trading in just tens of thousands of pounds.

Not that the money stayed there long. Cashiers at the bank had, by the end of September, become used to withdrawals by Scadlynn staff of around £20,000 each day. Then the amounts became larger, until on 23 October a surprised cashier was asked to count £55,000 out into a grubby plastic bag thrust across the counter. Further demands for similar amounts followed, then in November the withdrawals were again stepped up: £100,000 one day, £150,000 five days later and so on. Meanwhile the plastic bag had been replaced by a cardboard box.

December came, and the amounts escalated again. On 4 December a Scadlynn appointee turned up and asked for £200,000. He had brought a paper sack with him. Two days later he was back, this time asking for £270,000. In the middle of the month there were a further three payments, topping

£200,000 a time. By now so much money was leaving the branch that Barclays were forced to recruit more cashiers to deal with the Scadlynn account.

January saw yet another jump in the amounts involved. In the first week of the New Year the company phoned to say that it would need £300,000 later on that day. By now the extent and regularity of the withdrawals were becoming so spectacular that special arrangements had to be made with the Barclays Bullion Centre in Bristol to supply enough £50 notes.

At the same time the company's security arrangements improved slightly – Scadlynn recruited the services of a security firm. Chappell's informal manner of operating had cost the company dear when, on 17 December, a van that he had claimed at the time was carrying £97,000 of Scadlynn's gold was hijacked on the outskirts of Bristol. The van was later discovered at a motorway service station. The driver, Roger Feltham, the man who had unwittingly led customs investigators to Scadlynn, had been blindfolded and bound hand and foot. In fact, the gold on board was worth in the region of £250,000, although Chappell, concerned about the questioning he might face, chose not to admit that to police who investigated the robbery.

The incident also prompted a change in the method by which Scadlynn received the pure gold from its London connections. A code was devised to signify different pick-up points. A telephone instruction to meet at point number one meant Swindon railway station; two – the Plough pub; three – Parkway, a railway station on the outskirts of Bristol; four – the Post House Hotel, close to Heathrow Airport; five – Temple Meads railway station in the middle of Bristol; six – the plush surrounds of the Grosvenor House Hotel, Park Lane, in London's West End; seven – a motorway service station.

But the use of the security company for moving the gold back on to the open market, and for collecting the cash from Barclays, seemed at times a purely cosmetic exercise. The company's employees were horrified when, on their first job for Scadlynn, they arrived early in the morning to find the premises locked; Palmer turned up a little later in his Range

Rover and handed the gold over in the street. The next day, when he arrived with the gold in Harvey's pick-up truck, a security guard noticed that one of the bars was still warm to the touch.

The guards were equally flabbergasted when, on two occasions when they took money to the company offices – £320,000 in one instance and a cool £500,000 in the other – they were instructed to dump the notes in sacks on the floor until they could be counted.

And still the withdrawals continued, until Scadlynn felt obliged to warn the bank that the firm's requirements would soon top £1 million a day. The message was passed on by delighted officials to the Bank of England.

By the time the chain was smashed, the local Barclays branch, within a four-month period, had handed over a colossal £10.5 million to Scadlynn – but, incredibly, the authorities never got wind of it. As a result of pressure from conscientious staff, the small neighbourhood bank had been forced to bring in its own investigators to look into the transactions, but customer confidentiality ensured that the police were not informed. In the USA the law demands that any transaction involving $10,000 or more has to be reported to the federal authorities. In Britain the rules concerning bank secrecy at that time had hardly altered in the three hundred years since the founding of the first Bank of England – although the Brink's-Mat case was later to be cited as a major cause for reform.

Barclays took no action, but Chappell's gold dealings had excited suspicion in at least one quarter by the end of the summer. The problems arose when he contacted the Birmingham office of Engelhard Sales Ltd, the largest precious-metal refiners and dealers in the world and owners of some of the original Brink's-Mat bullion. He wanted to know what the terms were for gold 'scrap' showing less than 10 per cent gold. (By dealing in amounts of less than 10 per cent, Chappell ensured that, under the regulations then in force, the VAT payment from Engelhard would go direct to him rather than to HM Customs and Excise.)

A steady trade ensued, with the 'scrap' arriving in flower-pot-shaped lumps of metal. Then in August five bars of gold with a reddish colour arrived. Engelhard was concerned. The company suspected that the bars were melted-down krugerrands, deliberately adulterated with copper to disguise their source. Chappell was contacted and told that there were suspicions about the source of the gold. The Scadlynn boss was understanding itself. He too, he claimed, had been suspicious, and he arranged for the bars to be taken back. The following month, however, after accepting nearly £500,000 worth of business from Scadlynn, Engelhard decided to end the association. A director of the company felt that the spirit of the VAT regulations was being abused, and at the same time HM Customs withdrew the 10 per cent exemption rule.

It was a minor hiccup. Chappell turned his attention instead to Leeds-based bullion dealers Dynasty, which in October agreed to purchase gold from Scadlynn.

Scadlynn, as usual, claimed that what it had to sell was 'scrap' gold, so it was agreed that the 'scrap' would first be sent to an assay office in Sheffield for verification. Assay offices, set up by Act of Parliament, are empowered to hallmark gold, silver and platinum; without such insignia the metals lose value on the open market. The Sheffield office was also able to offer a quality-control service for analysing the purity of precious metals.

Scadlynn had already been using the assay office for some time for other transactions, but those had always involved small amounts. On 23 October, however, the first of the bars arrived.

As more followed on virtually a daily basis, the Sheffield metallurgists found that the ingots were very badly smelted, some so poorly that the copper was still clearly visible among the pure gold. All had to be resmelted, and staff at the assay office found it difficult to understand why Scadlynn had gone to the trouble of smelting the bars in the first place, knowing that the resmelting process would only add to the cost. They also noticed that when the scrapings from inside Scadlynn's melting pots were sent in for assaying, they often showed a much higher gold content than the bars; the proportion would normally have been about the same. And they knew that in the past the company had sent sovereigns and krugerrands in mint condition as scrap gold when they would have fetched a higher price in their original state. But whatever the suspicions of the assay office staff, they kept them to themselves until visited later by police and customs officials.

Dynasty collected the assayed bars from Sheffield and in turn sold them on to a Staffordshire-based company called TVA Noble Metals Ltd, but on 5 December, after the Leeds company had paid out some £3,099,616, Dynasty proprietor Neil Solden wrote to Chappell saying that he would no longer do business with Scadlynn. His suspicions too had been aroused.

TVA, however, continued receiving the Scadlynn gold, and began dealing direct with Chappell. Ironically, all the gold it purchased from Scadlynn was sold directly to Johnson Matthey, the original owners of much of the Brink's-Mat bullion. Between July 1984 and January 1985 Johnson Matthey purchased a total of £13,605,440 from TVA, the bulk of it spoils from the bullion robbery.

TVA, meanwhile, took one major precaution when dealing with Scadlynn; it informed HM Customs of the transactions. A VAT officer who called at the company's offices on 17 January 1985 watched deadpan as he was presented with details of the transactions, without alerting staff to the fact that the Bristol company was the subject of a large-scale investigation.

In all, Scadlynn was able to dispose of about half the Brink's-Mat gold, some £13 million worth, on the open market, although because it had been adulterated with other metals it fetched only £10.5 million.

Chappell, in masterminding the reappearance of the bullion, had anticipated that, somewhere along the line, at least one of the companies with which he was dealing would notify HM Customs, so he took his own precautions to guard against the suspicious VAT inspectors who he knew were bound to call.

A full account was prepared for their benefit: books showed

that £1 million worth of gold had been obtained from a Dorset gold company (which, in fact, had ceased trading two years earlier) and the rest from two of Matteo Constantinou's companies, the International Precious Metals Company and Shimmerbest Ltd. While the proprietor of the defunct Dorset company had no knowledge that his company's name was being used, Constantinou was a willing stooge.

He had been recruited by Chappell and had agreed that the names of his companies could be shown as suppliers of the gold to Scadlynn. To cover his own involvement in the deal, he was supposed to obtain invoices from elsewhere to show where he had purchased it. But this he never bothered to do. As he later explained to the police, he had been told by Chappell that the racket would be over by June of that year. Constantinou had banked on escaping the attentions of HM Customs VAT inspectors until then, when he planned to disappear to Spain with his wife and son and 'join all the others there'.

Putting together the pieces of this jigsaw puzzle was a complicated process for detectives, which was not helped by the lack of cooperation from some of the suspects they had rounded up. Constantinou was one of the exceptions. His first interview with detectives took place on the Tuesday evening at West End Central police station.

'Have you any idea what our inquiry is about?' asked Flying Squad DC Anthony Purdie.

'Well, I've been doing a bit of fiddling, yes,' said Constantinou.

'You say a bit of fiddling, but I consider it to be a lot,' said Purdie.

'Yes, the amounts are, but I've not made that much,' said Constantinou, and in that interview, and in one the following afternoon, he went on to explain that in September the previous year a broker had contacted him to propose a gold deal. He had then found Scadlynn's name in a trade paper as a possible customer and phoned Chappell.

That particular deal had fallen through, but two months later Chappell called and asked him to visit Bristol to discuss some business. There the Scadlynn boss asked to use the name

Constantinou's companies, offering to pay between £2,000 and £3,000 a week for the service, and sometimes more.

To satisfy the VAT inspectors, it was necessary to make some pretence of paying Constantinou for his non-existent gold, so money would be telexed from Scadlynn's bank account to Constantinou's. This happened on eight occasions, involving a total of about £600,000; Shimmerbest also received bank drafts amounting to £250,000. On each occasion Chappell would travel to London the following day and wait in a taxi cab outside Constantinou's bank while the elderly dealer withdrew the money, which was then handed back in the taxi.

That arrangement ceased when Constantinou's bank balked at clearing the repayments so quickly, and therefore the pretence was dropped, so Constantinou had to travel to Bristol every Friday to collect his week's fee, together with phoney receipts detailing the fictitious transactions. (His street cunning, however, rebelled at the idea of possessing anything on paper that linked him with the Bristol company, and the receipts were quickly destroyed by being flushed down the train lavatory on the way home.)

By the time police caught up with the chain, Constantinou had received some £30,000 for his help, and Scadlynn's sales ledger showed that it had purchased between £8 million and £9 million worth of gold from his companies. Constantinou maintained to detectives that throughout he believed that the gold had been smuggled in and was possibly melted-down krugerrands.

Constantinou's was a very different story from the one being told that Wednesday afternoon by Chappell at City Road police station.

'Exactly what do you want from me?' the Bristol dealer demanded of Flying Squad detective sergeants Daniel Conway and David Ryan.

He was told he would be asked questions about his company, his customers and his business associates, and the interview proceeded.

Chappell explained that Scadlynn specialized in purchasing precious metals by mail order, from trade customers and directly, over the counter. The company advertised in the Yellow Pages telephone directory all over the country. Some of the jewellery it purchased would be sold through shops belonging to John Palmer, who had resigned from Scadlynn in about March the previous year. The gold, however, would be sent to Sheffield for assaying, and the results of that process would determine how much the original owner was paid for it and how much it would be sold on for.

In recent months business had substantially increased because of dealings with a new customer – Shimmerbest. Constantinou, claimed Chappell, had phoned him the previous September and said, 'I'm looking to be paid promptly for gold bullion, of which I get large amounts.' He believed Constantinou had seen the company's advertisements in the trade press and had been attracted by the 97.5 per cent rate offered by Scadlynn.

The deals started, and amounts of money varying between £50,000 and £300,000 changed hands every time they met.

The interview then broke off, but was resumed at 1.55 the following morning. No, said Chappell, he hadn't asked Constantinou where the gold came from. 'It seemed impertinent, almost, to ask a man with such a well-established business,' he claimed. He, Palmer and others had on occasions driven to London to pick up the gold, while transactions had also taken place at a service station on the M4 and at Parkway railway station because Constantinou wasn't very familiar with Bristol. The gold they obtained was always smelted to 'do away with any foreign bodies and to stop pilfering'.

That interview finished at 4 a.m., but shortly after 6 a.m. Chappell was again faced with the same two officers. On this occasion he agreed that couriers would sometimes bring the gold to Scadlynn. Asked who they were, he declined to say 'because of security reasons'.

'What do you mean?' asked one of the detectives incredulously.

'I mean I'm not prepared to add anything to what I've already said,' said Chappell.

'I am a police officer. What do you mean, "security reasons"? Do you not trust me?' pressed the interviewer.

'I will, with respect, just repeat what I have said,' retorted Chappell. 'I am not prepared to make any further comment before seeing my solicitor, whom I tried to contact when first arrested and so far have not been allowed to do.' Chappell then denied knowing the names of Noye, Reader, Weyman, Adams, McAvoy, Robinson, White or the man who had been living in Noye's former home in Hever Avenue. Told that at another police station Constantinou was claiming that he had never supplied gold to Scadlynn, Chappell replied, 'That is untrue – it is untrue, I tell you,' but he declined to see a copy of Constantinou's statement.

Chappell went on to reveal that Palmer would do the smelting for Scadlynn, sometimes with the help of James Harvey and Lee Groves. The interview ended, but at lunchtime Chappell was seen again, and again refused to answer questions about couriers, with the exception of Patch who, he claimed, may have driven to Swindon to meet Constantinou. He claimed, however, that Constantinou would often bring the gold by train to Bristol.

'Are you telling me that Mr Constantinou, a man in his seventies and overweight, is capable of carrying 22 kilos of gold on his arm?' asked one of the detectives disbelievingly.

'Yes, definitely. I've seen him do it – he's a very powerful man,' broke in Chappell, too quickly to be convincing.

'I've met Mr Constantinou, and that man is ill and elderly,' remarked the detective.

Chappell made a forlorn effort to retreat behind his image of being a respectable bullion dealer by telling his interviewers that he was currently in the process of trying to raise £6 million to set up a deal with Arab customers, which would eventually total 100 tons of gold.

The detectives were unimpressed. 'Are you any good with telephone numbers?' asked one of them.

'Not particularly,' replied Chappell.

The detective read out Adams's telephone number, which had been found among Chappell's correspondence. 'Why would you have Adams's telephone number?' the detective wondered.

'I have no idea. I don't recognize the number.'

The suspect was then asked about the list of secret rendezvous spots that had been arranged for gold hand-overs. 'What are you trying to hide?' he was asked.

'I'm not trying to hide anything,' snapped Chappell, growing agitated.

'The gold you've been getting in large bulk recently is stolen, isn't it?' asked one of the detectives unexpectedly.

'If it is, it is without my knowledge. I have never thought of it as anything but completely legitimate,' replied Chappell.

'Mr Constantinou is a one-man show. He's elderly. How can he suddenly afford to produce £10 million worth of gold?' pressed the detective.

'He didn't suddenly produce it. It was done over a period of time in relatively small amounts.'

'Three million pounds' worth in one week is not relatively small.'

'I hadn't finished. I was about to say that Mr Constantinou has a reputation among the trade for being a wealthy man, made rich by his knowledge of uncut diamonds. I also believed Mr Constantinou to be a businessman of substance and dealt with him along those lines.'

And with Chappell still proclaiming his innocence, the interview ended. Constantinou, told later that Chappell was still insisting that he had legitimately purchased the gold from Shimmerbest and International Precious Metals, was scornful. 'That's stupid, ain't it?' he told detectives. 'I can assure you that I have never supplied him with one ounce of gold, no gold whatsoever.'

Patch was interviewed for the first time on the Wednesday, when his questioner was DS O'Rourke, who until then had been dealing with Brenda Noye. After initially stating that he didn't want to say anything, as his only involvement with the company was 'to sign cheques when no one else is about', Patch revealed that until December the previous year he had been sending the Scadlynn gold to the Sheffield assay office with Roger Feltham. After Feltham was robbed Palmer, although he had left the company, arranged with a security firm to make the journey. Patch would phone the assay office after each consignment to find out how much it was worth.

The gold, he believed, came originally from Shimmerbest. On occasions he had helped to pick it up, travelling to Swindon railway station or a service station on the M4 to exchange a briefcase full of cash for a case containing gold. He saw nothing suspicious about the manner in which the gold was handed over – the code was a straightforward security measure after the Scadlynn robbery.

Patch added that he received no payment for his services from the firm but was occasionally given odd bits of jewellery and allowed to use the office phones for his own business. He would also sometimes use the book-keeper to do his accounts.

Thomas Adams was interviewed by Flying Squad detectives some hours after his arrest. From the start it was apparent that he felt he had little to answer for. Refusing to leave his cell at City Road police station, he told DC Davis, who had arrested him, 'If you want to talk to me, it's here or nothing.'

Once again he denied any knowledge of the BMW parked outside his house. 'I have never seen the car before. I'll bet someone will say they've seen me in it, though,' he said.

'Why say that?' he was asked.

'Aren't you using C11 now, then?' was the sarcastic reply.

'We found a large quantity of jewellery in your house this morning. How do you account for it?'

'Do I have to?'

'If you're an asphalter, what are you doing with all that jewellery?'

'I used to be in the business.'

'When?'

There was no reply, and when asked how much a sovereign was worth and how much a krugerrand cost, he wouldn't answer.

'We found a gold bar in your house. Where is that from?' persisted Davis.

'You don't give up, do you?' replied Adams.

'We are investigating two very serious crimes and feel these matters need clearing up,' said Davis.

'I'm sure you do,' replied the prisoner. 'But you mustn't treat me like an idiot. I'm sorry that C11 man got murdered, and I was expecting a call from you lot, but give me a little respect.'

'How do you mean?' asked Davis.

'We all know the score. I'll either walk from here or walk from court after a six-month lay-down [remand period before the trial]. You've got nothing on me.'

And from that point on, throughout another three interviews, Adams refused to answer any questions.

As they continued searching his house, however, police discovered Patch's telephone number, plus the car-phone number of Chappell's Jaguar XJS and the telephone number of Scadlynn. They discovered his number among Chappell's correspondence and learned that a call had been made to Adams from Palmer's car phone. His address was also found on a sheet of paper in Brian Reader's home.

Before dawn on the Thursday police also moved in on Micky Lawson, the man who, thirteen months earlier, had purchased the furnace from William Allday and Co. Ltd in Stourport-on-Severn. His car had been seen visiting Noye's home, and one of his fingerprints had been found in Hollywood Cottage. Lawson's house was searched, and he was told he was being arrested on suspicion of dishonestly handling stolen bullion. 'I've already been through this once,' he replied, referring to his arrest the day after the purchase of the smelter.

At the police station Lawson admitted to Flying Squad DS Cam Burnell that he was a friend of Noye, having known him for years. Their children were friends, and their wives played squash together, but he couldn't remember the last time he had seen Noye or been to his house.

According to the police account of the interview, he initially stuck to the story about the furnace that he had given during his last arrest. A man named Benny had asked him to purchase it on behalf of someone he knew simply as the Turk, who wanted it for export, and it had been handed over in a road lay-by in Kent. He had seen neither man since.

'Can you explain how the operating instructions for the smelter you bought were found in Kenneth Noye's shed?' asked Burnell.

'No, I can't,' said Lawson.

At a later interview he insisted again that he bought the furnace under a false name for V A T purposes.

It was, according to the police account presented in court, on the Friday morning, half an hour after Noye had been charged with the bullion offence, that Lawson broke.

'I've been thinking about this all night,' he told Burnell.

'And what have you decided?'

'It's difficult. I've been friends with Ken Noye for a long time. I just don't know what to do.'

'The best way is just to tell the truth.'

'I want to but, like I said, it's difficult.'

'You got that smelter for Ken Noye, didn't you?' said Burnell.

'Not exactly.'

'What do you mean?'

'I knew where it was going.'

'To Noye?'

'Yes,' Lawson admitted resignedly.

Although Noye had never mentioned it directly, Lawson had assumed the gold that was to be smelted was from the Brink's-Mat job. He still insisted, however, that the smelter had been handed over in the lay-by to two men whom he refused to name. Later Lawson's barrister was to deny that the remarks attributed to his client were ever made.

*

The whereabouts of John Palmer were by this time no mystery to detectives. In the week after Fordham's death, while police were completing their mopping-up operation in the Bristol area, British journalists had made a bee-line for Tenerife, where Palmer was traced to a five-star hotel in the resort of Playa de las Americas.

In a series of television interviews – memorable for the few occasions when he would actually look directly at the camera – and talks with newspaper reporters, during which he was sipping either lager or brandy and looking tense and angry or bronzed and relaxed, depending on which report one read, the theme didn't vary. He was an innocent abroad.

'I've nothing to hide. The first thing I knew was that I had an urgent telephone call to ring home. They told me it was connected with some bullion robbery and the murder of a policeman. I was astonished and amazed when I heard what happened,' he said. 'I rang my solicitor, who was astounded. I can categorically deny I was involved in the bullion raid. And I have nothing to do with the gold from it.

'I have in the grounds of my house a smelting works, which was put there approximately two and a half to three years ago. This was connected with my former business, which was a bullion company. It's hidden only because of the valuable materials processed there.

'The police have found gold at my house. Some jewellery would have been mine, and the gold belonged to another dealer who often used my furnace. But it was legitimate gold. If someone came to me with a lot of gold which they wanted me to melt down, I would inform the police at once.

'The police could have found me here if they wanted to. We never made any secret of where we were going. Now I am considering action against them. They smashed down doors and have damaged the swimming pool and living-room floor. There is thousands of pounds' worth of damage. They over-reacted. It would have been quite easy to knock on the door.'

'My wife is very upset,' he added. 'She has a 6-month-old child to cope with and we have all been devastated by this.'

But Palmer dismissed the idea of returning immediately to sort things out. 'I don't think I could achieve anything by going back early. I think once I touch England, I will be arrested.'

He was right.

18. The trial

The murder trial of Kenneth Noye and Brian Reader took place at the Old Bailey the following November. At the request of the defence, the gold bullion charges were deferred to a later date. For more than two weeks the drama was played out in front of a jury of seven men and five women, press benches that were seldom empty and a packed gallery, in which were to be seen one or two faces, well-known in the criminal world, that were of considerable interest to police. Such was the security that each time Noye or Reader arrived or left in a prison van, streets around the court were closed and armed police posted at vantage points.

Surprisingly for a major Old Bailey murder trial, there were no challenges when the jurors were selected. Under British law a defendant has the right, generally exercised through defence counsel, to reject three jurors and demand replacements, without giving any reason. A practice has grown up, over many years, of defence lawyers challenging anyone who looks remotely middle-class. At some trials a collar and a tie on a male juror have been sufficient to have him asked to step down. The belief is that the more affluent and 'respectable' a juror appears, the more likely he or she is to accept the word of the police against the defendant. There is also thought to be a greater likelihood that such jurors will prove harsher judges, holding strong views on law and order, and viewing any suggestion of its breakdown with horror.

The practice of challenging jurors had, however, come in for close examination by the British media a month earlier, when seven British servicemen, alleged to have been recruited by Arabs to spy for Warsaw Pact countries while serving in Cyprus, were acquitted of all charges. On that occasion challenges were made until a jury was selected that included a young man whose appearances in the jury box were usually preceded by a flamboyant stage entrance.

Noye was able to use his wealth to provide himself with the services of John Mathew, QC, who was to leave virtually no police statement unchallenged in his bid to obtain an acquittal. Mathew had determined from the outset that there would be no suggestion that either defendant had anything to fear from a 'middle-class' jury. His client, and therefore Reader too, were innocent, and had no reason to resort to selection tactics.

Police, however, were fearful that the two defendants might resort to another kind of tactic, jury nobbling, and on day one, immediately after the jury had been sworn in, the court was cleared while the judge, Mr Justice Caulfield, outlined to the jurors the protection they were to receive, including a round-the-clock police guard and the interception of all telephone calls to their homes.

If before the trial police felt such measures might be necessary, they were even more convinced that morning, when one of the first people to take a seat in the public gallery was Reader's old friend John Goodwin, who in 1983 had been sentenced to seven years for nobbling the jury in a burglary trial in which he and Reader were co-defendants.

The nobbling – or, to give it its correct term, 'conspiracy to pervert the course of justice' – was said to have involved organizing approaches to at least four and possibly eight jurors in the burglary trial, who were offered £1,000 each to find Goodwin and Reader innocent. A team of Goodwin's accomplices were alleged to have followed jurors from the court to their homes and built up detailed information about their lifestyles. This came to light after a woman juror reported that an unknown man had approached her at a south London railway station and thrust £50 into her handbag 'to give the children a good day out'. A retrial was promptly ordered.

When Goodwin was convicted of conspiracy he was described in court as an 'arch Mr Fix-It'; the plot was said to be a 'determined attempt to poison the fountain of justice at its source'. Goodwin's conviction for jury nobbling was quashed by the Court of Appeal fifteen months later because of doubts about the evidence from two witnesses. An appeal court judge said, 'However suspicious we are, we have to look at the quality of the evidence and quality was lacking.'

The start of the murder trial brought an immediate objection from the defence to the use of photographs of the house and grounds of Hollywood Cottage, which were to be distributed to the jury. The photographs, Mathew pointed out, had been shot in daylight and could give a misleading impression – Noye had discovered Fordham at night. The judge agreed and asked if the defence wanted the jury to see the property for themselves in conditions similar to those of the night in question.

The offer was readily accepted, so at the end of the first day's hearing, while prosecutor Nicholas Purnell was still opening the case, the court was adjourned. Later that evening it reconvened in one of the most bizarre settings in legal history.

At 5.50 p.m., in darkness and a heavy rain storm, three limousines ferried the jury to the gates of Hollywood Cottage, the jurors pulling their coats over their heads as they alighted to hide their faces from the waiting television cameras. Ten minutes later, with blue lights flashing, two police cars arrived. Behind them was a green prison van containing Noye, and behind that a back-up police Range Rover. Reader had decided against attending, as was his right.

On the tarmac apron outside the gates, just yards from where Fordham had been found by his colleagues, the Old Bailey clerk convened the court, the official shorthand writer beside him sheltering under an umbrella while he painstakingly recorded everything that was said.

The judge, complete with bowler hat, Noye with an escort of four policemen and four prison officers, to one of whom he was handcuffed, the jury and a clutch of legal representatives were then shown over the grounds. Following, at a discreet distance, were some thirty journalists, straining to hear every word. Up at the house there was a scene straight from a Victorian etching as Brenda Noye and her two sons, grouped at a lighted window, waved forlornly to the head of the family, hemmed in on all sides by his escort. A coat and a pair of wellington boots that she handed out for her husband's use were carefully checked over in torchlight by two police officers before they were given to the prisoner, who was wearing an expression of aggressive confidence mixed with injured innocence that was to remain with him throughout the trial.

In the days that followed the cost to Noye of providing himself with the best counsel in the land proved money well spent. Mathew admitted that Noye had indeed carried out the stabbing – but insisted that it was justified defence *after* Fordham had struck Noye in the face when he was discovered. In that admission, much stress was laid on the way Fordham looked that dark night. Dressed in camouflage clothing and a balaclava, he would, said Mathew, 'have struck terror in the bravest of us'. Noye's reaction, according to Mathew, had been 'shocked terror. He froze, literally froze, terrified with fear. The next moment he received a blow in the face, in the left eye – he doesn't know with what, but he sprang to life, thinking in a flash that he had been struck with some kind of weapon and, having seen that apparition, he assumed that someone seen like that in his grounds at night would be armed. He thought he had seconds to live; he thought his end had come, and in a blind panic stabbed and stabbed.'

If self-defence is to work as the answer to a murder charge, the jury must find that the force used was reasonable. If they decide the force used was excessive, then self-defence fails as a defence, and the defendant will be guilty of murder unless the jury believes that the accused was so provoked by things said and done by the victim that he lost his self-control, as any 'reasonable' person might be expected to do. Then the jury can return a verdict of manslaughter.

In this case a manslaughter plea would have been appropriate if, for instance, Noye had alleged that he was so shocked by the figure he saw that in legal terms he was 'provoked' into losing his self-control and stabbed Fordham, inadvertently killing him in the process. Murder carries life imprisonment, but there is no sentence fixed by law for manslaughter. In most cases where provocation is accepted, however, a prisoner can generally expect seven to ten years' imprisonment. But from the outset Noye insisted that he used a reasonable amount of force to defend himself against attack, and manslaughter was never presented as an option for the jury to consider.

It was certainly not an option that the defence wanted to ask for. Noye's barristers knew that he would never sanction it. He was adamant: in killing the police officer he had been protecting himself. He was innocent of any crime. There is anyway a reluctance on the part of defence counsel in cases of this kind, where the degree of doubt is substantial, to play the manslaughter card. They prefer a clear-cut issue to be presented to the jury, not alternative charges that could allow the jury to sidestep determining a defendant's guilt. Doubts that should lead to a not guilty verdict for murder might be deflected into a finding of guilt for manslaughter.

The judge too could have introduced the manslaughter option had he thought it appropriate. Mr Justice Caulfield clearly felt it wasn't.

And, from the point of view of the police, manslaughter was not an alternative they wanted offered. One of their officers had been stabbed ten times: how could anyone regard that as a reasonable amount of force, particularly when medical evidence indicated that at least five of the stab wounds had occurred when the policeman was immobile? There was also the fact that the man who had carried out the killing appeared to be a major criminal, not an otherwise blameless member of society. Surely, with the discovery of the gold, which had to be Brink's-Mat bullion, a jury would see the motive behind the actions of Noye and Reader? Fordham was murdered to protect their illegal operations.

In countering the plea of self-defence, the prosecution pointed out that Noye had made no mention of an attack by Fordham when he was interviewed by police officers after the killing. Quite the opposite, in fact. A police sergeant who was giving Noye an exercise break at Bromley police station three days after the killing had specifically asked, 'Did he attack you then?', to which Noye allegedly replied, 'No, but what do you do when you are confronted like that?'

But, throughout, the prosecution failed properly to address the evidence on which Noye's plea was largely based – the injury to his eye. DC Manning said he saw a 'mark' around the eye when he first accosted Noye near the gates. Yeoman too mentioned a 'graze or small cut' when Noye was being held at Hollywood Cottage. And as a black eye it was plainly visible when the prisoner was examined by a police surgeon later that night.

But no suggestion as to how Noye came by that bruise was ever presented by the prosecution to the jury, not even the one made by a police officer when interviewing Noye after the killing – that it had been caused by Fordham defending himself. The possibility, even, that Fordham realized he was about to be stabbed, and so had struck out with a blow that might have landed first, was never mentioned. For the prosecution couldn't provide an explanation – they simply had no evidence, one way or the other. The only person who knew what had happened in the shrubbery was Kenneth Noye. It was a crucial weakness in the prosecution case, for there was nothing to counter his claims.

The black eye became even more damaging to the prosecution case when the pathologist, Crompton, under questioning by Mathew, seemed to agree that if Noye had been struck, it was likely to have been before the first blow from the knife, evidence that Mathew underlined when opening the defence case. The reason Crompton gave was that after the first knife wound Fordham would have been immobile and unable to deliver the punch.

But Crompton's answers seem capable of being read two ways, and in a later interview with Andrew Hogg he said he believed that his reply was misrepresented by Mathew to the jury. He originally mentioned the question of Fordham being immobile after the first wound only in relation to the group of five closely placed horizontal wounds; whether he thought this group preceded Fordham's other wounds was not established at any stage in the trial.

Fordham's immobility after the first of the horizontal wounds had been delivered was established when Crompton discussed three out of the five, which were to the front of Fordham's body. 'It would suggest . . . that the position of the deceased had remained constant; in other words, he had stayed still,' said Crompton. Of the two wounds that were in Fordham's back, Crompton repeated his belief: 'I would suggest that . . . the deceased had not moved between them.'

But a detailed analysis of Crompton's later evidence, when he was cross-examined by Mathew and supposedly claimed that the blow to Noye's eye was probably the first delivered, reads like this. Mathew, referring to the five horizontal wounds, asked, 'Those could have occurred very rapidly?'

'Yes,' replied Crompton.

'We are talking about literally one–two–three–four–five, like that?'

'Yes.'

'Indeed, all these blows might have taken place over seconds?'

'Yes.'

'Frenzied blows. Imagine for a moment: you have described the force required, the sort of force and the number of blows a man might use who had been attacked by a masked man in the dark and was fighting for his life or thought he was.'

'Yes.'

'You, of course, did not have the opportunity of examining Mr Noye shortly after this?'

'No.'

'For the purposes of my question, assume he had a black and cut eye and cut nose, among other injuries, and would you assume that that was a result of a blow to the eye. If from the time of the first wound, as I think you are saying, Mr Fordham would have been immobile . . .'

'Yes.'

'. . . if Mr Noye had been hit in the eye, it must have been before the first blow?'

'It would be likely.'

The phrase 'all these blows' was Mathew widening the questioning from the horizontal group of five wounds to all ten, and when he came to address the jury he left the lasting impression that immobility would have followed the first of the ten delivered.

After the trial Mathew maintained that Crompton clearly said that it was likely that Fordham would have been immobile after the first blow, irrespective of which blow that was. But Crompton told us, 'I assumed he was referring to the group of five throughout, not all the others. There were two other wounds in the chest – one went into the lung and the other didn't go anywhere. Fordham could easily have hit him after receiving those two. They were hardly incapacitating. It was a misrepresentation of emphasis. Mathew was extracting more from my answer than I had intended to give.'

Crompton appeared in court for the prosecution, but by the time he left the witness box he had been turned into a witness favourable to the defence, particularly after he also agreed that Fordham's immobility was not necessarily due to restraint – it could have been because he was unconscious, collapsed, or shocked.

Reader's counsel maintained from the outset that there was no case to answer. In fact, Reader exercised his right not to give evidence at all during the trial. And lest the jury might think this indicated that he had something to hide, the judge reminded them that it is only since 1898 that a person charged with any offence – including murder – has had the right under English law to give evidence.

He could be found guilty of murder only if, first, Noye was proved to have murdered and, second, if he, Reader, was proved to have given assistance, or participated, in an assault with the intention of killing the police officer or causing him serious injury. Hence in his case also there was no pressure for a manslaughter option.

It was true that Reader had been seen to make a kicking motion by Fordham's colleague, Murphy, but he did not see where the kick landed. And Murphy had made a statement claiming that the man who made that motion was the person *without* the shotgun in April, more than two months after his original statement, in which the question had been left open.

As well as admitting the killing, Noye's counsel was also quite open about the criminal activities in which he and Reader had been engaged that night. They were illegally dealing in gold. But it was gold that had nothing to do with the Brink's-Mat case. The bullion that had been found at Hollywood Cottage was the subject of proceedings to be dealt with separately, so in the interests of justice the full details of the involvement of Noye and Reader with the Brink's-Mat bullion had to be omitted.

The prosecution in the murder case was, however, able to mention it in explaining why the two defendants were under surveillance and to explain the motive for the killing. With Brink's-Mat, it was alleged, the stakes were so high that Noye and Reader had no compunction about murdering anyone who might have jeopardized their activities.

The suggestion that Noye was a major criminal who had gone out that night and murdered a man who was threatening his enterprise was firmly countered by Mathew. He drew the jury's attention to the fact that when Noye had left the house to attend to the barking dogs, he had openly walked down a well-lit drive calling to them. His actions, said Mathew, were not those of a man 'being surreptitious or bent on evil intent in any way'.

From the witness box Noye denied any knowledge of the Brink's-Mat raid, but Purnell attempted to show that he was lying by saying that Noye was involved socially with Brian Robinson. Noye denied knowing him. At the request of the defence the jury was then cleared from the court, and Mathew told the judge, 'Brian Robinson is the man in connection with Brink's-Mat. The only reason to bring it up is to link him with Brink's-Mat.' The prosecution claimed that the relationship could be a close one. A video of a charity night at a south London disco had been found at Noye's house, which showed Noye's wife dancing together with Robinson's wife. After seeing part of the video, the judge refused to allow it to be shown to the jury.

In court Noye provided a ready account of the gold transactions that he was involved in. The gold was part of regular consignments he had been receiving, smuggled in from abroad to avoid VAT payments. He would sell the gold at a price based on the daily 'fix' – the official gold price arrived at every morning and afternoon by the five companies that make up the London bullion market. The price they fix, based on a mid-point between the top price that customers world-wide are prepared to pay for gold and the lowest price that others are willing to sell it for, is the official value of gold at any one time.

The profit for Noye lay in how far below the fix he could buy gold for and how much he could mark up on top as the VAT he was supposedly going to pay to HM Customs. For the more links there are in a chain of people selling on illegal gold before it enters the legitimate market, the more the 15 per cent allegedly levied for VAT gets whittled down, for each link will take a slice as his share of the profit.

Noye claimed that his gold dealing had started between 1976 and 1978, and he could normally guarantee getting a couple of kilos a day – but he had never knowingly dealt in stolen gold. Two days before Fordham was killed, said Noye, Reader had visited him to buy some gold. Noye had been dealing with him for about four weeks, without realizing that he was a wanted man. But there had been a hitch. Noye had not received his usual delivery and had only eleven bars, reserved for someone else. The person they were reserved for had failed to phone and confirm the order, so Noye let Reader take them. He warned Reader, however, not to dispose of them until Noye had heard from the original purchaser. The original order was subsequently confirmed, so Reader was asked to return the bars, which he was doing that Saturday night, having missed a rendezvous earlier that day at the Beaverwood Club.

Both defence and prosecution made play of Noye's considerable wealth – the former to show that it had been made legitimately, the latter to show it could not have been.

Mathew mentioned Noye's first property deal and said that since then he had bought a number of properties, decorated them and sold them. He had also bought land, obtained planning permission for building development and sold it.

One particular deal was referred to: the purchase in 1983, for £545,000, of the Sun Garage in West Kingsdown, which Noye had sold for some £775,000. Purnell tried to counter this claim that the profits were large but legitimate by saying that Noye's share of that deal amounted to only 50 per cent. In response Noye revealed how familiar he was with the setting up of offshore banking companies. He claimed that the deal had been spread over three years to stagger the tax payments and that Purnell was looking at only one section of it. Noye was also said to have a business dealing in American motor homes and to have recently sold his haulage business.

Purnell then taxed him about his liquid assets, in connection with which Noye did not have such ready answers. Purnell claimed that Noye had millions of pounds in various bank accounts and referred to just one, an account in his wife's name at an Irish bank that contained £1.5 million.

'I have access to various bank accounts, but the money is not mine,' replied Noye.

Because of the stress that was to be placed on the Bank of Ireland transactions at the subsequent bullion trial, the suspicious manner in which the account had been set up and the deposits made was not fully revealed to the murder-trial jury. Had it been, the jury would have learned that in September 1984 Noye had approached a branch of the Bank of Ireland in St Michael's Road, Croydon, south London. There, conspicuous by his smart blue suit and gold jewellery, and using the name Sidney Harris, he inquired about the various facilities offered by the bank and its subsidiaries in the Isle of Man, Dublin and Jersey. Eventually he opted for an offshore account in Dublin, which, he said, would be in joint names, the other being Brenda Tremain (his wife's maiden name). He did not, he added, want the statements sent to him and left the branch no means of contacting him.

His first deposit, made on 4 September, was of £200,000, delivered in a small, black executive briefcase full of new £50 notes, divided into bundles of £12,500. He was shown into a private room on the first floor of the bank, and the money, which he claimed was the proceeds from property development, was fed into the bank's cash-counting machine.

Over the next four months a further four such deposits were made, earning something like 9 per cent interest, the claim being that Noye was in the building trade but had made a killing on the stock market. On one occasion 'Sidney Harris' even joked about buying a cash-counting machine himself but then decided it would be too expensive.

By admitting both the killing and the fact that he was engaged in a wholesale gold-smuggling operation, Noye was hardly presenting himself as a plausible figure to the jury. But after those two admissions almost every aspect of the police evidence, including the interviews with the two defendants and Brenda Noye, was vigorously challenged.

First and foremost were doubts about whether police had intended to execute the search warrant that night. Acting DI Suckling insisted that when he ordered the C11 team in, he was in fact executing the warrant and the search party would have arrived soon afterwards. Mathew, however, knew that, whenever possible, police prefer not to have to execute a search warrant in darkness. He believed that when the C11 team were ordered in it was to establish whether a raid would be worth while.

If no decision had been made to execute the warrant, Fordham and Murphy were unlawful trespassers, and a jury might be inclined to believe that Noye had behaved justifiably in stabbing a man who had no business being there anyway. It would also raise serious questions about how far police were prepared to bend the rules in their investigation.

Mathew pointed out that later that night Suckling was to record in a pocket book that he made the decision to execute the warrant at 6.25 p.m., ten minutes after Fordham and Murphy had gone into the grounds of Hollywood Cottage. And it wasn't until about 7 p.m., when a policeman lay dying, that Boyce had been notified of Suckling's decision, contrary to his express request that he be told as soon as possible. Boyce was at home, a quarter of an hour's drive away, at the time. If they had really meant to execute the warrant, Mathew implied, Boyce would have been told far sooner. As commanding officer, he would have wanted the option of overriding that decision. All it would have taken was a radio message to Scotland Yard, where Kenneth John, Boyce's deputy, could have contacted Boyce on his radio pager or phoned him. Cross-examining Suckling, Mathew said: 'There was no intention, or specific intention, to execute that warrant on that Saturday . . . The truth of the matter is that you gave instructions to move in because you wanted to be reasonably confident that there was gold there.'

Suckling claimed that the time recorded in his pocket book was an estimate; by looking at the log of radio messages, he could see that the time he gave the order was in fact 6.15 p.m. He added that he had notified Boyce as soon as he was able and that there was no way Boyce could have overridden a decision to raid Hollywood Cottage once it had been taken.

Mathew questioned whether the warrants that were in existence for other premises were ready to be executed at such short notice. Suckling admitted that they weren't but added that some or all of them would have been prepared that night. 'There were no other aspects of the operation in any way remotely identical with the circumstances at Hollywood Cottage,' he explained.

Boyce, when cross-examined, said that once Suckling made the decision to go in, he could not override him. He added that there were difficulties with radio communication between Kent and Scotland Yard. He admitted, though, that he had given three different times for when he was first notified of what had occurred. In his original statement he had said 7.15 p.m.; at the committal hearing he had said 6.45; now he believed it was about 7 p.m.

Implicit throughout Mathew's questioning was disbelief that after a three-week operation the decision to carry out a raid would be left to an acting detective inspector. In fact, Boyce could have been required at any time to attend other duties at Scotland Yard because of his involvement with other cases and so could not become too closely involved. Boyce may also have been falling back on his military training: operational decisions will often be left to the subordinate on the ground, while the commanding officer takes full responsibility for whatever is decided.

Mathew also questioned whether, during the Friday briefing, instructions had been given to Murphy and Fordham about their response if they were spotted. DCI Roland Heming, from C11, told the court that they had been told that if the dogs or people 'compromised' them, they were to withdraw. If they were discovered and could not withdraw, they were to identify themselves as police officers and show their warrant cards. Asked if Fordham had a warrant card on him, Heming said he had. It had been in his wallet, which Heming took from him in the ambulance. Murphy, however, said that no instructions on what to do if compromised had been given at the Friday briefing. 'There was no need to tell us what to do,' he said.

Bryan Moore, an ambulanceman who tended to Fordham in the back of the ambulance, then appeared as a defence witness to say that he saw no one take a wallet from Fordham on the way to hospital and didn't believe it would have been possible without his knowledge.

In court Mathew was also to question several aspects of Murphy's evidence, disputing that Murphy, Sinton and Matthews had been in a position to witness what was going on while Fordham was lying by the gate. Had they been, surely they would have made their presence known as police officers? The explanation that they were waiting for officers better equipped than they to arrive was also questioned. None of those who did arrive were armed, so how were they better equipped?

The defence also denied that Noye made a move towards Murphy while the detective was sitting on the fence after leaving the shrubbery, thus causing him to jump down out of the grounds of Hollywood Cottage. And it challenged the version of events given by detectives Manning and Childs, who were the first to go to Fordham's rescue. According to the two detectives, after entering the grounds they both leapt from the car to be confronted by Noye pointing a shotgun and shouting: 'Fuck off, or I will do you as well.'

Noye claimed in court that when the police car drove into the grounds, it went past the scene at the gate before quickly reversing. And, contrary to the detectives' evidence, at no stage while Noye was there did Childs get out of the car, so he could not corroborate the exchanges that Manning said took place.

The police video shot from the mock birdbox in the retreat was produced by Mathew to substantiate Noye's claims. The video did seem to show that the reverse lights of the police car remained on for some seven seconds after driving into the grounds, before going out again. The only way they would have gone out was if the car, which was automatic, had been taken out of reverse. But after the lights went off there was no sign of anyone leaving the police car by the driver's door. Instead the interior light was on and a shadow, which could have been a human form, could be seen in the driver's seat.

The defence also made great play of its suspicions that, in seeking to minimize the appearance of Fordham that night, the balaclava he had worn had been tampered with.

Noye was specific; the mask on the figure he saw had two eye holes. A shorthand writer he had employed to make a full note of the committal hearing had recorded Murphy, when cross-examined at that stage, saying that Fordham was 'wearing the green hood with the eye holes'. However, the first balaclava produced in court and shown to the jury was blue. It had just one cavity, through which a substantial part of the face would have been seen. Another balaclava, this time green, was also produced, but it too had just one cavity, torn and frayed, through which much of the face would have been visible. On being shown the first balaclava at her husband's trial, Brenda Noye said, 'That is not the mask at all.' On being shown the second, she remarked, 'No, I remember it was two holes. I don't remember it being split like that.'

Ann Priston, a forensic scientist from the police laboratory in Lambeth, said that when she examined the second balaclava it was clear there had originally been two eye holes. A piece of material separating them had been removed, possibly by cutting, but she wasn't able to say whether that had happened weeks, months or even a year earlier. It was clear to her, however, that the aperture was larger than when she had first examined it.

Boyce was first taken to task for refusing to allow Noye, his wife or Reader access to their solicitors while the initial Flying Squad interviews were taking place – although Kent police had allowed them to take legal advice immediately following the killing. Mathew reminded Boyce that there were rules and regulations that governed how prisoners in custody should be treated and interviewed. One of the rules was that, in ordinary circumstances, a person in custody should not be denied access to a legal adviser. Boyce agreed but said that, in his view, access at that time might have hindered the course of justice. He explained that a solicitor could have been used as an unwitting tool to pass on messages to people on the outside who were also involved in the illegal gold chain.

'It is nonsense,' retorted Mathew. 'The fact of the matter is that on the Sunday following this unhappy incident with Mr Fordham, the matter of the death of Mr Fordham received unbelievable publicity. Secondly, Mr Noye, on the Sunday afternoon, the day before you took over, had been allowed to see his solicitor, not once but twice. You were aware of that fact. Therefore if any innocent message was going to be passed, the opportunity to have done that was gone and finished.'

'When I took over, I also tended towards that same view,' said Boyce. 'But then I received certain intelligence that indicated that, further along the chain persons I was interested in had not, in fact, realized the significance of this incident. I had been proved right because on the Monday these same persons were operating, moving gold, elsewhere than in Kent or London. I took the view that he had already seen a solicitor; he had been advised of his rights; and that if he saw a solicitor again, either in private or otherwise, there was a real danger of the inquiry being hindered. I was acutely aware all the time that there was a balance between the right of the suspect and what I considered to be the public interest. I tried my best to balance that.'

Mathew then asked why access to a solicitor was not allowed during the police interviews. The object of a solicitor's presence then would have been to advise the prisoner about the answers to be given and to record what was going on. In those circumstances officers would have been able to hear anything resembling a message being passed.

'I felt the solicitor would then hear the questions being asked – the particular solicitor was also at the time acting for Mrs Noye,' said Boyce. 'The solicitor could then leave the police station with nothing to stop him telling other people the questions being asked and, as a result, the inquiry could have been hindered.'

Mathew was unconvinced. 'The truth is that you denied a solicitor to Mr Noye because you thought that he might have talked, and you didn't want a solicitor present advising him not to,' he said.

'The truth is what I have told you,' replied Boyce.

The defence also made capital out of the fact that Mrs Noye had been held in custody for eight weeks, despite repeated applications for bail, only to have the charges against her thrown out at the magistrates' court.

Flying Squad DS Kenneth O'Rourke was strongly attacked over his dealings with her. Mathew claimed that it was unusual that no policewoman had sat in while she was seen. He also said it was particularly important that she should have had legal representation because she was crying and in a troubled state.

'For a woman who had gone through that experience, I thought she was particularly cool,' replied O'Rourke.

'You went in there to bully her,' Mathew said.

'I don't think she is the type of woman that can be bullied,' replied O'Rourke.

'When she said she wanted her solicitor, one of you said she had been watching too much TV,' persisted Mathew.

O'Rourke denied it.

Mathew also claimed that in telling Mrs Noye that she had been seen at the boot of the car that night with her husband and Reader, and that Reader had made daily trips to Hollywood Cottage, 'you were misleading that lady, trying to get her to talk.'

'How can you mislead somebody who knows what happened?' replied O'Rourke.

Mathew also drew attention to the fact that while O'Rourke's notes of the interview on the Monday had been signed by a senior officer, police standing orders had been broken because a senior officer had not timed them. That could indicate that the notes were not made when it was claimed they were. It was only a minor point, but it indicated the thoroughness with which the defence had prepared the ground for battle; at the outset, enormous odds had been stacked against them.

To the police it was a familiar technique. Their old adage, that if things look hopeless for the defence, they attack the evidence, and if that doesn't work, they attack the police, seemed to be holding good. The denials of virtually every note that the police had recorded while interviewing the defendants was tantamount to an accusation of wholesale verballing. Add to that doubts about forensic evidence, a medical witness who is virtually turned into a defence witness and a confident 'I've nothing to hide' defendant, and it begins to look like a winning hand. It looks especially strong if the jury can be convinced that the figure Fordham presented that night looked truly terrifying – and they had a photographic reconstruction, commissioned by the defence, of a figure wearing a balaclava and camouflage dress, caught by torchlight at the foot of a tree, to tell them that was so.

After twelve hours and thirty-seven minutes' deliberation, not guilty verdicts were returned against both Noye and Reader. The jury accepted that the killing had been self-defence.

As the jury foreman announced the verdicts, there were screams of delight from Brenda Noye and Lynn Reader in the public gallery. Noye smiled, looked at his wife, then turned to the jury to say, 'Thank you very much. God bless you. Thank you for proving my innocence because that is what I am, not guilty.' Beside him Reader turned to the jury and said, 'Thank you for proving my innocence.' The impression was slightly spoiled a few moments later when Noye turned to the back of the court, by then packed with Flying Squad officers, and sneered and mouthed obscenities. He left the dock grinning, although it had not all gone his way. The judge refused an application that his defence costs should be paid out of public funds. (Reader was on legal aid.)

Anne Fordham, the widow of the dead policeman, a petite, 38-year-old New Zealander who had met her husband when he twice visited New Zealand with a view to settling there, left the court where she had sat every day, listening to the evidence, in tears. 'I am too upset to make any comment,' she said.

Outside the Old Bailey Brenda Noye told waiting reporters, 'I feel marvellous. I just want to get home to my children and start smiling again. I am deeply, deeply sorry for the Fordham family, but the death is down to others.' She would not specifically blame the police operation but repeated that 'other people' were responsible. She added that her husband was also deeply sorry for the Fordhams. 'He would say to Mrs Fordham that he was not responsible for what happened and it was the fault of other people,' she said – before retiring to a near-by wine bar for a celebratory bottle of champagne. Solicitor Ray Burrough later issued a statement. 'She is greatly relieved the trial is over, and she has never doubted the jury's decision from the word go. But she would ask you to consider the unfortunate Mrs Fordham and her children at this time, for whom she has great sympathy. She feels the responsibility for Mr Fordham's death is on the shoulders of others and not her husband.'

Reader's teenage son Paul was rather more belligerent. 'We are very happy. The whole thing was a complete fit-up,' he said.

Later that afternoon John Dellow, then Assistant Commissioner of the Metropolitan Police in charge of specialist operations, paid tribute to DC Fordham: 'John Fordham had been engaged in many other operations against very professional, organized criminals. He fulfilled his duties with bravery and with a quiet acceptance of the risks involved. There are many citizens alive in London today who owe their lives to John Fordham.' Dellow added that because of the nature of Fordham's work, it had been impossible for him to be part of the 'public face' of the Metropolitan Police. He declined to comment on the jury's verdict, saying it would be 'improper' to do so. And he refused to comment on the operation beyond saying that, despite the killing, there would be no change in police operational guidelines. 'I am satisfied that the operation was as professionally and properly conducted as it could have been,' he said.

In fact, over the following months a great deal of time and effort was spent by police on trying to ensure such a tragedy could never happen again. The military-style camouflage jackets worn by the surveillance unit were abandoned in favour of a more 'hunting, shooting and fishing' appearance, and clothing was introduced for winter conditions made from synthetic materials developed for astronauts in the American space programme. Technical experts also investigated whether the radio sets worn by Fordham and Murphy could have been operating on a frequency that might have attracted the dogs, with their highly developed hearing. No evidence was found to support that theory.

That evening Anne Fordham was ushered into the press room at New Scotland Yard. In a bid to win herself some privacy after the trial, she had agreed to a press conference in the hope that she would not be bothered subsequently by reporters calling at her house. With her voice breaking, and comforted from time to time by her 22-year-old son John, she said: 'Justice has not been done. It has not.' She described her husband as 'a professional policeman. The work that he did and the risks that he took were all for the good of the country.' Asked if she believed the operation had involved him in unnecessary risks, she shook her head and said in a forced whisper: 'No.' Her son intervened only once, when his mother was asked if her husband would still be alive if the operation had been carried out differently. 'We can't say that,' he said firmly. A reporter then asked her about the sympathy extended by Brenda Noye. 'Not accepted,' she whispered.

It was more than two years before DC Murphy would talk publicly about the events at Hollywood Cottage. Soon after Fordham's killing he suffered a minor nervous breakdown and was caught trying to leave a shop near his home without paying for some cassette tapes.

Some newspapers referred to the incident as the 'onion-field syndrome', named after a book by the former Los Angeles detective Joseph Wambaugh about a policeman who began stealing when tormented by guilt following the murder of his partner. It was a true story, and in the case of that officer a psychiatrist wrote that his behaviour 'reflects his need to manipulate the environment to agree with his obsession that he is an unworthy person, to punish himself and to relieve the anxiety of unconscious guilt, and to unconsciously avoid his police colleagues whom he felt looked critically at him . . .'

The incident involving Murphy was far less serious, but perhaps some of the components were the same. The store didn't prosecute, and he was allowed to retain his job with C11 after having psychiatric counselling. He explained that no dishonesty had been involved – his mind had simply been miles away.

In the first interview he gave after Fordham's killing he told Andrew Hogg: 'It was a good operation to be working on, but there was no particular excitement. A lot of the sort of work we do is fairly exciting.

'On the Friday night we went to look at the layout of Hollywood Cottage and saw the dogs then. We weren't particularly worried about them. I'm used to dogs anyway, and on previous jobs John had found that if you kept quiet and didn't move, after a while they just go away. I believe that is what he tried to do.

'When the dogs arrived they looked as frightened of me as I was of them. They kept coming forward and barking and then retreating. I realized straight away that they weren't going to bite.

'I threw the yeast tablets on to the ground, expecting them to start munching, but they ignored them totally. I looked at John and we had a little smile about it – and that was really the last time I saw him alive.

'To me it was obvious that we had to move away because somebody was going to come out of the house. We had to get out and try later. I have asked myself a thousand times why John didn't follow. The only thing I can think of is that he had got away with it with dogs before and just stuck it out. He was a very courageous guy. If he had had his way, we would have done the job from a dustbin outside the front door.

'Afterwards, all the problems I had were with what other people were thinking. Family and friends didn't know the full story and thought I had done something wrong, but I always felt I hadn't. There is nothing more that I could have done except perhaps at the end, when I saw what was going on near the gate, I could have run across. That's the only thing I reproach myself for, but I didn't want to jeopardize the operation. I thought perhaps he would get a bit of thumping and then they would kick him out.

'When I did go into the grounds . . . in normal circumstances I would have gone across to help him, but I just couldn't go near him. I felt then that I had let him down. But he was too brave for his own good in those circumstances – unnecessarily brave.'

Murphy's words were not a criticism. To many policemen, they seemed a fitting epitaph for any policeman willing to risk his life in the fight against armed crime in Britain in the 1980s.

19. 'I hope you all die of cancer'

It was a confident Kenneth Noye who strolled into the dock at the Old Bailey's Number Twelve court the following May, five months after his acquittal of murder. He had spent the intervening time in a prison cell, but it hardly seemed to have dampened his spirits as he prepared to answer the charge of conspiracy to handle stolen gold bullion. As his alleged fellow conspirators – Reader, Chappell, Patch, Adams, Lawson and the elderly Constantinou – lined up in the box beside him, the small army of fourteen defence barristers was also optimistic.

The trial, it was expected, would last two to three months. All the defendants denied handling the bullion, as they did a second charge, which all save Lawson faced – that of conspiracy to evade VAT. As far as the first, more serious offence was concerned, Noye was the principal defendant, as he had been during the murder trial. The gold-distribution chain had started with him – and if the jury couldn't agree that he was guilty of conspiring to handle stolen bullion, then it certainly couldn't convict any of the others. The judge, Richard Lowry, QC, underlined that fact on day one, asking the jury to be 'fair, decisive and courageous' in reaching its verdicts. Lowry was seemingly an ideal candidate for the case; his entry in *Who's*

Who listed 'fossicking' (searching for gold in old, disused seams) as one of his hobbies.

Noye's optimism, and that of all the defence counsel, was based on the belief that there was a crucial flaw in the prosecution case: quite simply, there was no tangible evidence that the gold he had been handling came originally from the Brink's-Mat haul.

True, no one would deny that there was a good deal of circumstantial evidence that he and the others had been engaged in illegal gold dealings. That evidence included the clandestine gold transactions that police had observed during the weeks preceding the death of John Fordham and the eleven gold bars subsequently found at Hollywood Cottage – an amount coincidentally covered by the receipt Noye had obtained from Charterhouse Japhet in Jersey. And there was also the Alcosa smelter leaflet discovered in Noye's barn, which seemed to indicate that he had been involved in gold smelting in a big way. But those factors alone didn't come close to proving a connection with Brink's-Mat.

Rather more damaging was the investigation into Noye's business dealings that had taken place following Fordham's death. Police knew that, after the Brink's-Mat robbery, Noye had deposited large amounts of money abroad, sometimes using a false name. And then there were the replies he had allegedly made when being interviewed by police, together with Reader's damning admission, shortly before he was charged, that 'of course' the gold he was handling had come from the Brink's-Mat haul. Perhaps the most significant piece of evidence against Noye, however, was some jottings in one of his diaries, which showed the daily gold-price fixes at the time of the Heathrow robbery. Why would he have made those if he was not involved in handling the gold?

But even the jottings, the defence believed, were not enough to link Noye, beyond all reasonable doubt, with Brink's-Mat. The prosecution case was circumstantial, and every allegation could be countered, either by explanations that had nothing to do with the robbery or by attacks on the credibility of the investigating police officers.

For their part, the defence believed they held two trump cards. The first was that none of the gold found at Noye's home carried anything to identify it as part of the Brink's-Mat haul. The second was that Noye was prepared to go considerably further than he had during the murder trial in putting his hands up to being a big-time gold smuggler. That way he hoped to escape the lengthier sentence that handling stolen gold was likely to bring.

Prosecuting counsel Michael Corkery immediately tackled head-on the problem of the gold's identification when he opened the case, claiming that, as the 'mainspring' of the conspiracy, Noye had re-smelted the bullion to remove its identifying marks before selling it on.

Corkery then described the robbery, the surveillance operation on Lawson, Noye's investments and his trips to Jersey, the Bristol gold runs, the killing of Fordham, the arrests of the men in the dock and their subsequent interviews with police. In respect of the second charge, Corkery added, not content with the vast amount they were making on the gold, the gang also charged 15 per cent V A T when they sold it on to the open market, which they pocketed. Even with the running costs to take care of, that provided an extra 12 per cent profit.

Corkery was a more experienced prosecutor than Purnell, who had appeared for the Crown in the murder case, but even so, as his case progressed, it was soon apparent that the defence's optimism seemed well placed. The prosecution was not having a smooth ride. Perhaps it was because of the amount of time police had spent investigating the killing of Fordham, coupled with the sheer size and complexity of the gold investigation, or perhaps the detectives simply lacked the business expertise to unravel the case properly. Whatever the reason, the defence were soon watching with delight as important prosecution points appeared, under cross-examination, to fall apart at the seams.

The problems began with a disagreement between two of the Crown's principal witnesses, police forensic scientist Trevor Oliver and John Williams, a bullion instruction manager at Johnson Matthey, who were called to provide evidence about the purity of the Brink's-Mat gold and to reinforce the Crown's case that the eleven bars found at Hollywood Cottage were part of that original haul.

The gold stolen in the raid had consisted largely of either Johnson Matthey 9999 bars, so called because of the 99.99 per cent purity of the gold they containined, or 999 bars, known as 10-tola bars, which have a 99.9 per cent purity. According to Oliver, a margin of error was allowed for in both categories: 9999 gold incorporated everything from 99.985 per cent up to 99.99 per cent, while the other ranged from 99.85 per cent to 99.985 per cent. The assay values of the eleven bars found were: bar one, 99.95 per cent; bar two, 99.94 per cent; bar three, 99.89 per cent; bar four, 99.98 per cent; bar five, 99.96 per cent; bar six, 99.95 per cent; bar seven, 99.985 per cent; bar eight, 99.99 per cent; bar nine, 99.98 per cent; bar ten, 99.98 per cent; bar eleven, 99.90 per cent. Bars four, seven, eight, nine and ten, said Oliver, were pure enough to fall into the 99.99 per cent category, while all the others were pure enough to be 10-tola bars.

But Williams, under cross-examination, denied Oliver's claims. He said that although the 0.015 per cent margin was commonly applied on the international gold market, Johnson Matthey insisted on greater precision. As far as he was concerned, only one bar, number eight, would qualify as a 9999 bar, and only one bar, number eleven, qualified as a 10-tola bar. The rest were above the 10-tola level but below the 9999 category, with the exception of number three, which fell below even the 10-tola level.

The levels of impurity were an indication, said Williams, that the bars could not have come from Johnson Matthey. The company, he explained, purified gold in batches, and all bars from the same batch would show the same level of impurity. The 4,000 10-tola bars stolen from the Brink's-Mat raid would have come from more than two, possibly three, batches, but there were seven different levels of impurity in the eleven bars found at Hollywood Cottage. Had they been Johnson Matthey gold, they must have come from seven different batches.

The impurities could, of course, have resulted from a resmelting process, but Oliver, in evidence that was not disputed, made it clear that was highly unlikely. The impurities found in gold that pure are minute. To add even a copper farthing is to push the purity level a long way down the scale. Instead the impurities must have been in the original gold, and, if so, the nine bars that didn't meet the Johnson Matthey specification could not have come from the Brink's-Mat haul. It was an important point, which had some of the defendants in the dock exchanging satisfied smiles.

The second problem for the prosecution was their contention that Noye had bought eleven kilo bars of gold in Jersey to provide himself with a receipt to explain away gold from the Brink's-Mat haul if it should be discovered in his possession. When buying the gold from Charterhouse Japhet, the prosecution claimed, Noye had specifically asked that the receipt did not show the identification numbers of the bars.

Not so, said Crown witness Martin Coomber, a director of Charterhouse Japhet; it was the other way round. When the bars had been shown to Noye at the bank they were marked and scratched. Noye, said Coomber, 'was obviously concerned about it. He raised the question, therefore, of the identification numbers of the bars not being on the receipt. He wanted them on, so that if it turned out subsequently that this was not fine gold, he had the receipt for these particular bars and nobody could say it was not these bars we sold. He was assured that it was 9999; that it was not customary to put numbers on the receipt; that he could totally rely on Charterhouse Japhet; and that the bank kept its own records. That satisfied him.'

Noye's counsel, John Mathew, QC, who had defended him in the previous trial, went on to damage the prosecution case further by pointing out that Noye had, in fact, left the receipt in Jersey, in the safe-deposit box where he had stored the bank's gold. It was therefore hardly going to be much help in satisfying an inquisitive policeman on mainland Britain. Even if it had been in Noye's possession, said Mathew, it would have done little good. It was clearly from a Jersey bank, with nothing to show that any VAT had been paid in Britain. If he had wanted a receipt to allay suspicions, asked the barrister, why didn't he simply obtain one by purchasing the gold in Britain? It would have cost only another 15 per cent and would have been far more convincing.

The only reason why Noye had purchased eleven bars, said Mathew, still driving home the attack, was because he had walked into the bank and asked for £100,000 of gold. He hadn't specified how many bars he wished to purchase. Also the receipt was for only 11 kilos of gold, whereas the eleven bars at Hollywood Cottage weighed 13 kilos.

The defence were also able to capitalize on discrepancies in the accounts of three police officers about the circumstances in which the Alcosa smelter leaflet was found in Noye's barn and the timing of its discovery. Anthony Phillips, a senior scenes-of-crime officer, said he discovered the leaflet on the Tuesday after Fordham's killing and immediately summoned DC John Bull and DS Alan Branch to the barn. Both Bull and Branch said that had occurred at 9.30 a.m. It was 'a staggering find', added Bull.

In spite of the importance attached to the leaflet, however, Phillips, when in the witness box, seemed less than precise about when it was found. He said he only started examining the contents of the barn at 9.30 a.m., and it had taken him some time to work his way across the shelf on which the leaflet was lying. He was unable to remember exactly when that was – it could have been the morning or even the afternoon.

While giving his evidence Phillips also claimed that he had found the leaflet partially obscured by a plastic bag. In cross-examination, however, he said it was 'staring me in the face'. And in an earlier statement he had made, of which he was reminded by Mathew, he had said that the leaflet was 'partially covered by other papers'.

Mathew, clearly implying that the leaflet had been planted by police, reminded the jury, with more than a hint of sarcasm, about the circumstances in which Lawson had allegedly picked up the smelter for Noye's use. It had obviously been important, said Mathew, as Lawson had sat in a pub while it was collected for him. He had then driven home with it sticking out of the boot of his Rolls-Royce for anyone to see, and there it had remained all night, in the car parked outside his house.

As a means of disposing of 3 tons of Brink's-Mat gold, Mathew added, the smelter was laughably small. It could take only 30 kilos at a time and had just one small ingot mould. He also pointed out that after purchasing the smelter, Lawson had been arrested, then released without charge. Had it been obtained to dispose of stolen gold, both he and Noye would have been at panic stations – but instead they continued to see each other socially almost every week.

Noye was in no doubt about how the leaflet appeared in the barn: 'I have never seen it before,' he told the court. 'If it had been there, I would have seen it. It wasn't there. There was no reason for it to be there. If I was handling stolen gold, or if anybody was handling stolen gold, you don't think they would be as careless as that? Therefore I can only draw one conclusion.'

By that time, of course, Noye's definition of what does or does not constitute carelessness on the part of a person handling stolen gold had gained a certain authority, for he had spent two days in the witness box outlining his dealings in another field of criminal endeavour – gold smuggling.

Throughout most of the prosecution case, the Crown, it is fair to say, had been losing on points: the defence had been able, on occasion, to drive a coach and horses through the allegations. Two factors changed all that. One emerged five days before the end of the prosecution case, when customs officers presented Corkery with new evidence about how the gold-disposal chain operated.

Following their involvement in the Bristol raids, HM Customs had found themselves frozen out of Scotland Yard's Brink's-Mat inquiries and had been forced to content themselves with quietly investigating the breaches of VAT law that they believed had taken place.

In the weeks immediately preceding the trial, however, detectives, believing they faced an uphill struggle if they confined themselves simply to charges of conspiracy to handle stolen bullion, invited customs investigators to inspect the evidence and to see if there were grounds for a VAT prosecution as well. The customs officers who sifted through the enormous amount of documentation that the police had picked up in the raids leapt with alacrity on various documents, the significance of which had been lost on detectives.

A VAT charge was duly prepared, and, as the trial progressed, customs men continued going through the documents, building up their case. Thus, in the nick of time, they were able to give Corkery a new set of schedules detailing the fresh evidence, which included papers, found in Reader's possession, showing gold fix prices that matched exactly others seized from Chappell.

The second factor that turned the tide in the Crown's favour was the appearance of Kenny Noye himself as principal defence witness. Fighting against a long prison sentence, he had been alive to every nuance and change of mood in the court room. Heartened by his previous acquittal, when at times it had seemed as though the case against him was hopeless, his confidence second time around had grown every time the prosecution found themselves on the ropes.

Even the fresh evidence was not enough to cool his defiance as, in brash, occasionally scornful tones, he went into the witness box to deny the charges with an extraordinary story in which he claimed that the gold found at the Hollywood Cottage was from a massive smuggling operation that he had been running for years. Veering between candid roguishness and injured innocence, Noye's performance was to fall entirely flat on the listening court – a fact that the prisoner didn't discern until it was all over.

Telling the jury that he never did business without a deal on the side, Noye explained that he was a gold smuggler who obtained his supplies from two principal sources, Brazil and Kuwait. The gold, which he would buy at 3 per cent under the fix, as no tax had been paid on it, would be taken first to his office in Holland and then sold on, at 3 per cent above the fix price, to other dealers, usually 'frummers' (Cockney slang for Orthodox Jews). Those dealers – based mainly on the Continent but also in Britain – would then charge tax when selling it on to the open market and take that as their profit.

Noye's gold-smuggling business began in an inauspicious manner in 1976, when he started to bring into Britain gold krugerrands, which at that time were not liable to VAT. Their gold content was taxable, however, so the coins were melted down and sold with a 15 per cent mark-up.

Then in 1980 a friend in the construction industry introduced him to a man named Lorenzo Ferreiro, who lived in Barcelona. Ferreiro, a mining engineer, was a technical adviser to the United Nations and travelled frequently to Africa, particularly Rwanda, from where he claimed he could arrange for gold to be smuggled.

The following year the smuggling started, with Noye's construction-industry friend arranging for the gold to be taken to the Al Humaidu company in Kuwait, where it was refined. Noye, using the name Sidney Harris, put up £50,000 to finance the first deal. He had been wary of investing more because of 'the risks of going into a Third World country – being shot or robbed'. Following that run, claimed Noye, Al Humaidu drew up a contract with Ferreiro and 'Sidney Harris', guaranteeing the two of them commission if they could find purchasers for more of the company's gold.

Noye had the right contacts, and early in 1981 he set up an office and a smelter in Eindhoven, in the Netherlands, where he knew people through his transport business. Two Dutch colleagues ran the operation from a ground-floor office, and a smelter brought from West Germany was installed in the basement. The gold would arrive with a courier from Kuwait, who would be paid in dollars from an Amsterdam bank.

'Over the next four years,' Noye told the court, 'we received in Holland about £3 million worth of gold from Kuwait,' which resulted in a profit averaging between £350,000 and £400,000 a year. 'Most of the gold,' he added, 'was sold to one friend on the Continent, and he was an Orthodox Jew.'

Noye's problem in telling the story was that he was unable to produce any real corroborative evidence to back it up. He refused to name his friend in the construction industry, saying,

'I'm not prepared to involve others in my sort of trouble.' Ferreiro, he added, had been willing to give evidence on his behalf until frightened off when he learned that Noye faced a VAT charge (a claim that drew the retort from Corkery that an offer of immunity would be made). He refused to name his two Dutch colleagues or give the address of the Eindhoven office, and he refused to identify the Orthodox Jew who was his principal buyer.

Noye also claimed that no records of the gold transactions had been kept in the Netherlands, and when he had attempted to get them from the Kuwaiti company, he found that computer tapes for the relevant period had been wiped. Detectives knew, in fact, that while there was indeed a Kuwaiti company called Al Hamaidu that dealt in jewellery, its activities were not of the kind that Noye alleged.

It was the same story when Noye came to describe the Brazilian operation. The court heard that in the mid-1970s he went on holiday to Florida, where he met two Americans (he wouldn't name them) with whom he struck up a business partnership. It was a profitable relationship. In 1978 he had returned to Miami with £50,000, which the two Americans invested for him in 90 acres of land. Planning permission for two houses per acre was obtained, and 50 acres were sold off at a vast profit – some $800,000 each for Noye and his two friends. The two Americans had subsequently learned of his Dutch operation and told him they had contacts with a Brazilian company that was already smuggling gold into Belgium. Noye understood the company to be government-sponsored. In court Corkery expressed surprise that the Brazilian authorities should have colluded with gold smuggling, to which Noye replied, 'Well, the government of Brazil at that time was a military government, and military governments are always on the fiddle. This one certainly was.'

He had told his American partners that Belgium was no good to him, so arrangements were made to get the gold to Eindhoven, with Noye agreeing to buy it at 3 per cent under fix price.

In 1982, said Noye, the combined total of the smuggled

Kuwaiti and Brazilian gold amounted to £20 million; his profit was £1.3 million. In 1983 the total reached £32 million, although his profit went up to only £1.6 million, and in 1984 it climbed to £35 million, although his profit that year dropped to £1.5 million.

'Quite a lot' of the gold eventually reached Britain, added Noye, but he was largely uninvolved with smuggling it in. That was left to the people who had already purchased it from him.

As far as his dealings with Reader were concerned, they had started in 1981, when Noye had provided him with £1.5 million worth of smuggled gold. Then in November 1984 Reader approached him at Brenda Noye's squash club and again asked if he could supply smuggled gold. They agreed that the price would be 3 per cent above the fix price and that deliveries would start after Christmas. Because of the number of £50 forgeries flooding the market at that time, it was also agreed that payment would be made in new £50 notes that could be easily verified.

As Reader was willing to pay 3 per cent above the fix, it was 'absolutely clear' to Noye that a VAT fraud was going on, but he didn't ask where the gold was going or who was buying it, as he didn't want to get involved. 'That requires organization, and a different type of organization to that which I have got. It is a very, very huge business; it requires a lot of other people to help you. You cannot do it for more than six to nine months, and then you get caught up with,' Noye told the court. 'I have got my own business, which had been going on for three or four years. I make a nice 3 per cent turnover and don't want to spoil that.'

Reader went on to receive gold worth £3.66 million from Noye during January 1985, the consignments being smuggled into Britain in a less than glamorous manner. In Holland the gold would be put on lorries bound for Britain, hidden in the driver's Tupperware lunchbox. The driver would take the lorry to the quayside and leave it to be shipped over to Britain unaccompanied – with the Tupperware box still on board. A British driver, whom Noye also refused to name, would pick the lorry up when it arrived and take it to its destination. He would then take the gold back to his home in south-east London, and Noye would collect the contraband later.

But, sticking to the story he had told during the murder trial, Noye claimed that the Thursday before Fordham's killing, the gold supplies from Holland had dried up. The last to arrive were the eleven bars found at Hollywood Cottage, and their small size indicated that they were 'bin ends' – all that remained from various smelts. They had been intended for another buyer, but he had let Reader take them away on the understanding that he could get them back if the original purchaser contacted him.

Noye endeavoured to counter another prosecution claim – that prior to the Brink's-Mat robbery he had relatively little money in his bank account but was soon dealing in much larger amounts – by producing as a witness his bank manager, Michael Bryan, from a branch of Barclays Bank in Dartford, Kent.

Bryan told the court that in 1984 Noye had come to him and said that in the past he had been taking money out of the country in suitcases to deposit in one or other of his offshore banking funds. Bryan knew that his wealthy customer had access to such accounts. On two occasions earlier that year Noye had deposited a total of £600,000 at the bank, the money being handed over in plastic carrier bags. He then asked for banker's draft orders totalling the same amount to be sent to an account in the Isle of Man. (Noye followed up those deposits with at least another £200,000, which were transferred to the Isle of Man by another bank.)

Following Noye's claim to have suitcase deposits abroad, Bryan suggested, 'It would be more convenient and safer to send the money through the bank.' This, he told Noye, could be done by telegraphic transfer orders, without its going through, or being reflected in, his bank account. The proposal evidently met with Noye's approval, for in October that year he arrived at the bank with £150,000 and asked for transfer orders covering the amount to be sent to a Swiss bank with instructions that the money should be retained until collected by a Mr I. M. Bottom, bearing British passport number B158417 as identification.

It was Noye, travelling with a passport stolen from Essex lorry driver Ian Bottom, who later travelled to Zurich, collected the money and then deposited it in a Swiss bank account. In fact, although the transaction did not show up on his bank statements, the bank retained a record of them, which formed part of the prosecution case against him.

There was, however, no corroborative evidence of Noye's earlier suitcase deposits. There couldn't be: the manner in which they had been transacted had seen to that.

Noye went on to claim that £800,000 of the money that he sent to the Isle of Man, and the £1 million that he deposited in the Bank of Ireland during September, had been sent over by his Florida partners. They controlled one of the accounts in the Isle of Man, said Noye. The money had come from their 'large illicit profits from property and gold', which they couldn't bank in the States because of the law stating that all amounts over $10,000 must be reported to the authorities. Investing in sterling in the Isle of Man, added Noye, had been an attractive proposition as the dollar was low against the pound, which meant a very good rate of interest. 'I'm not going to pretend,' insisted Noye, 'that this came from gold dealings, which I could well. The fact of the matter is that it came from them.'

Noye added, 'When the police saw the bank manager in the Isle of Man he told them that I was doing this on behalf of people in the U S A.' The manager, Alexander Thompson, who was produced to support his story, told the court that Noye, when setting up the account, had explained he was acting for a syndicate that required offshore incorporated companies. The shares were to be held by a trust and the syndicate's funds used to finance property deals.

Asked why the Americans should trust him in this fashion, Noye replied, 'Well, we had reciprocal powers of attorney. I had money and property and so on in Florida; they had money here, which I was looking after, or had the means of looking after, in these various bank accounts. They could do what they wanted with my property over there, and I had control of their property here. Therefore there was mutual trust, but there was always that safeguard.'

Noye added that the false passport in the name of Sidney Harris, which he had obtained with the assistance of his accountant Subhash Thakrar, was now held by the two Americans to give them the right to 'deal with those monies in the Bank of Ireland if anything should happen to me'. (In June 1985 Thakrar, who operated out of Woolwich High Street, south-east London, had pleaded guilty at Lambeth magistrates' court to making a false declaration on the passport application form, which resulted in a fine of £100 and costs of £150.)

The defence went to great efforts to counter the most crucial pieces of evidence against Noye: the paper giving the gold-fix price at the time of the Brink's-Mat robbery, the circle drawn around the *Guinness Book of Records* entry in his house and the asterisk alongside the date of the raid in his wife's 1983 diary.

Noye claimed he had obtained the paper showing the fix prices from Johnson Matthey's London offices in January 1985 and, to back this up, pointed to the fact that the paper also bore the gold-fix price for 23 January 1985.

He claimed that a few days before 23 January he had been approached by a person acting as a middle-man for others, who had offered him £5 million of gold at 10 per cent discount. Noye believed that it was stolen gold that could have come from Brink's-Mat. Before meeting the middle-man's principals for a discussion, Noye first decided to check the date of the robbery and obtain the gold-fix prices at the time in an effort to discover whether the figures might indicate that it came from the Heathrow raid.

He had looked first in his sons' copy of the *Guinness Book of Records*, where Brink's-Mat was recorded as Britain's largest robbery. That accounted for the circle drawn around the entry in the book. He had then gone to Johnson Matthey in Hatton Garden to obtain the relevant fix prices. He could prove that he had been in Hatton Garden on the day he claimed because his car had received a parking ticket, and he had ordered a radiator from another shop in the area.

Said Noye: 'I asked for the fix and they produced the book for the back fixes. They gave me that piece of paper and I wrote on it. In fact, it transpired that 26 November was a Saturday. I didn't even know that and so they gave me, and I jotted down, [the fixes for] two days before and two days afterwards.' He had also written down the fix for the day of the visit, and a forensic scientist was produced to testify that the November 1983 details had been written with the same pen and apparently at the same time as the January 1985 price.

'If you had a guilty conscience,' said Mathew, 'Johnson Matthey would be the one place you would not go to because they were the start of this gold.' He added that if it was accepted that the prices were not obtained until the week before the killing at Hollywood Cottage, then 'It has got to mean Noye had not been dealing in that gold for the previous weeks and months.' Noye was unable to explain, however, why the date of the Brink's-Mat raid had an asterisk placed against it in his wife's 1983 diary, with a doodle drawn alongside, although Mathew said that an examination of Brenda Noye's 1984 diary showed a similar asterisk every twenty-five to twenty-eight days, and 'It is clear what those asterisks relate to.'

Mathew's almost bitter attack was reserved for the police accounts of interviews conducted with Noye while he was in custody, particularly the one on the Wednesday morning after Fordham's killing, when he was seen by DS Suckling and questioned specifically about the gold. Noye had apparently admitted knowledge of the Brink's-Mat raid and clearly implied that it was that gold he was handling.

Picking up on a description of the police given by Corkery as the 'thin blue line standing between law and order and anarchy', Mathew told the jury: 'If the thin blue line, with all the power that it has when people are in their custody, acts dishonestly, they should be exposed because such conduct is anarchy in itself. It invariably leads, or can lead, to a miscarriage of justice. We suggest that the falsity of the Crown's case generally is typified by the evidence of Detective Sergeant Suckling.'

Mathew said that Noye had been denied a solicitor for the interview in order to avail Suckling of an 'opportunity to invent admissions', and he reminded the jury that the same officer had allegedly obtained a confession from Tony White, said to have taken part in the actual Brink's-Mat raid, who was later acquitted after doubts had been cast on police evidence.

Mathew added that during the fifty-minute interview no notes were taken, yet afterwards Suckling and a colleague were able to reproduce 'twenty-six and a half pages of manuscript, eighty-odd questions and answers, with no corrections, no alterations, no disagreement between the police officers about what was said, when and in what order, and how the answer had been framed and so on; they had accurately recorded a verbatim conversation over fifty minutes, even as to who asked what question.'

The admissions, said Mathew, 'were born of incredible feats of memory or the fertile and practised imagination of Mr Suckling, whose evidence you may think was so clearly embarrassing for the prosecution that uniquely not one single question was put to Mr Noye about that interrogation in cross-examination, no doubt for fear that fallacies and falsehoods so obviously told by that witness would have been made even more apparent'. Mathew added that in his final interview Noye had apparently agreed he had been to Jersey in a private plane, saying, 'Yes. So what?' Said Mathew: 'That cannot possibly be true because how would Noye conceivably have been agreeing he went to Jersey in a private plane to buy gold when he went on a chartered airline?'

It was a blistering assault.

Claiming that police witnesses were lying and important evidence had been planted, was, Mathew knew full well, not quite enough in a case in which the defendant was asking the jury to believe that he had been engaged in criminal activities, but of an altogether different kind from the ones he was charged with.

As Mathew summed up, he asked for the jury's understanding. 'Kenneth Noye may have been a wheeler-dealer; he may have evaded his tax responsibility; and he may have had trouble over the years (but not for some years) with the law, but at least one can say he has never been an idle lay-about,' he told the court. 'As he has said, "I don't do any transaction without a deal on the side." Not paying your taxes and smuggling, in this day and age, you may think possibly unhappily, are looked upon by many as being in a totally different bracket to the offences of theft and handling stolen property. You may think that most of those people, if not all, who do not declare their profits or all their earnings for tax would probably cut their arms off before they would put their hand in the till and steal even a 10p piece.'

It was an appeal that was misjudged, as Noye was soon to find out.

As the trial progressed, his was not the only account to strain the credulity of the jury to breaking-point. Reader too insisted that the gold had been smuggled.

Chappell put it bluntly: 'A child could see that it was smuggled rather than stolen gold,' he told Corkery, and he stuck to his story that he really had purchased the gold from Matteo Constantinou. 'Mr Constantinou supplied me with £9 million worth of gold. He would carry it to my office, and as far as I was concerned, it was a legitimate transaction,' he said. And, with the benefit of hindsight, he claimed, 'Opposite my office the VAT people and Customs and Excise people set up an office to keep constant observation on me. Do you think that I would be so silly as to deal with stolen gold with those people on my doorstep day and night?'

Patch admitted to the court that he had carried out some book-keeping for Scadlynn but said he usually acted just as a driver and errand boy, helping out in exchange for the use of the office and telephones. He claimed that he had been kept totally in the dark about the company's shady dealings.

Adams didn't appear in the witness box at all. His counsel, Robert Banks, was so confident that the case against Noye would not stand that he contented himself with simply outlining his client's involvement in a closing speech. Adams, said the barrister, was an innocent courier acting as a trusted agent for jewellers and other dealers in the Hatton Garden area and was unaware of, and unconcerned about, the contents of the packages that he was handling.

Constantinou also denied the charge, as did Lawson, whose counsel told the court that his client's alleged admission that he had bought a smelter for Noye was a fabrication.

Two and a half months after the trial began the court rose, and the jury retired to consider its verdicts. The break occurred on a Thursday, when the eight men and four women jurors were told that, under the supervision of court bailiffs, they would be looked after at an £80 a night London hotel. No discussion of the case would be allowed outside the jury room.

It quickly became apparent that arriving at the verdict was not going to be an easy task, and on the Friday Robert Bishop, the loss adjusters handling the Brink's-Mat insurance claim for Lloyd's, decided that they weren't prepared to take any chances. If the accused were not convicted, they wanted a chance to sue them through the civil courts – where, instead of proving beyond reasonable doubt that they had been handling bullion from the raid, they would have to show only that, on a balance of probabilities, they had done so.

In a High Court action on the Friday morning a judge agreed that the assets of all seven accused – including the £3 million owned by Noye – should be frozen pending the outcome of the civil hearings. It was an unusual move but not unique in British law.

On Saturday, when several of the jurors were looking noticeably tired, messages were sent to their families to expect them no earlier than Monday. They were, however, promised a day out in the country the following day, although the judge refused a request from the predominantly young jury that they, not the court bailiffs, should decide what time they went to bed at night.

It had not been an easy two and a half months for the eight men and four women hearing the case, and during the days they spent deliberating their verdict rumours abounded about their behaviour. One story claimed that a woman juror had offered sex to three of her male counterparts, while another couple had apparently asked bailiffs if they could sleep together. A male juror was allegedly so drunk one morning that he had to be carried into court, and another was said to be on the run from the police. Eventually the stories reached the judge's ears, and he ordered an inquiry. A court administrator who was ordered to take statements from three senior bailiffs told the judge, 'I am satisfied they are a rumour.'

Despite the strength of the defence case, it was clear that the circumstantial evidence, coupled with Noye's performance in the witness box, had had a damning effect. It was the following Wednesday that the verdicts were at last returned. Hysterical scenes broke out as the jury foreman announced that Noye, Reader and Chappell had been found guilty both of the conspiracy to handle stolen bullion charge and the VAT charge. By the time Constantinou's conviction for evading VAT was announced, the judge had to shout to make himself heard. Patch, Adams and Lawson were all acquitted.

'I hope you all die of cancer,' screamed Noye at the jury as the truth sank in, visibly distressing some of them. Anybody who had wondered what kind of man could stab another ten times in self-defence had, in those words, a graphic answer.

'Never has such an injustice been done. There is no fucking justice in this trial,' shouted Brenda Noye from the public gallery.

Pointing to the jury, Brian Reader called, 'You have made one terrible mistake. You have got to live with that for the rest of your lives,' while his 20-year-old son Paul scuffled with police officers after shouting, 'You have been fucking fixed up!' at the jury. He was arrested for contempt of court and later bound over in the sum of £100 for twelve months to keep the peace.

Lynn Reader struggled out of court crying, 'It's not true. It's not true.' Outside she told reporters, 'There has been a terrible injustice.'

Down in the cells customs officers immediately slapped a £1 million writ on Noye for the VAT he had evaded. A six-page High Court writ was also served on him from the Inland

Revenue, claiming nearly £1 million in back tax. Mathew, controlling his anger with difficulty, told Noye that his outburst from the dock was hardly likely to influence the judge in his favour when he went up for sentencing.

In court Judge Lowry told the jury, 'It is plain you have worked hard and long, and the case has not been an easy one, culminating in a great burden of decision. But you have shouldered that burden.' Referring to the constant police guard they had been placed under, he said, 'I am conscious it has been an added problem that you have been under surveillance, but you know the purpose: to avoid worse problems. It may be that in retrospect you will understand why I ordered it.' He then excused them from jury service for the next twenty years.

The following day, in a bid to make amends, Noye, casually dressed in pale-blue sweater and open-necked shirt, apologized to the judge before sentence was announced. The curse, he said, had been made 'in the heat of the moment', and then he stood resignedly as Judge Lowry, who had adjourned for nearly an hour to consider the sentences, told him the worst. He was to be jailed for thirteen years for plotting to handle the gold and fined £250,000. He was also fined a similar amount for evading VAT, plus an extra year's imprisonment, and ordered to pay £200,000 towards the cost of the case, which was estimated at £2 million. Noye also received another two years' imprisonment for failing to pay the two fines. He couldn't pay – his assets had been frozen. But the judge was less than sympathetic.

Fourteen years was the maximum for the handling plot, which, said Judge Lowry, 'I must and do observe.' Noye's guilt, added the judge, fell 'well and easily into the top band of crime'. The fine, he added, could be considered 'paltry' compared with the sums of money involved in handling the gold.

Chappell, said to have been an 'essential element in turning gold into cash', was jailed for a total of ten years for both offences, fined £200,000 and ordered to pay £75,000 towards the cost of the prosecution, while Reader, described by Lowry as Noye's 'vigorous right-hand man', was jailed for a total of nine years. Constantinou was given a year, suspended for two years, on the VAT fraud.

After the sentencing Brenda Noye called from the public gallery, 'I love you, darling.'

Noye blew her a kiss and shouted, 'I love you too.'

Lynn Reader shouted to her husband, 'I will wait for you, Brian.'

Outside the court violent scenes followed the sentencing as friends and relatives of the convicted men, including an elderly woman with a blanket over her head and Brenda Noye surrounded by four minders, left the building. Leslie Lee, a freelance photographer working for *The Times*, was knocked to the ground and kicked when he tried to take pictures.

The following day Corkery told the court that Noye, his wife and two others were to face trial over the Meissen china found in a secret compartment at Hollywood Cottage and at Hever Avenue. The china, worth £3,000, was part of a haul stolen three years earlier. As Noye's assets had been frozen, legal aid was applied for and given. (He later received a four-year concurrent sentence for receiving the solen property. No evidence was offered in the case against Brenda Noye, and she was discharged, but one of the other defendants, who pleaded guilty to assisting in the retention of stolen property, was fined £500 and ordered to pay £150 costs.)

At the same time Corkery announced that the Crown was dropping the charge of conspiracy to handle stolen bullion that had been hanging over Brenda Noye. It was, said Corkery, a 'merciful course to follow', and the judge agreed. But the court also heard that Noye's sister, Hilary Wilder, and her husband Richard, a legal executive, both of whom lived in West Kingsdown, faced trial for receiving £50,000 from the proceeds of the Brink's-Mat gold. (Both were later cleared of the charge, although the money was reclaimed by the Brink's-Mat insurers.)

Meanwhile Home Office officials were busy briefing political correspondents that in future banks would be encouraged to tell police about suspicious large-scale cash deposits and withdrawals. The Home Secretary was expected to announce that they would be given immunity from 'breach of confidentiality' actions by angry customers when tipping off the police. The new measures, to be announced in the Criminal Justice Bill that autumn, were intended to stop British banks from being used as clearing houses for large amounts of cash generated by crime syndicates.

20. The runaway returns

The passenger sitting in the economy-class seat of Varig Brazilian Airlines flight 706, a non-stop flight from Rio de Janeiro to London's Heathrow Airport, seemed to have a lot on his mind. There was a subdued look about him, and the DC10 stewardess noticed him occasionally sigh with resignation. The in-flight movie, *The Desperado*, broke the monotony of the eleven-hour journey, but afterwards the passenger returned to his state of complete preoccupation. As the plane landed at Heathrow and taxied to a halt in bright summer sunshine, he seemed particularly glum.

Suddenly an unexpected announcement was heard over the cabin speakers. Would Mr John Palmer please identify himself? Faces the length of the plane craned round as the fugitive, smiling self-consciously, raised his hand.

The date was Wednesday, 2 July 1986. At the Old Bailey Noye and his six co-defendants were answering charges of conspiracy to handle stolen bullion. But the return of Palmer, after a seventeen-month absence, meant that, for the next few days at least, the court-room drama was forgotten.

Goldfinger had come home to face the music.

*

Minutes after he had identified himself, two airport security men boarded the jet and asked the West Country jeweller to accompany them. He was the first to leave the cabin, and as he walked on to the gangway, he saw there was a reception party waiting for him.

'You are John Palmer?' asked Scotland Yard Detective Superintendent Ken John.

'Yes, I am,' replied the tired arrival.

'So that we are absolutely correct: you are John Palmer, born in Birmingham on 3 April 1950, and up until your departure from this country in January 1985 you were residing at Stable Block, Coach House, Battlefields, Bath?'

'That's right,' replied Palmer.

'I am arresting you for the offence of conspiracy with others to dishonestly handle stolen gold bullion, the proceeds of the Brink's-Mat robbery at Heathrow in November 1983.' Palmer then received the usual caution, but made no reply. 'You will now be taken to Kennington police station, where you will be detained.'

Palmer had expected nothing less and, grim-faced by now, he said nothing as detectives grabbed his arms and bundled him into an unmarked police car.

The jeweller had been the first person to feel the effects of a new aliens' law in Spain, which came into force in January 1986. Aimed at cracking down on fugitive Britons who had fled to the sun, it stipulated that they could only stay provided they had valid passports.

In December 1985 Palmer's name had featured on a list of twenty of Britain's most wanted fugitives drawn up by Scotland Yard at the request of Spain's interior ministry. Fate had then intervened, and two days before Christmas his passport ran out.

The British official in the Canaries had been politeness itself as he declined to renew it. He wasn't totally unaccommodating, however. Her Majesty's Government was prepared to provide Mr Palmer with an emergency travel document – but that, of course, would be valid only for a trip to England. The offer was refused.

The Saturday before his return to Britain, Palmer had been arrested in Tenerife, flown to Madrid and told that he was to be expelled as an 'undesirable'.

Allowed to select the destination of his choice, he opted for Brazil, but, unlike the Great Train Robber Ronnie Biggs, he received a frosty reception in the South American republic. Although Brazil has no extradition treaty with Britain, the authorities there had been told of Scotland Yard's interest in the fugitive jeweller, and when he landed at Rio airport he was told he would be refused entry, as his passport was out of date. Asked where he wanted to be sent, Palmer had thrown in the towel and said that he would return to Britain.

'I think I may have some trouble in London,' he told Brazilian police official Senhor Giovanni Azevedo, adding that he hoped to clear it up within a few months.

'Does the problem relate to the Brink's-Mat robbery?' asked Azevedo.

'Yes, the press have tried to accuse me of that, but I had nothing to do with it,' said Palmer, and with that he signed a declaration saying that he was leaving for London voluntarily.

'He is jet-lagged and dog-tired,' said a police officer as Palmer rested in a cell at Kennington police station, close to the headquarters of the Brink's-Mat investigation team at Tintagel House, across the River Thames from Scotland Yard. 'He is being allowed to have a short sleep before more interviews take place.'

London solicitors Ralph Haeems and Co. then spoke on behalf of the prisoner, telling reporters that he denied any involvement in the bullion robbery and other allegations related to evasion of VAT. Mr Palmer, they said, was anxious to clear up any misconceptions with the police without delay.

Palmer's entrepreneurial spirit had ensured that the seventeen months he was out of the country were not wasted. Following his televised denials of any involvement in the Brink's-Mat robbery in the days immediately after Fordham's death, he had faded out of sight in Tenerife, leaving his hotel secretly at the end of his three-week holiday and moving to a plush £100,000 four-bedroom villa close to San Eugenio Bay.

The next that was heard of him were reports that he had gone into the timeshare business in Tenerife, a burgeoning industry catering for tourists wanting to reserve themselves several weeks each year in an island villa. In April 1985 it was claimed that he had invested some £250,000 in a luxury villa development. With high property prices on the Canary Islands, simply selling the villas would have recouped him at least £1 million, but timeshare's attraction is that, by selling individual weeks in a villa, the amount made from all the weekly bookings is much greater than the actual real-estate value of the property. Palmer was said to be helping to finance the project by selling some of his jewellery stock and a number of his properties in and around Bristol; associates took the cash out to him.

By early 1986 business was obviously booming, for by then Palmer was reported to have invested £5 million in 450 timeshare villas; the sale of the weekly units would bring in about £160,000 per villa, amounting to a staggering £72 million.

The sales technique was a familiar one used by a number of timeshare development companies in the U S A, Britain, Spain and Portugal. A sales army of more than a hundred touts, mostly British youngsters who had gone to the Canaries rather than remain unemployed at home, were luring prospective buyers off the street with the promise of free bottles of champagne and presents for their children. Taken to the 25-acre Island Village site in a fleet of cars and taxis, they were given a lightning tour of the white-washed villas containing a variety of mod. cons., including jacuzzi baths, and then subjected to a hard sell that gave them just two hours in which to make up their minds. The money they were paying in hand over fist was then banked offshore on the Isle of Man.

Palmer's wife Marnie and their two daughters had remained on the island for just four months after their holiday before returning to Battlefields so that the elder child could resume her schooling.

'They were missing home so much and they wanted to see their grandparents,' the dutiful mother told reporters. Asked about her husband, she said, 'He's a good businessman, and we have a lot to keep going over there.' Rumours that their marriage was on the rocks were denied by both parties, and later that year Marnie received a new Porsche, paid for by a cheque for nearly £20,000 from Tenerife.

'Looking at this document, it appears that you were actually appointed a director of Scadlynn Ltd on 3 September 1981.' The detective leaned across the table and showed the prisoner the paper he was referring to.

'Yes.'

'Are you still a director?'

'No.'

'When did you resign'?

'I don't know.'

The man sitting beside the prisoner, solicitor Philip Alberry, answered for him. 'Approximately three years ago.'

It was 10.30 a.m. In a classroom on the top floor of Kennington police station the Canary Isles seemed a million miles away. Palmer, having spent his first night in the cells, was now facing the grilling he had spent many months avoiding.

'I'll show you a complete bundle of documents referring to Scadlynn. Can you find any document in which you notified the registrar of companies of your resignation?' asked DCI Ronald Smith.

'No,' replied Palmer.

The solicitor broke in. 'I can produce minutes of a meeting at which Mr Palmer notified the company of his resignation,' he said.

The detective didn't reply but began taxing Palmer about his activities when he did work at Scadlynn, before moving on to discuss the smelter found hidden behind Palmer's home. The prisoner was quite open about it – some of the bullion he had smelted had come from Scadlynn.

And there, having studied the prisoner and obtained a chance to gauge how cooperative he was likely to be, the detective left it. One factor was immediately apparent: there was a lot Palmer couldn't remember. The question now was whether that was simply due to the length of time he had been abroad or whether it indicated a refusal to answer truthfully.

That afternoon Palmer saw his wife Marnie for the first time. The couple hugged and kissed, then spent ten minutes together before Marnie was driven away sobbing and lying on the back seat of a police car to avoid waiting photographers. Soon afterwards her husband was also driven away to face his first court appearance. At a ten-minute hearing *in camera* at Horseferry Road magistrates' court, the jeweller, in a pink T-shirt and grey trousers, listened impassively while police applied, under the Police and Criminal Evidence Act, for a twenty-four-hour extension to the thirty-six-hour period during which they can detain suspects without bringing charges. The request was granted.

By now Philip Alberry, the Bristol solicitor who had sat in on the police interview, was representing Palmer, telling reporters that his client was very angry at the London solicitor who had claimed to be acting for him when he first arrived back in Britain.

Shortly before 5 p.m. that afternoon Palmer was escorted back into the classroom to face another interview.

'What do you know of the company Shimmerbest Ltd?'

'Nothing.'

'The company International Precious Metals in Holborn?'

'No, nothing.'

'Read that to me, please.' The detective, Smith, passed across a small piece of paper on which the words 'Fatey Shimerbest' were written. Police claimed it was among the correspondence that had been seized from Palmer's home at Battlefields.

'Is that your writing?' asked Smith.

'I don't know. I can't say.'

The detective then came to the events in the weeks before the police raided his home. 'In November you obtained the assistance of Harvey to operate a smelter in your garden shed. About twelve bars a week were produced. If you were not working for, or with, Scadlynn, where did this gold come from?'

'I was acting purely as an outside contractor, if you like. I owned a furnace. I was asked to undertake different types of melting work,' replied the jeweller.

'You were an outside contractor for whom?'

'You have to explain the question.'

'Where did you get the gold from?'

'What particular gold are you talking about?'

'The gold,' said Smith patiently, 'that was melted by you, assisted by Harvey – melted in your garden shed.'

'It could possibly be Scadlynn gold. I often did melting work for Scadlynn . . . It usually came sealed in Cellophane bags bound tightly with a dark plastic tape which would be put in a crucible as it came.'

It was almost enough to take the wind out of the detectives' sails. No denial – just a straightforward statement of fact. It wasn't just the smelter that Smith was interested in, though, and further questions followed about Palmer's handing over of gold to a security company on behalf of Scadlynn and about a call, made on his car telephone, that resulted in the boss of a security company used by Scadlynn travelling to Barclays Bank, Bedminster, to pick up £320,000 – money that was taken back to Scadlynn.

Palmer was also asked about a call that had been made from his car telephone to Adams in London. Palmer denied that he knew the man, saying he couldn't account for every call made from the phone, as the car was often used by Scadlynn staff. Questions then followed about the jeweller's shops Palmer had owned. By then police had been able to take a lengthy look at their accounts, and Smith was unequivocal: 'Mr Palmer, I am investigating the realization [fencing] of £26 million worth of gold stolen from the Brink's-Mat warehouse on 26 November 1983. We have examined some of the books which clearly relate to purchases in respect of scrap gold for one or more of your jewellery shops. I am of the belief, having looked at the books, that the total value of scrap for all your shops in one year would be under £100,000. Why do you need a smelter in your garden to melt these relatively small amounts of scrap?'

'The smelter you talk about was purchased first for Scadlynn. When I split from Scadlynn, it was agreed between me and Mr Chappell that the furnace would become mine. It was extremely useful in small tests and melts and, had my businesses not been closed down, perhaps my turnover would have increased.'

On that note of ready explanation, the interview was terminated.

The following morning Palmer was allowed to consult alone with his solicitor. He was then seen by Smith and asked if he wished to say anything.

'Only that I am sorry I cannot answer any more questions, as I feel it has been such a long time and such a bad experience for me, I cannot give the correct answers at this present time.'

Smith was not rebuffed so easily. 'This is a photocopy of a telephone dialling book seized by police when your house at Battlefields was searched. On the front is written in manuscript . . . the telephone number of Kenneth Noye. How come Noye's telephone number is found in your home?'

'This is the last question I will answer. I do not know Kenneth Noye. This is not my handwriting and I do not know how it got there,' said the prisoner emphatically.

'I have had time to study the notes of the interview overnight. I do not believe you have told me the truth at all,' rejoined Smith. 'I believe that you, together with Garth Chappell, your fellow Scadlynn director, and Terry Patch, conspired with Kenneth James Noye, Brian Reader, Thomas Adams, Michael Lawson and Matteo Constantinou to dishonestly handle stolen gold bullion between November 1983 and February 1985. I inform you that you will be charged with that offence . . .'

An hour later and it was the turn of customs investigators.

'We are making inquiries about VAT, and we wish to ask you some questions concerning the company Scadlynn Ltd and, possibly, other business interests you have,' said senior officer Wayne Welch. 'You don't have to say anything if you don't wish to do so, but what you say may be given in evidence. What is your connection with Scadlynn Ltd?'

'I'm sorry, but I will not be answering any questions at the present time. However, I will give my full cooperation in the near future,' said Palmer, replying, 'No comment,' as he was shown various documents.

Later that day, after a four-minute court appearance, he was remanded in custody, where he was to stay until he went on trial at the Old Bailey. A month after he was charged he applied for bail, offering to provide three sureties of £500,000 each, as well as a £100,000 cash deposit to the court. The magistrate said it was a 'strong' application but none the less turned him down. 'I had three gentlemen before me the other day who had seventy-five passports between them,' he said by way of explanation.

Five months later another Brink's-Mat suspect gave himself up. Shortly before lunchtime on 18 December 1986 gold dealer Christopher Weyman, the man seen with Reader and Adams during the gold-chain surveillance operation, walked into the foyer of Cannon Row police station in central London, accompanied by his solicitor, to meet Flying Squad DS John Redgrave.

Weyman had been missing since the police raids that followed Fordham's death. After the acquittal of Adams, however, he was confident that police had little evidence against him. He was also, by now, tired of the life of a fugitive. The detective recognized him instantly as the man whom he had seen outside Farringdon station nearly two years earlier. He was, in fact, the owner of the white Mercedes that had been used in a number of the gold transactions.

'I am arresting you for dishonestly handling stolen gold bullion,' said the detective, and Weyman was marched off to be interviewed. It was almost a formality – the prisoner claimed that he hadn't known that the gold he was handling was stolen. His home had been searched three days after Fordham's death, however, and a paying-in book in the name of the jeweller seen during the surveillance operation had been found.

At 12.32 p.m. Redgrave charged Weyman with conspiring to handle stolen bullion. Weyman was also cautioned.

He replied, 'I've been advised by my solicitor not to say anything.'

Later, in his cell, police claimed that Weyman was slightly more communicative, asking whether there was a warrant out for the owner of the paying-in book.

'Why?' said Redgrave.

'He's abroad, isn't he?' the dealer replied. 'Was it you that was out there looking for him?'

'What do you mean?' asked Redgrave.

'Someone went looking for him, but I know you missed him. You haven't been looking too hard for me, have you? But I've been at all my normal addresses. I was even home last night. People will come to court on the day and say I was around all the time.'

'Where were you then?' asked Redgrave.

'I'm not saying that, am I?' said the prisoner. 'I didn't go abroad. Am I going to get bail?' he added.

'We'll explain the situation to the magistrate, and it's up to him then,' said Redgrave.

'I don't want to use up one of my goes if I'm not going to get it . . . I didn't think you were going to charge me, otherwise I wouldn't have given myself up before Christmas, would I?'

Redgrave was interested. 'Why did you give yourself up?' he asked.

'I've got nothing to worry about. Adams got off, didn't he?' replied Weyman.

Six weeks later, with Weyman now in Wormwood Scrubs prison awaiting trial, he was visited by customs officers to discuss possible V A T offences that he may have committed. He wouldn't reply to any of their questions.

*

The trial of Palmer and Weyman took place in March 1987. Both were accused of conspiring with Noye, Reader, Chappell, Constantinou, Derek Larkins and 'other persons unknown' to dishonestly handle stolen bullion. And both were accused of conspiracy to contravene V A T regulations. Both men denied the charges. By now a number of the lawyers in court were veterans of the Brink's-Mat hearings. Representing Palmer were John Mathew, and his leading junior Ronald Thwaites, who had both previously represented Tony White and then Noye at his two trials.

Prosecuting was Nicholas Purnell, who had handled the Noye/Reader murder case for the Crown. The defendants, he claimed, had played an 'essential part in turning the gold into money'.

The prosecution knew that in the case of Palmer it was essential to prove that, although he had resigned as director of Scadlynn at a meeting in March 1984, he was still closely connected with the company. In Weyman's case, they had to prove that he knew it was stolen gold that he had been handling.

Part of the case against Palmer rested on the evidence of Pauline Drake, Scadlynn's part-time book-keeper between June 1983 and September 1984. She told the court that Scadlynn's books 'only reflected the business the majority of the time'. Asked why that was, she replied, 'False invoices were written out. It was mostly Mr Chappell who asked me to do that, and Mr Palmer once or twice. There was no gold coming in.' (By that she meant no gold that she was aware of.)

Pauline Drake added that she knew both men used false names: 'Mr Chappell used Higgins and Cooper, Mr Palmer would use Mr Paton and Mr White and a friend of his who was a builder.' Even though he had resigned as a director, she added, Palmer would call in every day, 'sometimes for half an hour, sometimes for a couple of hours'.

Cross-examined, however, Pauline Drake admitted that she knew Palmer had bought jewellery shops in Bath, Bristol and Cardiff and that invoices he had asked her to fill in could have been for material that was bought and sold without actually coming into Scadlynn.

Arthur Cooling, the branch manager of Pritchard Security Services, the company used by Scadlynn in January 1985, was then called to the stand. He told how on 18 January he had visited Scadlynn's offices and been introduced to John Palmer, who had instructed him that he was to talk to him and no one else, as he was the company's security officer.

Three days later Cooling and a security-van crew had collected a consignment of gold from Palmer in the street for delivery to the Sheffield assay office. The following day Palmer had called at his house with a further consignment of gold, which was followed by three more consignments that week. He also received instructions from Palmer by telephone to go to Barclays' Bedminster branch, where he picked up £320,000 for delivery to Scadlynn.

In an attempt to show that Palmer was basically dishonest, Purnell also drew attention to his lucrative timeshare business in Tenerife, referring to it as a 'legitimate gold mine'. The jeweller had built the business into a multi-million-pound development from an initial shareholding of £30,000, which he had borrowed from his brother.

But Purnell revealed that a substantial number of deposits from customers were needed before the development could be completed. 'Did you tell them that if you didn't successfully market a substantial proportion of this development, there wouldn't be a development?' he asked.

'No, but that is not the attitude to take. The fastest growing developments are in the Canaries,' replied Palmer.

'What would have happened if you hadn't sold enough?' persisted Purnell.

'I don't think like that. I know what's happened and that's all,' snapped the jeweller.

Asked by Judge Richard Lowry if he thought the timeshare operation had been a gamble, Palmer replied, 'I wasn't selling a gamble. It was too good to be true.'

Back on the question of the gold again, Purnell said that Palmer had been smelting £200,000 worth a time in the shed behind his house. It would be delivered by car at around midnight in what was clearly an illegal operation.

Palmer, however, told the court that he was convinced the gold that he was handling was legitimate and that it was part of a massive 20-ton consignment that Chappell had told him he was purchasing.

Palmer explained that he had left Scadlynn because it was not on a very firm financial footing and that he had wanted to concentrate on jewellery items rather than scrap gold and silver. He had taken over a shop in Bath, the lease of which was owned by Scadlynn, while Chappell had taken over the premises in North Street, Bedminster, where he owned the freehold.

It was arranged that he would continue to carry out some smelting for Scadlynn, in return for which he would have the opportunity to repair and re-sell, at market rates, damaged pieces that came to him via Scadlynn, which would charge him only scrap prices for the pieces. The smelting work for Scadlynn would take place in the shed in his grounds before he went to work.

In December 1984 the amounts he was asked to handle increased greatly and, to make sure they were '100 per cent legal', he questioned Chappell, who replied, 'Remember the Smith deal? Well, that is now going through.'

The contract with a man named John Smith was one that Chappell had been talking about for a long time. Palmer had seen documents referring to the deal, one of which mentioned 'tons of gold', and he knew that Alberry, the solicitor, had helped in the negotiations. So he had gone to Alberry and 'asked him if he would tell me about the 20 tons of Smith's gold. Could he give me some details about it? But he wouldn't give me any details because I was no longer part of Scadlynn. I said, "Does this man at least exist?" and he said he did exist, but he wouldn't give me any details.'

When Palmer had asked Chappell about the funding of the deal, he was told that much of it came from Patch, whom he knew to be wealthy.

The gold would be delivered to him in a briefcase or in

canvas bank bags, with the bars wrapped in tape. They would be dropped, tape and all, into the crucible, so he had no way of knowing if the bars were marked.

The negotiations for the Smith deal had, in fact, been genuine enough, as documents produced for the court proved. But after Chappell's conviction Palmer had been very confused. Asked if he believed that his former partner was guilty, Palmer replied, 'I didn't know. My mind kept telling me that he wasn't, but he must be. I couldn't believe that he would deceive me.'

While carrying out the smelting, added Palmer, his home had been fitted with an alarm system wired to the local police station, with 'panic buttons' in every room. The police 'asked if they could tap the phones and put a radio transmitter in the house', added Palmer, and this had been done.

The case against Weyman, said his counsel, Robert Banks, amounted to 'next to nothing' and, as a result, the 36-year-old gold dealer was not called to the witness box. Instead Banks told the court that the evidence against Weyman rested on a single piece of paper said to contain calculations on his 'cut' from the deal, some 'unremarkable' surveillance operations, a palm print on a single bank note and evidence from a conversation with a witness. 'They have got a few little straws,' said Banks. His client, he claimed, had been an honest courier who was completely unaware of the source of the gold.

Palmer's and Weyman's explanations seemed to suffice. Even the discovery of Noye's telephone number at Palmer's home did not help the prosecution. The defence called a handwriting expert who testified that it was not Palmer's writing. After a three-and-a-half-week trial the jury took just three hours unanimously to find both defendants not guilty. Palmer stood with his eyes closed and hands clasped in front of him while the verdict was announced. He then blew a kiss to the six men and six women in whose hand his fate had rested, while Marnie, his wife, shouted out, 'Thank you,' to the judge.

The happy couple later drove from court in a silver-blue Mercedes, leaving Palmer's solicitor, Henry Milner, to tell reporters that his client was 'pleased and relieved at the verdict'. He said Palmer had remained in Tenerife and then flown to Brazil only in order to avoid a year in custody. 'That is the only reason he stayed away,' he told reporters with a smile.

21. Operation Cougar

In the summer of 1985, while Noye and Reader and the Scadlynn chain awaited trial, two men met in London. One was an urbane financial consultant with considerable charm called Patrick Diamond, who ran a successful Isle of Man business setting up companies for clients anxious to take advantage of the island's offshore banking facilities. The other was a 27-year-old man said to be the 'chief enforcer' for a Florida drugs racket. His name was Scott Errico, and he was in trouble.

As the hitman for a Miami-based, 100-strong marijuana-smuggling gang known as the Thompson Organization, Errico was alleged to have carried out three execution-style killings. Two of his victims, who had tried to leave the Organization, had apparently been put on a yacht, taken several miles out into the Caribbean, tied with ropes and chains, shot and dumped overboard. The third victim was said to have suffered a similar fate after stealing a safe containing about $600,000 from Raymond 'Little Legs' Thompson, the leader of the gang.

The discovery by police of the links between Errico and Diamond was, nearly two years later, to mean that scant regard was paid by the British public to the acquittal of Palmer and

Weyman. For by then the Brink's-Mat case had acquired an entirely new dimension. British detectives were convinced that some members of the Heathrow robbery team were, despite their south London background, linked with international organized crime. The discovery was to cause a fundamental change in Scotland Yard's response to serious crime in London.

Ray 'Little Legs' Thompson was arrested in January 1985 in Miami after a lengthy grand jury hearing, with the US Drug Enforcement Administration (DEA) claiming that between 1978 and 1981 his smuggling ring had brought thousands of tons of marijuana, worth a staggering $700 million, into the country aboard ten luxury yachts. Errico, who was on the run, was also indicted for murder, kidnapping and drug smuggling.

It had been an ingenious trafficking operation. The yachts would be manned by khaki-uniformed crews, while the 'owners', sitting on deck drinking cocktails, were in reality pensioners hired to allay the suspicions of coastguards. One favourite was a man with a wooden leg, attended by a nurse who was in reality a prostitute dressed up to look the part.

The drug, which came from Colombia, would be unloaded from the 'mother ship', generally a trawler or other large vessel, off the Bahamas and taken aboard one or more of the yachts, which would return to the Amity Yacht Center, a marina at Fort Lauderdale owned by Thompson. From there it would be sent by van all over the USA.

By the time Thompson was formally charged, Errico was long gone. In the early 1980s, aware of the attention that DEA agents were beginning to take in Thompson's organization, Errico decided to go freelance and began working for another marijuana-smuggling outfit using the same yacht basin.

It was then that he came into contact with Diamond, for the proceeds of this second gang were laundered by a number of American attorneys, including Michael I. Levine of Miami, through Patrick Diamond in the Isle of Man. Levine and

Diamond, it has been alleged, offered a similar service to a Florida-based cocaine-smuggling racket.

The laundering of money is essentially turning dirty money into clean. The fortunes to be made from drug smuggling, or even from a major armed robbery, are of little use unless they can be successfully explained away if challenged. In addition, in the U S A it's difficult to bank such money because of a law stipulating that bank deposits of more than $10,000 have to be reported to the federal authorities.

In the U S A the cash can be salted away in dribs and drabs, but that is time-consuming and expensive, and there is no guarantee that it won't eventually be traced. In Britain it can be put into legitimate enterprises, but that makes it difficult to use in future illicit transactions. Far better, then, to put it in an offshore banking haven.

The advantages are generally myriad. First, there will be no tax on capital gains resulting from switching investments. Second, no taxes will be paid on interest accruing on the account. And, third, most offshore tax havens have secrecy laws. The register of investors is not always open for inspection and, when it is, professional money managers will offer the services of a nominee company to disguise the true beneficiaries.

The cash thus hidden away can be channelled back at a later date in one form or another (perhaps as an investment in a building project) as legitimate foreign capital. The later sale of the building project places the money in the hands of the owner as 'clean' money. The web of companies through which it will have passed, ending back at the offshore banking centre, makes discovery on the part of the authorities a formidably difficult task.

On the Isle of Man, a self-governing Crown dependency that is also a major offshore banking centre, Patrick Diamond, for a fee, was only too happy to set up 'shell' or 'front companies' with nominee directors into which the money would pour. And in 1983, it has been alleged, Errico began to make full use of his services. In May that year he deposited $750,000 in various safe-deposit boxes in New York and met with Levine to discuss transferring the cash to the Isle of Man. Two months later Diamond visited New York to meet the alleged hitman, who was using the name Craig Jacobs, at the Helmsley Palace Hotel. Within a week Diamond and Errico had flown to London with $250,000, which was deposited at a branch of the Midland Bank in an account that Diamond had opened for Errico in the name of Castlewood Investments Ltd, a company set up under the nominee ownership of a Liberian company called Hemstead Investments Ltd. The two men flew back to New York immediately and returned a day later with another $275,000 in cash.

Safely back in Florida, DEA agents claim, Errico concentrated his attentions on various marijuana-smuggling runs for the Levine syndicate, sending a further $600,000 across to Diamond in August 1984.

With the arrest of Thompson in early 1985, however, and Errico's indictment for three murders, a kidnapping and taking part in Thompson's drug-smuggling operation, the hitman, realizing that he could face the electric chair if caught, went on the run.

Several months later he arrived in Britain to consult with his financial adviser.

It was an ill-fated meeting, for by that time Diamond had plenty of problems of his own. A divorcé well-known in Isle of Man social circles, where he was regarded as something of a charming rogue who had a way with women, in London he was none too fussy about the company he kept. In February 1984 he had been staying at a flat in West Kensington, London, when late one night members of Scotland Yard's drug squad burst through the door.

They were investigating a Chinese syndicate believed to be importing heroin into London and Blackpool and had picked up two members of the syndicate elsewhere in the city. Information that the two members had given led to the flat in which Diamond was staying, where a party had been in progress most of the day.

Diamond, who later declared to Andrew Hogg that he had stopped off for only one night at the flat prior to flying out to the USA, was woken up, and the room in which he was sleeping was searched. Hidden among clothes in a drawer, detectives found a small amount of cocaine.

Although Diamond argued that he had not been to the drawer – all his clothing was in his suitcase in readiness for his flight – detectives were convinced that he was part of the drug syndicate. The $4,000 cash he had on him, and a copy of a Blackpool local newspaper that he had acquired while travelling down from the Isle of Man, only increased their suspicions.

After a week-long trial Diamond was found guilty of possession, given an eight-month prison sentence, part of it suspended, and fined £4,000.

Diamond's business activities were also causing him problems – particularly in the case of an off-the-shelf company that he had formed for a group of West German businessmen called Nettleville Investments Ltd. This company attracted a substantial amount of West German investment from citizens wishing to speculate on the futures market, a hit-and-miss business that involves speculating on the supply of various commodities around the world before they have been produced. No such market exists in West Germany, largely because it is only one step removed from gambling. Businessmen, however, were queueing up to place money in Nettleville, which would invest it for them.

The investors should have looked more closely at the company's credentials. The directors were listed as Dr Johannes Weissmuller (the late actor who made his name playing Tarzan) and Dr Phillipe Marlowe (named after the fictional detective).

The company brochure even showed a red London bus with the name Nettleville emblazoned on the side, but in reality it was a straightforward confidence trick; the businessmen running the company simply pocketed the investors' money.

Eventually, however, their West German customers became suspicious, and when a group of them investigated they would not accept the suggestion that Diamond had not played a part in the deception. As a result, the West German Police Authority took out a Mareva injunction, so called after a legal dispute in London in 1975 involving a Panamanian company by the same name, freezing a number of his accounts. (Diamond later complained to the authors that the West Germans had got it all wrong: the money that was frozen was the assets from the American marijuana-smuggling ring!)

Police interest in Diamond was still considerable. They were aware of the concern of the West German investors; they were interested in a number of his London acquaintances who were still thought to be involved in large-scale drug smuggling; and they knew that, a month after the Brink's-Mat robbery, he had met with at least one suspected member of the robbery gang.

He was therefore put under surveillance, and when Errico appeared in London to check on his investments and plan his future, he was soon spotted. At first detectives did not know the identity of the 27-year-old, good-looking young jetsetter staying at an exclusive address in Cheyne Walk, Chelsea, who called himself Stephen Marzovilla.

A full-scale surveillance operation was mounted, however, to identify all his associates while he was in Britain. Early in September it appeared that the mystery man was making plans to move on – and those plans somehow seemed to tie in with the Brink's-Mat gang. On the afternoon of 5 September he arrived at Heathrow Airport with the intention of catching a plane to Spain. One of the people whom he had been advised by Diamond to visit out there was a man named John – believed by Boyce and his team to be a south London robber who had taken part in the theft.

There was no way that the detectives were going to allow the trip to be made, for there was no guarantee that, once out of Britain, he would not simply disappear again. In the event, he got no further than the security body-scanner device at the entrance to the departure lounge. There a warning signal sounded, and he was searched. Inside his coat pocket security guards found three switch-blade knives. He was immediately marched off to a private room and his suitcase was retrieved from its journey to the plane. When it was opened, hidden under his clothes £15,000 and two false passports were found. He was taken into custody, where his true identity was rapidly discovered. The 'enforcer' had been found. Soon afterwards the U S authorities started extradition proceedings for his return.

It was a desperate Errico who was interviewed by officers investigating the Brink's-Mat case. Realizing that in his own country he faced the death penalty, he was anxious to discover whether any kind of deal was possible. It was a hopeless attempt, but in the process he talked, confirming his association with Diamond. Of his own activities he appeared largely unrepentant, saying, 'Joseph Kennedy was a bootlegger during prohibition – I deal in marijuana. There's no difference. It will be legalized soon anyway. I don't deny I deal with marijuana and that homicides are part of it. But that is only the word of snitches. There are some bad people around . . . but I'm a very nice guy. We're all college-educated white boys – no Cuban boys here.'

Errico was later to contest his extradition, claiming that because the first two killings took place 7 miles beyond the coast, they were in international waters, outside the jurisdiction of the U S A. He claimed that he had not been present when the third murder was committed.

As police began trawling through the affairs of the sinister Scott Errico, they soon discovered the $1.3 million he had stashed away in bank accounts in London and the Isle of Man. It was another six months before police moved in on Diamond, for he was much more valuable going about his normal business. He was followed, and his associates were monitored. His business life was truly astonishing.

Working from an office in Upper Church Street, protected by video cameras trained on the entrance, Diamond had over the years arranged the formation of literally hundreds of 'front companies'. He was known to have an association with Levine and his alleged accomplices, but he was also known to have participated in various other questionable business deals, including the bizarre case of the Vincent Foundation, a small charity based in Stoke-on-Trent in Britain, which, without the knowledge of its founder and organizer, had been used to launder millions of pounds of 'hot' money from around the world. Two of those said to have used the charity to hide large sums of cash and gold were ex-President Ferdinand Marcos of the Philippines and his wife Imelda. Diamond was the founder of the company Fairhurst Investments that turned the charity, which had been set up to help women in trouble with the law, into an organization secretly laundering millions. Detectives were also intrigued by some of the company Diamond kept when he visited Northern Ireland, where the IRA's terror campaign is largely funded by racketeering.

The problem confronting Scotland Yard was just how many of Diamond's companies were being used for illegal purposes. For they knew they had stumbled on a major money-laundering operation for organized crime. The situation was considered so serious that the Yard's top brass ordered a major reappraisal of its resources.

By March 1986 DAC Brian Worth, in charge of C Department, had decided that the most effective measure was to set up a Specialist Operations Task Force of officers to investigate the links between British criminals and international organized crime. The task force, because of Diamond's connections with at least one of the Brink's-Mat robbers, woud be under the control of Brian Boyce and would include the detective team investigating that particular robbery. But it would also include officers drafted in from the fraud squad and C11.

Desperate measures were obviously needed, for also drafted in to help was London's most controversial detective, Detective Superintendent Tony Lundy. Lundy had achieved spectacular results as a Flying Squad officer in north London during the 1970s, but his relationship with one of his informants had led to criticism of his methods, apparent in a video produced by John McVicar, the former armed robber turned journalist.

The film revealed how after a £3 million silver-billion robbery in London in 1980, which Lundy had investigated, twelve bars, worth £127,000, went missing in questionable circumstances shortly before the haul was retrieved. A house burglar was also shown repeating allegations, made in court, that during a break at Lundy's house he had found an attaché case full of Spanish and American currency.

In 1983 DAC Ronald Steventon, who had investigated the circumstances surrounding the silver-bullion raid, submitted an internal report stating: 'It is my belief that Lundy is a corrupt officer . . . Consideration should be given to removing him from duty.'

Following that indictment, Lundy was transferred from Scotland Yard to a Metropolitan Police division, but such was his knowledge of top-class London criminals and the reputation he enjoyed among certain sections of the force for his prowess as a thief taker that, as the Brink's-Mat inquiry progressed, he was soon drafted back to C11 to help the task force.

Thus it was to Lundy that the job of interviewing Diamond after his arrest fell, with the Isle of Man authorities only too anxious to help. The Manx government had long been sensitive to media reports of the criminal activities of the operators of Manx-registered companies, particularly following the collapse of the Isle of Man Savings and Investment Bank to the tune of £40 million, with every appearance of malpractice and continuing allegations by depositors who lost money of lax control and supervision by the government.

In his 1985 annual report the island's Chief Constable, Frank Weedon, had warned: 'Evidence is increasing that large amounts of money from major crime like illegal drug transactions are being laundered on the island, and it is essential that trained investigators are appointed . . .'

Diamond was arrested in March 1986, and Scotland Yard detectives were sworn in as special constables to give them full powers on the island to untangle the web of companies that he had created. It was an unusual but necessary move – the Tynwald, the Manx parliament, jealously guards the Isle of

Man's independent judicial system. The officers, led by Lundy, established themselves in a hotel on the Douglas seafront and, on 12 March, raided Diamond's home and business addresses. As they read through mountains of paperwork, they also learned an intriguing piece of information. In previous years staff at a local travel agency had been puzzled by Diamond's frequent purchase of air tickets for different young women. They would always fly tourist-class to Miami or elsewhere in that area of the United States and return a few days later, flying first-class from New York. Their job, detectives soon discovered, had been to bring large sums of cash back to the Isle of Man.

At first Diamond refused to help the police, but when they told him that they already knew a great deal about his activities and threatened to freeze the assets of every bank account of every company he had ever set up, he decided to open up. The detectives' biggest breakthrough followed soon afterwards.

That was the discovery that Diamond had not been acting alone in laundering the proceeds of the drug-smuggling gangs that had made use of his services. He, and the drug gangs, also had a cash conduit through to an office in the British Virgin Islands. The islands, some of Britain's few remaining dependencies, have a colourful past. Discovered by Christopher Columbus on his second voyage to the New World in 1493, practically every European country has at one time or another laid claim to the thirty-six islands in the group. It was Britain, however, that eventually established a rule of law there, after routing the pirates who had been attracted to the island's strategic position 800 miles north of the Venezuelan coastline. One of the islands, Norman Island, is said to have been visited by Robert Louis Stevenson during the last century and to have inspired his classic *Treasure Island.*

The real treasure of the islands, however, did not become apparent until the advent of the notion of offshore banking. The Virgin Islands' low tax rates and banking secrecy laws ensured that they too received a slice of the action. In the 1960s British businessmen began buying property on the islands, and investors moved in to take advantage of a favourable tax treaty that existed at that time with the UK. In the 1970s they were followed by American investors, particularly those seeking a shelter for their equity earnings.

By the early 1980s both Britain and the USA had taken action to stem the flow of cash to the islands. During a ten-year period from 1973 deposits at the four major banks in Tortola had increased from $30 million a year to hundreds of millions. The Virgin Islands, however, were not about to let anything interfere with the flow of capital, and they drew up new tax laws deliberately designed to attract foreigners wanting to move investments into and out of the USA. These were followed in 1984 by the introduction of zero taxation for trust companies.

Foremost among those handling this largely illicit cash was a former Manx accountant by the name of Shaun Patrick Murphy, who had settled on the islands in 1977 and worked in an office above an electrical equipment store in a wooden, two-storey building standing in front of the main church in Road Town, the capital of Tortola, the largest island. There, with Union Jacks fluttering from the flag poles in the street outside, and even red pillar boxes to complete the colonial picture, Murphy, the son of a Liverpool bookmaker, through his company Financial Management and Trusts, would receive millions from the drug dealings of his overseas clients. Companies would be formed and the cash placed in especially created bank accounts designed to thwart the most inquisitive tax investigator. To ensure his position, Murphy went straight to the top, encouraging the island's chief minister, Cyril Romney, to buy up ninety-nine of the issued 100 shares of Financial Management and Trusts and become a director.

In 1985 Murphy's office was described by the *Financial Times* of London as the 'nerve centre of the islands' financial services industry'. The accountant, while discussing the colony's new zero-taxation laws, was reported as saying, 'Now we have something to sell.'

One of his companies even had a vaguely sentimental ring to it, Ballabeg Trading Company, named after the village near

Castletown on the Isle of Man, where he had lived and met his wife Jennifer. Murphy's ostensible respectability, enhanced by his keen membership of the island's rugby club, was not enough, however, to deter Lundy and other Brink's-Mat detectives. A preliminary look at the paperwork in Murphy's office gave them the evidence they needed, for there they found documented his dealings with Michael I. Levine in Miami and with Diamond on the Isle of Man.

Proof of the American connection now meant that it was time for Scotland Yard to take the U S Drug Enforcement Administration into its confidence. Said one detective later: 'At first when we told the D E A what we had found, they didn't believe us – it was just too large. But after we showed them the evidence, we started a joint operation.'

That combined effort, code-named Operation Cougar, was to earn the Brink's-Mat inquiry team an enormous amount of praise and publicity on both sides of the Atlantic.

On Wednesday, 23 April, Murphy was arrested and charged with assisting in the breaking of U S drug laws. He was held under armed guard at his luxury mountainside home awaiting trial. But with the writing firmly on the wall, and anxious to spend as little time as possible in the island's 200-year-old prison, he decided on a dangerous gamble. He would reveal everything he knew in return for immunity from prosecution. It was a deal that the D E A jumped on with alacrity – promising the 33-year-old accountant protection: if he kept his side of the bargain, he could chose to have his features altered by plastic surgery, and new identities and a safe house would be provided for him and his family in the U S A.

Once the agreement was struck, Scotland Yard and the D E A set about analysing, with renewed vigour, just how far his business dealings stretched. It was not an easy job – there was so much paperwork that a jet had to be chartered to transport the files to the D E A headquarters in Fort Lauderdale.

News that he had turned supergrass was initially suppressed, for obvious reasons, but on 15 July his former accomplices were left in little doubt about what had happened. That day the acting attorney general of the British Virgin

Islands, Jack Smith-Hughes, issued a statement saying: 'I have decided to exercise the powers conferred upon me to discontinue the present criminal proceedings against Shaun Patrick Murphy.

'Scotland Yard detectives whose inquiries led to the arrest of Murphy have more recently concentrated their investigations in the United States of America, where they have been working in collaboration with the Drug Enforcement Administration. These inquiries have now reached a point where the DEA have decided that they prefer to treat this accused man as a witness rather than as an accused. It would be inconsistent were the BVI to seek to maintain any charges against him in such circumstances. He will not be returning to the BVI. His business has ceased to trade and his family have now departed also.'

Later Paul Teresi, head of the DEA in Fort Lauderdale, said, 'He came to Miami to be interviewed voluntarily. The drugs monies involved are the proceeds of marijuana and cocaine trafficking in the United States.'

The revelations about Murphy's activities had meanwhile caused considerable embarrassment for Cyril Romney. He was interviewed by Scotland Yard detectives but was subsequently cleared, claiming that he had only been a nominee director of Murphy's company. Murphy, he said, had appeared to him to be a 'very bright, intelligent man'. However, Romney was forced to call a snap poll to avoid defeat after a no-confidence motion was passed against him in the eleven-man Legislative Council, the islands' parliament. 'There is little doubt that the drug traffickers have been using the islands. We have been trying to stop it. I have had no dealings with drug dealers or with the Brink's-Mat robbers,' insisted Romney, but it didn't do him much good. The election brought the opposition party to power, and although Romney was re-elected to the council, he lost his position as chief minister.

In Miami, Operation Cougar soon began to enjoy the assistance not just of Murphy but of Diamond as well. He had agreed to accompany Lundy and a group of Brink's-Mat detectives, together with an officer from the Isle of Man, to Florida to identify various addresses where inquiries could be usefully made.

Later Diamond was caustic about the activities of the police officers. 'It was a circus,' he told Andrew Hogg. 'You had the DEA determined that the British were not going to teach them anything; you had Scotland Yard convinced they were the best detectives in the world; and the guy from the Isle of Man was desperate to make sure that nobody thought he was a hick. They all seemed to think I was in danger, and I was checked into a hotel under a false name. When the DEA agents arrived at reception, however, they asked for Mr Diamond, which caused considerable confusion.

'When we flew out, the team all bought spy books to read on the plane – they were really into it as some kind of major undercover operation. But when I asked on one occasion what they would all do if something did happen, one of the Scotland Yard detectives said, "You're a smooth bastard – you can talk your way out of it." I had virtually given up by then. On the flight out I couldn't believe it when I saw them sticking airline teaspoons in their top pockets as souvenirs of the flight.'

Despite Diamond's cynicism about the operation, Murphy was being extremely forthcoming as he outlined details of his relationship with Levine and Diamond to the DEA.

He revealed that in September 1981 Levine had flown to the Isle of Man to discuss with Diamond the setting up of offshore companies. The Miami lawyer then flew to Tortola and asked Murphy to form a shell company, named Murphy Investments Ltd, for the alleged purpose of buying real estate. Murphy then purchased Tillworth Investments Ltd, an Isle of Man corporation, in which the shares of Murphy Investments were placed.

Two months later Murphy mailed certain documents to Patrick Diamond, including a declaration of Trust and Indemnity acknowledging that the company was owned on behalf of Tillworth Investments Ltd. Diamond had the document legally validated and sent it back.

The method by which the laundering worked was simple.

Whenever a member of Levine's syndicate wanted to move cash out of the United States, Murphy was contacted and a bogus company formed. Similarly, when the drug traffickers needed money to buy fast boats, Murphy formed another company. Money would then be moved into the company's new bank account, and the fleet of power boats or whatever was necessary would be purchased.

Later, as the profits from the drugs organization began to mount up, Murphy was ordered to buy property, acres of it. In Fort Lauderdale this included warehousing, a country club and houses, while in Miami the proceeds went on an industrial park, an apartment building, more warehouses, company offices, agricultural land and houses.

At times Murphy was also able to play a part in the actual logistics of the smuggling operation. On one occasion a lawyer attached to the syndicate travelled to Jamaica to organize a drugs consignment, then flew to Tortola with a false birth certificate to lease another vessel under a bogus name. It was the ever-obliging Shaun Murphy who made the necessary arrangements.

In all, Murphy set up a total of 150 bank accounts to help his clients. On the Isle of Man Diamond had done slightly better, setting up 170.

As far as the Brink's-Mat case was concerned, Scotland Yard detectives, while investigating Diamond's affairs, were particularly curious about payments he had received from a man called John in Spain. John was the person Errico had been flying out to see when he was arrested at Heathrow Airport, and now a series of cash transactions were discovered that, police believed, involved money made from the Brink's-Mat raid.

The discovery led to Diamond's final downfall. He was charged with handling £100,000 – proceeds from the Brink's-Mat robbery – and bailed in his own recognizance of £10,000, plus another surety of £10,000 from his sister Margaret.

When he appeared in court in Douglas in September 1986 Diamond was said to have set up five 'front' companies to enable John (whose surname was never mentioned in court) to establish himself in Spain, even though he knew he was a wanted man.

The money was handed over to him by John in £50 notes in February 1984, and then all but £9,000 was transferred out to Spain. One sum of £41,000 had been used to help buy an expensive villa and a cruiser.

Lundy took the unusual course of appearing for the defence, telling the court, 'Due to the things he [Diamond] has told us, a world-wide operation has taken place involving police agencies from a number of countries.' Then – the comment was to infuriate Diamond – he said, 'He cooperated to such an extent that he was often putting his life in danger by confronting certain individuals in America.' Lundy added that it was 'one of the biggest world-wide police operations I have ever been involved in', and said that the inquiries were likely to last at least another two years. Defence advocate Mark Moroney argued that the monies had been held 'on a client basis' and that Diamond had merely looked after the cash. He added that the defendant and his family had been placed under great mental and financial strain.

Passing sentence, the Deemster (the Manx equivalent of a judge) Jack Corrin told Diamond, 'You were a willing vehicle to look after and organize the distribution of the money, in which you were prepared to indulge for personal gain. What I find even worse is that a criminal could rely on you for their ill-gotten gains.' He added, however, that the sentence would be considerably reduced because Diamond had cooperated with the police and had pleaded guilty. 'I can't imagine the costs to the taxpayer if you had contested this charge and the case had gone to trial,' said Corrin.

Diamond was given an eighteen-month prison sentence, half of which was suspended. He was also fined £10,000 and given a year in which to pay. Astonishingly, Diamond's conviction went virtually unreported by the British press. Such was the secrecy surrounding his part in Operation Cougar at that stage that the only mention of his court appearance, apart from those in Isle of Man newspapers, was two paragraphs in the northern edition of the *Daily Telegraph*.

That silence was not to last, for the following month the DEA arrested Levine and ten other Florida-based individuals, including a professional racing driver and a group of Miami attorneys, charging them with racketeering, drug trafficking and money-laundering offences. They were alleged to have smuggled a total of 100,000 pounds of marijuana from Colombia into the USA, valued at $30 million.

By now the opportunity for the DEA and the Brink's-Mat team to gain some credit for their achievements was too good to pass up, and a joint press conference was organized at the DEA's Miami office on 22 October.

Teresi from the DEA told the conference that Operation Cougar had become the largest single drugs operation in US history. 'The laundering took hundreds of millions of dollars from all corners of the US,' he added, including Mafia money from the East Coast. Explaining how the gang operated, he said, 'The huge bulk of cash generated presents the drug traders with a problem of disguising the source of their income. The drug distributor takes it to a man in the UK who specializes in laundering money. He arranges to get it out of the country and into the Caribbean. Phoney shell companies are set up, and the money is invested through a number of these companies until it is reinvested in a legitimate corporation and transferred back to the US.' He explained that attorneys were used to set up the shell companies because they could claim confidentiality in any discussions with their clients.

Lundy told the conference that in Britain a number of solicitors and at least one senior official in a London merchant bank were likely to be arrested within the next few weeks. He added, 'The scale of the problem is immense. It stretches from the United States to the Caribbean, London, the Channel Islands, the Isle of Man, Europe and the Far East. London, being one of the major money markets, is an important centre for the transfer of cash.

'The money comes from all sorts of crime, not only drugs. It represents the proceeds from armed robberies, drug dealing and every other aspect of criminal activity.

'We have broken through the surface of it now, and down into the labyrinth, but the operation could go on for another two years.'

The arrests had taken place, he added, because 'The Americans had information that some of the people they were after were up and running. People were disappearing and sinking boats.'

Later Teresi told the authors that the $30 million on the indictment papers was 'just the tip of the iceberg'. He said that $50 million worth of assets, including property and boats, had been seized. A further $50 million belonging to the syndicate had been traced, and attempts were being made to recover it. The inquiry now stretched as far as Panama and Hong Kong.

In Britain Deputy Assistant Commissioner Worth issued a statement saying: 'The Specialist Operations Task Force, together with American agents, have made significant inroads into organized crime and money laundering. This operation is teaching us that we must be truly international in our approach. I am determined that the American experience of legitimizing of the proceeds of crime will never become a simple or profitable process in London.

'We cannot be sanguine. Our current inquiries establish that the international laundering of the profits of crime has grown beyond infancy. Our intelligence strongly indicates that known criminals, on both sides of the Atlantic, are conspiring in the realization of illicit funds from all aspects of major crime, particularly drugs.

'The activities of the task force in London, which, as I have said, have led to the current successful initiatives in Florida, are now directed to seizing the problem in London. We are in the process of attacking a number of targets which I am convinced will lead to further arrests and the recovery of very substantial illicit funds amassed by organized crime.' The press conference, and Worth's comments, attracted worldwide publicity, and in his cell on the Isle of Man Diamond became a deeply troubled man, particularly when he learned that officers from C 11 were alleging that, while assisting police in Florida, he had worn a microphone when meeting some of his contacts.

He insisted that a statement be issued immediately on his behalf, and the following day it duly appeared. 'The only information Mr Diamond has been in a position to supply to the authorities is financial information in relation to companies he has formed on behalf of a lawyer in the United States, and an accountant in the British Virgin Islands, and Mr Diamond has been happy to supply this information.'

To distance himself further from any suggestion that he was a marked man because of information he had given, Diamond also disputed Lundy's claim, at his court case a month earlier, that Diamond had occasionally risked his life during the police inquiry. 'Mr Diamond is not in fear of his life, has no reason to be, and at no time has he advised the police, or anyone else, that this was the case,' the statement stressed. 'After police inquiries were completed, Mr Diamond was released on bail for a period of four months; during such time he had a well-publicized holiday in Northern Ireland.'

Diamond was not the only one who was embarrassed. The Manx government was also anxious to counter what it regarded as adverse publicity about the island's role as a centre for illegality.

A day after the news broke Tynwald's executive council hastily drafted a statement to ward off criticism. It read: 'The Isle of Man government has noted the recent news reports relating to Scotland Yard's investigations into an international network of lawyers and accountants who are alleged to have laundered large sums of money through the United Kingdom, the Isle of Man, the British Virgin Islands, Hong Kong, Panama, the United States and elsewhere which have been derived from drug trafficking. The network was discovered during investigations into the £26 million Brink's-Mat gold bullion robbery at Heathrow in 1983.

'The Isle of Man government wishes it to be known that the Isle of Man police force has worked very closely with Scotland Yard and the Drug Enforcement Administration in the United

States from the outset, and the authorities in the island have given every assistance to the authorities in the United Kingdom and the United States in these investigations. Members of the Manx police force have actively participated in the inquiry and have travelled extensively in the course of the inquiry.

'The Isle of Man government also wishes it to be known that it is determined that the island will not be used by drug traffickers or other criminals and is doing everything in its power to prevent this from happening.'

22. No case to answer

The British *señor* living it up on the Costa Blanca in Spain was a popular figure in the bars and discos that he frequented with a small crowd of cronies. He liked a drink but, despite his boxer's face and build, was never any trouble. Instead he could at times be the life and soul of the party, particularly at the Penelope disco in the package-holiday resort of Benidorm, where he would often put up the prize money for 'Miss Topless' and 'Miss Big Boobs' competitions, generally inviting the winners back to his luxurious villa at the near-by town of Altea for a private party afterwards.

It was, it's true, sometimes difficult to know just how to address him, as he seemed to have several names, including John Smead and J. J. Barham. And no one knew for certain just where his money came from. There was a Barcelona company dealing in furniture, boats and cars in which he had a financial interest, but there were also the cash transfers from London, Liverpool and the Isle of Man into an account at the Banco Hispano Americano in Alicante – the proceeds of successful investments, the *señor* claimed. His choice of a nightspot also raised the occasional eyebrow, including as it did a piano bar in Benidorm set up, it's believed, with money from the Union Corse, the Corsican organized-crime gang based in Marseilles.

But in the live-and-let-live atmosphere of Spain's Mediterranean coast the *señor* was just another well-heeled foreign businessman enjoying the good life.

It hadn't always been like that for John Robert Fleming, born on 8 October 1940 in Burgess Hill, West Sussex. In 1983, for instance, while living in Denmark Hill, south-east London, he was apparently just another family man with a bank overdraft to contend with.

But at the end of 1983 his luck had taken a dramatic turn for the better. For between December and July the following year sums amounting to £56,000 were deposited in his bank account. Then, in February 1984, John Fleming travelled to the Isle of Man to meet a financial consultant, to whom he gave a large amount of cash to be deposited in a bank account in Florida. Further substantial investments followed in unit trusts, oil and commodities. After the failure of several of these investments, he turned his back on Britain in favour of a life in the sun, and purchased a villa for £60,000.

In Spain Fleming remained undisturbed for more than a year, living off the money transfers from Britain.

Flying Squad detectives scouring south London for clues to the whereabouts of the missing Brink's-Mat gold soon became aware of Fleming's sudden wealth. He had been placed under surveillance, but, despite his spending spree, nothing conclusive was found to link him with the robbery or the handling of its proceeds.

Scotland Yard had watched with a degree of concern as Fleming settled in the south of Spain, but detectives were not unduly worried, for they knew that the Spanish authorities would be very interested to know the true identity of the man who had arrived on a false passport. And in summer 1985 – anxious to have him somewhere where he could be brought to justice if evidence of a connection with Brink's-Mat was ever discovered – C11 contacted the Spanish authorities.

The big-spending Briton, the Spanish were told, was in reality the John Fleming who in 1970, while in Gerona, to the north of Barcelona, had been convicted of fraud and trafficking in false US dollars worth several thousands of pounds. Fleming had been sentenced to thirteen years' imprisonment for that particular escapade, of which he served six before being expelled from Spain and made the subject of an exclusion order.

The Spanish now spent the next few months investigating Fleming and his associates, then in November raided his villa. A search of the premises quickly revealed a false passport and a false birth certificate, and he was told that police would apply for his expulsion.

The bureaucratic process that then moved laboriously into gear meant that it was a further nine months before the order was granted, but when it was, the instructions from the Ministry of the Interior were unequivocal. Fleming had just fifteen days in which to leave the country.

A condition was also imposed stipulating that Fleming had to report to local police and state his intended destination, but for two weeks nothing was heard from him, until eventually Spanish detectives were forced to visit his villa to find out his plans. They discovered that the place was deserted; a note left by Fleming indicated that he was going to Brazil.

At his office in Alicante his lawyer, Adolfo Valor Gil, when asked if the note was genuine, told reporters, 'I can only say that he is not planning on returning to Britain.'

In fact, Fleming had secretly flown out to Costa Rica, a Central American republic that, because of the lack of an extradition treaty with Britain, had been widely predicted as the probable bolt-hole for fugitive Britons forced out of Spain. There Fleming moved into a hotel in the capital, San José, with a Spanish girlfriend, seemingly determined once more to enjoy a lotus-eating existence.

But Scotland Yard moved fast. With Lundy and officers from the Specialist Operations Task Force already in Florida and the

Caribbean for Operation Cougar, it was a small matter to dispatch Detective Inspector Antony Brightwell down to Costa Rica to inform the authorities about the identity of their visitor. Fleming was promptly arrested as an 'undesirable' and his girlfriend sent back to Madrid. 'His background does not make him worthy of staying in the country,' said interior minister Guido Fernandez.

At Scotland Yard's request all his possessions, with the exception of his genuine passport, were confiscated – including his gold Rolex watch and Cartier sunglasses – and after a supreme court hearing, at which his lawyers attempted to present a writ of habeas corpus, he was taken in handcuffs to San José airport and expelled on the first available flight, which Brightwell had ensured would be one to Miami. The Scotland Yard detective travelled on the same plane, claiming later that shortly before take-off he had been able to question Fleming briefly about the Brink's-Mat robbery. It had not been a cordial exchange; Fleming allegedly told the detective: 'The world and his fucking wife knows I had something to do with it, but you have fucking nothing. If you want me, you will have to drag me back in fucking chains.'

Arriving in Florida on 20 August 1986, Fleming was immediately taken into custody by immigration authorities. 'What is your purpose here in the U S?' asked a brisk official.

'No purpose at all. I'd prefer to leave. I was brought here forcibly,' replied the dejected detainee.

A little later, however, he decided to apply for permission to enter the United States officially but was told that because of his criminal record he was an 'excludable alien'. There were also doubts about the authenticity of a visa in his passport. Instead he was asked which country he would like to be sent to and, after insisting vehemently that he had no desire to return to Britain, on Wednesday, 27 August, an immigration judge gave him a week to find a country that would accept him. His lawyers were confident that they could meet the condition – by then Panama had indicated that he would be allowed entry. At the same time the court acceded to a request from officials of the U S Immigration and Naturalization Service (INS) that Fleming had to leave on a scheduled flight rather than by private plane as a guarantee that he would go to the destination stated, and reasonable warning would have to be given.

The thinking behind those two conditions was at first lost on Fleming. In fact, they marked the opening of a game of cat and mouse that was to last eight months and take Fleming's U S lawyers to a number of Central American, South American and Caribbean countries, closely pursued by British detectives.

For Scotland Yard had no intention of applying for Fleming's extradition from the U S A or anywhere else – detectives were far from sure that they had enough evidence on him to bring charges. Instead they contented themselves with trying to ensure that eventually the U S authorities would have to deport him back to Britain because no other country could be found to accept him.

It was a long-drawn-out process. Scotland Yard had already notified all Interpol countries about Fleming's background and his suspected involvement in the Brink's-Mat robbery. And now quietly the INS in Miami did everything it reasonably could to assist the detectives in their efforts, without leaving itself open to the charge that Fleming was being denied his basic rights.

Every time Fleming's lawyers found a foreign government that did look amenable, immigration officers would tip the wink to Lundy and task-force officers in Miami, who would then impress on that country's diplomats just what the case was against Fleming and how badly Scotland Yard wanted him back. Their overtures would be backed up by approaches from British diplomatic staff.

That the U S authorities did not plan to make life easy for Mr Fleming became apparent immediately after the 27 August court hearing, when a grand jury investigating drug smuggling and money laundering issued a subpoena for Fleming's passport, saying they wanted it to help their inquiries, a demand that was passed on to the INS by the U S Attorney's Office.

At eight o'clock the following morning, Thursday, Fleming's

lawyers notified the INS that their client had booked a scheduled flight to Panama and gave INS officers the ticket to ensure that he was taken to the airport on time. But six hours later the lawyers were told of the grand jury subpoena. Without the passport, the flight to Panama was one Fleming couldn't take.

The following day one of Fleming's lawyers, John Berk, went to a federal court to plead: 'An obvious abuse of the grand jury system is taking place here at the behest of Scotland Yard that clearly exceeds any sense of fundamental fairness that should be afforded to John Fleming, an individual who was brought here against his will and only wishes to leave with that only possession not taken away from him by Costa Rican authorities: his passport.'

In a counter plea, the US Attorney's Office argued that it was perfectly prepared to obtain from the British consulate in Miami temporary travel documents that would enable Fleming at least to fly home to Britain. Like that made to Palmer in Tenerife, the offer was not taken up.

The intervention of the US Attorney's Office was highly unusual but thought to be the result of the anger the Justice Department felt about the refusal of the Spanish courts to extradite a major Colombian cocaine smuggler to the USA a month earlier to face charges in Miami. Instead of being sent to the USA, the alleged trafficker, Jorge Ochoa, was returned to Colombia, where he was promptly released on bail – and disappeared. In the light of that, the US government was thought to be anxious to re-endorse the principle that there should be no hiding place for suspected major criminals.

At the end of the day's hearing it was apparent that the cards were now well and truly stacked against Fleming. For the federal judge adjourned without making any ruling, despite the fact that it was a Labor Day weekend, which meant that there was no possibility of a judgment until the following Tuesday – which, if Fleming did get his passport back, would give him less than a day to leave before the deadline imposed by the immigration judge had expired. And by now Panama was out: the attendant publicity surrounding the trials and tribulations of Mr Fleming had caused the country to have second thoughts about playing host.

It was a despondent Fleming who, dressed in a bright-orange, pyjama-like uniform, was led back to a 4- by 8-foot isolation cell at Krome detention centre, where he spent most of his time reading, watching television, going for solitary walks and answering phone calls from his friends in Britain.

In the event, the lack of a court ruling was not as serious as it had first appeared. The Wednesday deadline came and went without comment, then on the Thursday judgment was at last issued. Fleming's passport had to be returned within eight days. But the judge imposed two conditions: first, Fleming's lawyers had, within that period, to produce a written agreement from a foreign government allowing him entry; second, he had to travel on a commercial airline ticket.

Six days later Fleming's lawyers told the court that he had obtained 'provisional consent' from an unnamed foreign country and that full consent would be forthcoming 'by the end of the week'. The judge therefore ordered both Fleming and his passport to be surrendered to the court on the Friday – the eighth day. If it was apparent that all the conditions had been met, he would be placed on a plane to whichever destination he had chosen.

He almost got away with it. After appearing in court on the Friday, he was sitting on an Eastern Airlines plane at Miami International Airport, waiting to fly to the Dominican Republic (from where it was believed he planned to head for Brazil), when he heard the Dominicans had rescinded their permission for his entry. With just minutes to go before take-off, he was marched off the plane and taken back to Krome.

The Dominicans' change of mind was due to the persistence of Detective Superintendent Lundy and a consul with a suspicious mind who was not afraid to make unilateral decisions.

The Dominican Republic, which shares the island of Hispaniola with Haiti, was an obvious choice for Fleming's lawyers because it broke off diplomatic relations with Britain over the Falklands War. But the lawyers did not reckon on the fact that a new government, which wanted to restore links with Britain, had recently come to power.

The new Dominican consul in Miami, Frederico Antun, aged 70, a grandfather of eight, who had twice been a government minister and was a close friend of the republic's new president, Joaquin Balaguer, was just settling in at the consulate in early September when he received a surprise visit from the son of one of his country's army generals. 'He told me that he had a very rich English friend who wanted to visit the island and who might make investments there,' said Antun later.

The consul was immediately suspicious because all that most visitors need to enter the republic is a tourist card, which costs $15 and can be bought at the airport. But the general's son was adamant; he wanted a written commitment from Antun saying that his 'friend' would be welcome.

The consul refused to provide it without firm evidence of the Englishman's identity, and two days later a lawyer who said his name was Conrad de Voronof turned up at the consulate with a photocopy of Fleming's passport and birth certificate. Voronoff said that Fleming himself could not appear because he was 'in Atlanta'.

But still Antun refused to put anything in writing. 'If he's rich, he can just take the plane there,' he told Voronoff.

Realizing that Antun was not going to change his mind, the day before Fleming and his passport were to be surrendered to the judge Fleming's lawyers went back to court and asked for a subtle amendment to the conditions the judge had imposed. Instead of a written promise from a foreign country to accept Fleming, the lawyer offered his own sworn statement that such a country existed.

When Fleming was taken to Miami International Airport early on the Friday afternoon, however, he had to show the immigration service his airline ticket, and within minutes British officials knew exactly where he was heading.

In a race against the clock, Lundy phoned Antun telling him Fleming was a suspected criminal. Peter Spiceley, the British consul, also phoned Antun to urge that Fleming should not be allowed to enter the Dominican Republic.

Without consulting anyone, Antun telephoned Eastern Airlines and bluntly warned, 'Your plane is not going to land if you take that man.' Despite protests from a senior Eastern Airlines executive, he refused to give in, and Fleming was removed from the plane minutes before it left the ramp.

Soon afterwards an immigration judge ruled that Fleming should be deported back to Britain. Fleming's lawyers immediately started the lengthy process of launching an appeal. In December 1986, while that appeal was still being considered, the Brink's-Mat suspect again attempted to leave Miami – this time for Peru. His visa, however, was cancelled the day after the INS made the news public. Further approaches were also made to Colombia, Mexico and Argentina, but in all cases alert officials in the respective consulates in Miami spotted cancelled visas in Fleming's passport and turned him down.

The following February saw Fleming's appeal rejected by the Board of Immigration Appeals in Washington, but his lawyers were still not beaten. They discovered that a plan existed to put Fleming quietly on a plane back to Britain and immediately decided to take the matter to the Eleventh Circuit, the regional appeals court, one step down from the Supreme Court. That appeal also failed, and in March he was ordered to return home.

On this occasion it was the immigration service, anxious to be seen to be playing everything by the book, that stopped him leaving: officers rushed on to the London-bound plane, after he was buckled into his seat, to tell him that his lawyers had obtained him a visa for Venezuela.

Ironically, this one occasion when immigration officials did intervene on his behalf was to prove the last round in Fleming's desperate fight to avoid deportation to Britain – and delivered him into the hands of Scotland Yard.

The problems began for Fleming the morning after he was

taken off the flight. The Venezuelan consul in Miami cancelled his visa. Fleming's lawyers fought back strongly, successfully challenging the legality of the move by making a dramatic call to a Venezuelan official in Caracas, who said the visa had been approved by a higher authority than the consul, who therefore had no power to cancel it.

Faced with that 'seed of doubt', a federal court that day ruled that Fleming could not be deported to Britain for at least another week while inquiries were made. What the court did not know, but what the *Sunday Times* had by then established, was that the 'official' in Caracas who planted the 'seed of doubt' and the man who obtained Fleming's Venezuelan visa in the first place were brothers.

The story had begun two weeks earlier when a young Venezuelan businessman and lawyer, who called himself Leon Puppio, turned up at the consulate general of Venezuela in Miami saying that he had a prominent British friend who wished to go to Caracas and needed a letter indicating that he would be welcome.

The Venezuelan consul, Benjamin Ortega, duly wrote a 'To whom it may concern' letter saying that British nationals were welcome in Venezuela.

A few days later Puppio said that the letter was not good enough and must contain his friend's name. Again Ortega obliged. But when Puppio returned a third time and said he needed a visa stamped in his friend's passport, 'in case he has some immigration problem', Ortega became suspicious: British nationals do not require a visa to enter Venezuela, merely a tourist card which is obtainable from any airline office. In what the consul later described as a 'moment of weakness', however, he told Puppio to go to Caracas and ask for the visa there.

On the day that Fleming was to be deported back to Britain Ortega, much to his surprise, received a telephone call from an official of the Venezuelan foreign ministry, whom he refused to name, ordering him to issue a visa to Fleming. He had no option but to comply.

Ortega had never heard of John Fleming, but he rapidly found out about him when Fleming's last-minute stay of deportation was shown that night on TV. At the same time the British embassies in Washington and Caracas began hitting the phones, and Ortega was told by his Washington embassy the following day to revoke the visa.

But cancelling it proved much more difficult than issuing it. Fleming's lawyers challenged the right of a mere consul in Miami to cancel a visa issued on the direct orders of the Venezuelan foreign ministry. The judge then demanded that clarification be sought from Caracas.

It was one of Fleming's lawyers, Oscar Levin, who suggested they might call a Dr Antonio Puppio, whom Levin described as a 'legal adviser to internal relations', in Venezuela's foreign ministry. According to Perry Rivkind, director of the INS in Miami, the US government had no choice but to accept Dr Puppio's credentials and his advice, given through an interpreter, that he knew of no legal authority for a consul to cancel a visa. This was the 'seed of doubt' that caused Fleming's stay of execution.

After learning of the *Sunday Times* investigation, however, Rivkind was furious and told the US State Department to conduct an immediate inquiry. The State Department reported that Fleming's Venezuelan visa had been issued 'in error' because of 'false information' supplied to the ministry of internal affairs by a young Caracas lawyer named Leon Puppio. The Venezuelan government told the State Department that Dr Antonio, Puppio's brother, was a legal consultant for the interior ministry and 'is not authorized to speak officially for the government or even the interior ministry on this matter'.

'It's outrageous,' said Rivkind, and when several days later Fleming's lawyers appeared in court to say that they now had permission for their client to go to Nicaragua, Rivkind told the federal judge that as regional director of the INS he had authority to expel anyone he chose.

'I'm now going to use my discretion and deport Fleming back to Britain,' he said. The judge refused to intervene, as did a federal appeals court in Atlanta, and five hours later, on 26 March 1987, Fleming was being flown across the Atlantic accompanied by U S immigration officials and detectives from Scotland Yard.

'I have had time to consider the evidence against Mr Fleming, and I consider there is insufficient evidence. He is therefore discharged.' It was Thursday, 25 June 1987, and stipendiary magistrate Norma Negus, after considering overnight the case against John Fleming, had taken less than two minutes that morning to deliver her judgment.

He had been appearing at a committal hearing in which the case against him was examined by a magistrate to ensure that the evidence was strong enough to put before a judge. The charge had been that of dishonestly handling £840,000 – proceeds of the Brink's-Mat robbery. The case against Fleming was based on the substantial change in fortune that he had enjoyed from December 1983 onwards. It was denied that the source of his funds was either illicit or part of the robbery. A claim that Fleming was linked with Kenneth Noye – the gold handler had spent a night at Fleming's villa in 1984, and his telephone number had been found among Fleming's possessions – was described as 'guilt by association'.

At the end of the first day's hearing Mathew had submitted that there was no evidence linking Fleming's money with Brink's-Mat and asked for the defendant to be discharged. 'It was a formality,' Fleming's solicitor, Henry Milner, admitted later to the authors. 'It was a very slim case, but we didn't really expect a magistrate to have the guts to throw it out at that stage after all the publicity there had been about Fleming.'

Magistrate Norma Negus, however, was used to controversy. Two years earlier she had dismissed a case against a man alleged to have been a fund raiser for the notoriously brutal Irish National Liberation Army after deciding that she was unhappy about police handling of the prosecution.

Astounded, police and DPP officials who had fought a three-year legal battle to have the suspected terrorist extradited from the Irish Republic had rushed off to the High Court to obtain clearance for his immediate committal for trial. It was granted, and detectives had sped to Heathrow Airport to re-arrest him, only to find that they had missed him by ten minutes.

After the discharge of Fleming, Negus declined to speak about her decision.

Leaving the dock and collecting his belongings from police, Fleming congratulated his lawyers, then walked out to face the waiting press. His bitterness became quickly apparent. 'It's like a dream,' he said. 'It's a great relief. It did take me by surprise. It has been a bad year, uncomfortable, expensive and unnecessary. I don't know how I shall be celebrating. I shall probably have a quiet drink with my family. All I would like now is a bit of peace and quiet.

'Justice has been seen to be done. It was an incredible case, full of scheming and dirty tricks by four governments, the Costa Rican, the Spanish, the British and the American – a conspiracy full of illegal acts. They just broke all the rules – threw the rule book out of the window.

'The police made it increasingly difficult for me after I repeatedly stated that I had nothing to say to them. Almost a full page of alleged confession by me came to light in corridor conversations.'

Asked where the money he had enjoyed came from, he replied, 'No comment,' then added, 'Where the money came from is a private matter. They have put enormous pressure on me to try to make me divulge the source, but I have not told them and I will not tell you now. I expect the tax man will want to know, but that's a matter between me and the tax man.'

The dismissal of the charge against Fleming was greeted with resignation by Scotland Yard, which pointed out that it had always been aware of the weakness of the case against him, otherwise it would have applied for his extradition from the USA, rather than waiting for him to be deported.

American immigration officials and British diplomats in the USA were not so phlegmatic and expressed dismay at the months of wasted effort. Scotland Yard's failure to ensure that the case would stand up in court was described as 'inefficient' by Perry Rivkind. The INS, said Rivkind, had given the case top priority and later had to cope with a sizeable backlog of more than a hundred other cases. He declined to comment when asked if the immigration service would be prepared to take on a similar operation for a foreign government in future.

Spiceley, the British consul in Miami, was also staggered when told the news. 'God Almighty – after all that work!' he said.

Another British official said, 'Next time Scotland Yard wants to do something like this we should be a little more careful.'

One happy man was attorney Oscar Levin, Fleming's immigration lawyer in Miami. 'I'm very pleased for Mr Fleming. He is free at last.'

In London Henry Milner, Fleming's solicitor, when asked why his client had not returned to Britain voluntarily after his expulsion from Spain, replied that Fleming was 'not over enthusiastic about the facilities at Wormwood Scrubs' for prisoners awaiting trial.

Aftermath

The failure of the prosecutions against a number of those allegedly involved in the Brink's-Mat case was seen in various quarters as proof that there was something fundamentally wrong with the professional expertise of Scotland Yard's detective force.

There were darker whispers too. It wasn't the ability of those investigating the robbery that was at fault: instead, the spectre that had haunted Scotland Yard since the early 1970s was to blame – police corruption! For how else could so many reversals be explained? Detectives, for a fee, must have doctored some of the evidence to safeguard certain defendants.

Those who had followed the case from the beginning, however, knew just how unlikely that theory was. At the outset the only thing that had distinguished the robbery from any other armed raid was the sheer size of the haul. Brink's-Mat was, and still is, the largest proven robbery in British history. (The Knightsbridge safe deposit-box robbers in July 1987 were said to have escaped with more than £30 million, but the figure is an estimate, and so far less than £20 million have been recovered.)

There was another ingredient in the Brink's-Mat case that gave it a unique status in the annals of British crime and explained why police, on occasion, brought prosecutions that were less than watertight. For the case presented Scotland Yard, for the first time, with unassailable proof that the top echelon of armed robbers in the country, those who had graduated from the streets of south London, had links with international organized crime.

Detectives knew that within weeks of the robbery a number of the stolen traveller's cheques had been skilfully disposed of outside Britain. Diamond's subsequent role in laundering a proportion of the proceeds also showed just how sophisticated the armed-robber fraternity had become. 'We were led into other areas of organized crime, drug running and conspiracy between our criminals and Italian, French, Spanish and American criminals. There were some pretty close connections. It was a watershed for us,' said D A C Worth later. Detective Chief Superintendent Boyce added, 'If a group of criminals have £26 million of gold in their coffers, they have probably got more power than some Third World countries. That makes them a very potent danger to our society.'

As a result, the Specialist Operations Task Force was formed. It was the first coordinated response to organized crime in the history of Scotland Yard, and by setting up the squad the Yard ensured that no one connected with the Brink's-Mat raid could rest easy. For the case was the Yard's first major breakthrough into the area that it was now targeting and, as such, it was not about to be overtaken by other priorities. It would be vigorously pursued, and charges would be pressed where and when possible. The evidence, however, given the criminal expertise of those that were convicted, was in most cases largely circumstantial, placing a greater onus on juries to decide whether or not the police had got it right. And in some cases, they made it clear that they believed that the police had been mistaken.

The core of this new task force consisted in the main of Flying Squad officers who had investigated the Brink's-Mat robbery, and their resolve to track down everybody connected with the raid and the disposal of the gold was strengthened by another factor – the killing of John Fordham.

For Kenneth Noye had made an enormous error in stabbing the undercover policeman to death. A jury had accepted that the killing was in self-defence, but that did little to excuse Noye in the eyes of the Metropolitan Police. A policeman had died while investigating Brink's-Mat. As a result, Fordham's colleagues and their superiors felt duty-bound to bring to justice all those involved in the case on which he had been working.

As they continued the search for the gold, detectives found an unexpected ally in the form of Micky McAvoy, who, once the prospect of spending twenty-five years behind bars had sunk in, was eager to explore ways of reducing his sentence. Detectives had regularly seen the prisoner in the hope that he might talk, and after one such visit word came back that he was planning to appeal against sentence and might be prepared to cooperate. Meetings took place with Deputy Assistant Commissioner Worth, who indicated that if the gold was forthcoming, the appropriate authorities would be told that McAvoy had assisted police.

McAvoy told Worth he knew where at least half the gold had gone. As one of the organizers of the robbery, he had received a large proportion of the proceeds, as well as some of Tony Black's share. Associates had been entrusted to look after his interests, and he knew some of the gold had already been passed on to a fence. Now McAvoy was prepared to get a message out to another associate, who would be instructed to arrange the return of the money that had been made and all the gold that was left.

In vain, Worth attempted to persuade the prisoner that the associate would be unlikely to carry out the instructions. On discovering the whereabouts of the cash and the money, he would in all likelihood vanish with what he could get his hands on. But McAvoy was adamant: there was no way that he was going to place anyone at risk by telling police exactly where to go to retrieve the haul. The middle-man would have to be trusted.

The detectives didn't bother to try to convince themselves that the prospects looked good – they knew they were within an ace of returning a substantial amount of money to the

Brink's-Mat insurers, but they were under no illusions about their chances of success. Sure enough, like the Great Train Robbers before him, McAvoy discovered a marked reluctance on the part of those outside who were administering his money to give up what they had got.

Detectives now began a major operation to identify all those outside with whom McAvoy was known to be associated and, before long, found evidence of an enormous chain of financial transactions involving offshore accounts and property deals amounting to more than £10 million. The earliest pre-dated the Noye/Chappell gold chain, and the later ones, detectives believed, reflected the profits made from that operation too.

As a result, a total of eight people, including a solicitor, were subsequently charged with conspiracy to handle the proceeds of the Brink's-Mat robbery. Their cases have yet to come to court, so the precise details of what is alleged to have taken place is, at the time of writing, *sub judice.*

In general terms, however, police allege that deals included the depositing of enormous sums of money in Irish banks in London, as well as banks in Jersey, the Isle of Man and Switzerland. On one occasion a married couple from Britain were stopped by German border guards at the Swiss frontier, and £500,000 in new £50 notes was found in the car. It was part of a consignment of £710,000 that they planned to deposit in Switzerland.

While the deposits were made, companies were set up, in Panama, the Cayman Islands, Spain and London, to purchase property. Money was then transferred from bank to bank until it arrived back in London to fund the purchases. By the middle of 1985 between £6 million and £7 million was floating around in myriad bank accounts and a trust fund in Liechtenstein. That figure grew rapidly, however, after a series of impressive property deals in London's booming docklands area. One plot bought for under £3 million was later sold for more than £4 million. Land was also purchased for development at the exclusive Cheltenham Ladies' College, and a series of houses were bought. When police raided one of them, two Rottweiler dogs were found, one called Brink's, the other Mat.

Following the failure of his plan to gain an early release, McAvoy once again began refusing to cooperate with police. Ensconced in Leicester jail, in June 1987 he got married in the gymnasium, in the company of warders and armed police, before returning to his cell where he whiled away the time, inexplicably still convinced that a romantic code of loyalty existed among criminals and wondering what had gone wrong.

Robinson, meanwhile, although he had been party to the offer to return the gold, had accepted his fate more resignedly. Nothing that happened to him, he claimed, could be as worrying as the time he had spent after the robbery when Tony Black was in custody and he had been left in no doubt by those who knew the security guard well that he was weak and liable to crack. As for Black, the man who had put Robinson and McAvoy in prison in the first place, he was released from jail early in 1986. He and his wife then assumed new identities, and began a fresh life away from London. Late in 1987, however, there were reports that he had visited at least one old acquaintance who, horrified, had told him to make himself scarce. There was still a contract out on him.

Tony White, who had been acquitted of the actual robbery, was in 1987 to have a further brush with the law. Prior to the raid, he had lived in a council house, drawing unemployment benefit. But following his release from custody after his acquittal, for which he had received compensation from the police, he had opened a shoe shop and made substantial investments in property. A house in Brockley Road, south-east London, was bought for £33,000; another in Sandhurst Road, Catford, south London, was bought for £40,000; while a third, called Mona Lea in Beckenham, Kent, was bought for £146,000 and renovated at a cost of more than £200,000 before being sold on. White and his family then went to live in Spain.

Police, curious about where all the cash had come from, applied for details of the purchase of the house in Brockley Road, which had been carried out through his conveyancing solicitors. DC Bernard Clarke went to court in February 1987 to claim that police were entitled to the information under the Police and Criminal Evidence Act 1984. The Act provides that

'A constable may obtain access to . . . special procedure material for the purposes of a criminal investigation . . .' The conditions upon which such access can be granted include reasonable grounds for believing that a serious arrestable offence has been committed, that the material is likely to be of substantial value to the investigation, and that it is in the public interest that it should be produced.

The court agreed, but White and his solicitors appealed to the Queen's Bench divisional court and, the following July, successfully stopped the application. They argued that the judge in the original hearing had been given information by the police containing 'highly prejudicial statements which ought not to have been there', while copies of that information had not been made available to White, his solicitors or counsel acting for them. Lord Justice Watkins and Mr Justice Kennedy agreed that it was clearly wrong of the judge to have had the constable's information without showing it to counsel for the solicitors, adding that the quality and kind of evidence provided by the constable was unsatisfactory.

His Lordship, with the agreement of Mr Justice Kennedy, therefore quashed the application but said that it did not prevent the constable from applying afresh for the material he wanted in order to further investigations into the serious arrestable offence of dishonest handling.

Kenneth Noye, meanwhile, locked up in the maximum-security prison of Albany on the Isle of Wight, was also of considerable interest to police – but for an entirely unexpected reason. They wanted to know whether he could help their investigations into a police officer he had named to Boyce as a man who, he believed, would give him a character reference. Noye had told Boyce that an officer called Ray Adams would vouch for the fact that he wasn't a 'cold-blooded killer'.

Early in 1987 Adams, with a reputation for being an ambitious, shrewd and streetwise officer, had been appointed commander of S O 11, the criminal intelligence branch. Within two months of his appointment, however, he had become the subject of a full-scale inquiry by the Yard's Complaints Investigations Bureau, the successors to Robert Mark's creation, A 10. The investigation, under the supervision of the independent Police Complaints Authority, is believed to have started after a detective constable arrested a drugs dealer in south-east London who made allegations against various officers.

In Adams's case, it is believed that the investigation centred on his relationship with his informants – one of whom was Kenneth Noye. The two men had known each other since the mid-1970s. It was the questioning, however, of a police officer living close to Adams, Alan 'Taffy' Holmes, that was to push the inquiry firmly into the public eye. For Holmes, a member of the task force, shot himself dead after two interviews with Complaints Investigations Bureau officers. Friends claimed that he was told that if he did not assist the inquiry, he could face action over his relationship with the wife of a south London criminal. On the other side of the criminal divide there were claims that he had been killed because he knew too much.

As the press went to town on Adams, revealing that he lived in a £450,000 house in the exclusive millionaires' row of Bishop's Walk in Shirley, Surrey, had a villa abroad and a wife – reputedly from a wealthy family – who ran a boutique, Deputy Assistant Commissioner Peter Winship, in charge of the complaints bureau, went to see Noye. It was an unproductive meeting; Noye refused to help but used the opportunity to complain bitterly about his imprisonment.

At the time of writing, the inquiry into Adams, by a 'team within a team' of handpicked officers based at Tintagel House, still continues, and Adams has been moved to another department until its outcome is known.

Adams's connection with Brink's-Mat rested solely on his relationship with Noye, and his subsequent position as head of SO11, but in 1987 another officer, more closely connected with the case, was suspended from duty. He was Detective Superintendent Tony Lundy.

Lundy's latest problems began in November 1986, shortly after his return from the Operation Cougar inquiry in Florida, when Granada Television's *World in Action* team put out a programme called *The Untouchable*, which investigated the relationship between Lundy and a north London businessman who had been one of his key informants. It alleged that the informant had escaped prosecution for serious crimes, despite being described in court as one of London's most dangerous criminals. Following the programme two Labour MPs – Clive Soley, the Hammersmith MP and front-bench spokesman on police affairs, and Chris Smith, MP for Islington South and Finsbury in north London – used parliamentary privilege to call for a full investigation into the relationship between Lundy and his informant.

Unlike Adams, who has consistently refused to discuss the inquiry into his activities, Lundy came out fighting. In a lengthy press statement two days after the programme, he said: 'I wish to reply to the false allegations which have been made against me over the last few days. These allegations are a repetition of malicious and unfounded allegations which have been going on for a number of years. They have already been investigated and I have been fully exonerated.

'I have been in the front line of operational detective duties for more than twenty years. During the last ten years in particular I have been responsible for the arrest and conviction of numerous major criminals, including murderers and armed robbers.

'I have frequently had to withstand attacks on my integrity at Crown Courts, and, as with most officers, that situation is looked on as inevitable when dealing with the type of criminals being prosecuted.

'In addition, I have been subjected to intolerable intrusions into my private life. My house was burgled and then further allegations made. Visits were made by the media demanding interviews and TV cameras filming my premises. This resulted in having to change my address in 1984.

'I have recently been responsible for probably the biggest breakthrough into money laundering of drugs and organized-crime syndicates in the USA and throughout the world and have spent many months away from my family.

'Because of confidentiality and the Official Secrets Act, I

have remained silent during the past few years and have continued to do my job with outstanding results.

'However, the latest series of allegations on my character have taken different and sinister lines of attack. I am not in a position to detail some of the devious and determined methods because of *sub judice* rules, but I will be in a position to do so in the near future.

'The fact that Members of Parliament can irresponsibly make unsubstantiated general allegations that I am corrupt whilst hiding behind parliamentary privilege is absolutely disgusting.'

Notwithstanding the vehemence of Lundy's statement, Sir Kenneth Newman, Commissioner of the Metropolitan Police, asked the Chief Constable of South Yorkshire, Peter Wright, to investigate the allegations that an improper relationship had existed between Lundy and his informant.

At the outset of the South Yorkshire inquiry, Lundy was allowed to remain on duty, but in June 1987 his North London informant was arrested by customs officers and charged with the illegal importation of cocaine worth more than £13.5 million after a raid in Harley Street. The informant had only just been released from prison after customs officers had successfully prosecuted him for a £2 million V A T fraud involving the smuggling of krugerrands from the Channel Islands. Following the cocaine charge, in July 1987 Lundy was suspended from duty for a 'recent breach of discipline'. The results of the South Yorkshire inquiry are not yet known.

The success of Boyce and Lundy in cracking open the Patrick Diamond/Shaun Murphy money-laundering racket led to further developments. Levine struck a plea bargain with the authorities, saying he was prepared to take the stand and testify against the other defendants. In the end, however, there was no need for him to do so, although the evidence he provided was crucial in convicting the others. He was sentenced to nine years' imprisonment and a $35,000 fine, as well as the seizure of a number of assets, including his $400,000 Florida home. He also lost the right to practise as an attorney.

Levine, however, fared rather better than another of the

defendants, Patrick Bilton, who despite pleading guilty received a seventeen-year sentence.

Bilton had faced a drugs-smuggling charge before the Levine case but arranged for a man named Elton Gissendanner, director of Natural Resources for the State of Florida, to have the charge against him reduced. Gissendanner, who ran the Florida Marine Patrol, responsible for law enforcement on the borders of the state and inland waters, was eventually tried on four charges and pleaded not guilty. Halfway through the trial, however, he agreed to plead guilty to one count – obstruction of justice – and was sentenced to three years' imprisonment and a $15,000 fine.

In November 1987, with Murphy still helping the authorities, a second wave of arrests took place, and $14 million of assets, including a Los Angeles casino, a yachting marina and a corporate jet, were seized from another alleged drugs-money-laundering ring.

Miami lawyer Melvin Kessler was said to have set up companies, in Liechtenstein, the Caribbean and the United States, to handle cash transfers of millions of dollars in illegal profits from marijuana trafficking.

The actual drug trafficking was said to have been carried out by a power-boat racing fanatic named Ben Kramer and a man also said to have been involved in the Levine case, former Indianapolis racing-car driver Randy Lanier. They were accused of smuggling thousands of pounds of marijuana into the United States.

Kessler was said to have set up companies, in consultation with Murphy, in the Virgin Islands to hide the profits. After the money was transferred out of the USA it would arrive back again, usually in the form of loans.

Some of the money was said to have been transferred to the Fort Apache Marina, Apache Offshore Racing and Engineering Inc. and Lamborghini Apache Racing Team Ltd, all companies that supported Ben Kramer's hobby. The drug profits also allegedly went to buy the casino (with the unlikely name of the Bell Gardens Bicycle Club), the jet, a small fleet of boats – and an 85-foot, $1.7 million motor sailboat named the *Sea Witch*.

As for Scott Errico, the hitman's two-year campaign to avoid extradition from Britain ended on 24 July 1987, when he suddenly abandoned plans to appeal to the European Court of Human Rights. Errico was flown out of Britain amid intense security after rumours that he had offered up to $1 million to anyone who could rescue him.

Handcuffed and guarded by armed Scotland Yard detectives, he was flown by helicopter to the USAF base at Mildenhall in Suffolk. There, as members of the Yard's blue-beret firearms team stood watch, he was handed over to a team of DEA agents and US marshals. After extradition papers were signed, he was placed on a USAF jet for the seven-hour flight to Florida. Errico is now held in a top-security prison in the USA facing federal charges of conspiracy to import marijuana and charges, brought by the state of Florida, of murder while working for the Thompson Organization.

The events in the USA had not gone unnoticed by Whitehall, where the laundering taking place in Britain and some of its offshore dependencies was viewed as an increasingly worrying phenomenon. In the USA the law specifying that deposits of more than $10,000 have to be notified to the federal authorities had created problems; so many deposits were reported that a massive backlog built up in dealing with those that warranted investigation. But the law had enabled the authorities to investigate swiftly deposits considered particularly unusual, and it created a climate in which no one could, with impunity, simply walk into a bank and hand over carrier bags full of cash with no questions asked.

The British government took the first steps towards introducing similar safeguards in 1986; drug traffickers were the first target. The Drug Trafficking Offences Act 1986, which came into force at the start of 1987, contains, one minister has boasted, 'the toughest powers in the Western world for depriving drug traffickers of the profits of their ghastly and exploitative trade'.

Under the terms of the Act it became an offence to help a drugs trafficker retain the proceeds of his crimes and money laundering was punishable by up to fourteen years' imprisonment. So seriously was this clause taken that in November 1986, shortly before the Act came into force, the London Stock Exchange wrote to every stockbroking firm in the City warning them of the consequences they could face if they assisted traffickers hiding their money in City-style investments. The Act also gave the banks statutory protection from any breach-of-confidence law suits brought by customers whom they did report.

Other provisions in the Act were equally swingeing, enabling a judge to order the confiscation of assets in any case where the defendant's proceeds of crime total £10,000 or more and where £10,000 or more is likely to be recovered by the authorities. Any of the defendant's assets can be sold to raise an amount ordered by the judge, even if the actual proceeds of the crime cannot be traced; and a defendant refusing to give up assets is liable to imprisonment in addition to the penalty he is already serving. Courts also have the power to freeze assets at an early stage in an investigation; receivers can be appointed to trace funds; and police and customs officers have the right to seize assets during an investigation, whether they be cars, boats or houses, if they believe that there is a risk these may be sold or smuggled abroad.

The Act rapidly proved an enormous success. In the first few months that it was in force 110 defendants had their assets frozen by the courts – a total of more than £5 million – and by the end of 1987 more than £20 million in suspicious deposits had been notified to police.

It was natural, then, that pressure would mount to expand it further. Sir Kenneth Newman paved the way when, in March 1987, in a speech to the Police Foundation, he criticized the Bank of England, Barclays Bank and Sheffield assay office for failing to report the business activities of Scadlynn. 'It is noteworthy that at none of the institutions in this chain were any alarm bells sounded about the massive quantities of monies being moved,' he said. 'There was such a rise in the number of notes supplied by the Bank of England in a month to its regional office in Bristol that the point was reached at which the bank was obliged to notify the Treasury.'

Lack of information from the banks, he added, had allowed the Brink's-Mat gang to pursue their aim of becoming 'robber barons' – 'That is, to convert money into substantial property, which is their base, and to gain respectability'. They had also sought to invest where they would be brought into respectable company, particularly in the City.

Later a spokesman for the Bank of England said it was 'simply not true' that extra notes had been issued to cope with demand from the Bristol office or that the Treasury had been informed. 'There was nothing for us to raise alarm bells about, as far as we knew,' said a spokesman. Barclays refused to comment on the speech, but at Sheffield assay office, a spokesman said, 'It is not unusual for us to deal with large amounts of gold because we do that every day. We were only concerned with our job of testing the quality of the bullion.'

None the less, when the Criminal Justice Bill was introduced late in 1987, the bank-reporting, seizure and confiscation measures were extended to cover all major crimes, although, temporarily at least, the penalties for assisting in money laundering remained confined to drug trafficking only. The Home Office had no doubt that that particular aspect of the legislation would be difficult to enforce and wanted to see how many successful prosecutions were brought under the Drug Trafficking Offences Act before extending it further.

The banks, sensitive to the prevailing climate of opinion, kept what doubts they had about the efficacy of the law to themselves. The only hint of public criticism came from Derek Wheatley, QC, chairman of the legal committee of clearing banks and legal adviser to Lloyds Bank; he reflected the views of many in the financial world when he said the proposals were 'ill-considered' and 'could trigger an avalanche of reports on the financial affairs of innocent bank clients whose instructions awoke the suspicion of a young and inexperienced bank clerk' as well as threaten the reputation of London as an international financial centre. An unusual transfer of funds to, say, the Cayman Islands could arouse suspicion but 'might just be the result of an unexpected windfall', he claimed.

Such views were a surprise to no one, and John Patten, the

Home Office minister, was unrepentant as he reported to a meeting of Tories in Oxfordshire in July that the new provisions 'will mean that all large-scale convicted criminals will face the prospect of having their ill-gotten gains stripped from them', as well as preventing them from stashing their profits away. 'The new provisions will bite hard on organized crime and offences like armed robbery, racketeering, blackmail and fraud,' he claimed. 'When the Criminal Justice Bill is enacted, the courts will be able to ensure that when they send someone to prison, the offender will not be able to sit smugly in his cell dreaming of a life of luxury at the end of his sentence. We are acting to ensure that crime does not pay.'

Meanwhile, in July 1986 a two-man fraud squad was established on the Isle of Man. Its staffing was recognized to be inadequate, but Chief Constable Robin Oake promised that the squad would be enlarged as soon as financial constraints allowed. In his annual report in March 1987 he noted a 'disturbing continuous upward trend' in the incidence of fraud and acknowledged that funds obtained through major crime and drug-related activities were being laundered on the island. 'Manx institutions are being used to facilitate the perpetration of fraud,' he said. 'There are no geographical limits to the source of these problems, and it is clear but sad that the island is being used for unlawful purposes by some people in other parts of the world.'

The Criminal Justice Bill, which is expected to become law in 1988, could include two other far-reaching changes in English law: the abolition of the need to present a prima facie case in an English court of law before suspects can be extradited abroad, and an end to a defendant's right of silence when being questioned by police.

Changes in the extradition law, which would mean the first redrafting of extradition laws in England since 1870, were proposed by the government in the belief that some countries found the prima facie requirements so difficult that Britain could become a haven for foreign criminals. Instead the government proposed a new procedure under which foreign governments would be required to provide a warrant, a statement of facts about the crime and details of the law under which the individual would be prosecuted. Implicit in its reasoning was a desire to prevent the recurrence of an event such as the abrogation of the extradition treaty with Spain.

There was a vehement outcry from all sides of both the House of Commons and the House of Lords, however, and claims that any change of the law would be an infringement of civil liberties. Despite assurances from the government that the new arrangements would apply only to countries with 'similar judicial standards' to Britain's, the fate of that particular clause is at present undecided.

There was equally fierce criticism of the plan to abolish a defendant's right of silence. The call to end the right came initially from the Home Secretary, Douglas Hurd, who said in a lecture to the Police Foundation: 'Is it really in the interests of justice that experienced criminals should be able to refuse to answer all police questions, secure in the knowledge that a jury will never hear of it? Does the present law really protect the innocent, whose interests will generally lie in answering questions frankly? Is it really unthinkable that the jury should be allowed to know about the defendant's silence and, in the light of other facts brought to light during a trial, be able to draw its own conclusions?'

Peter Imbert, who became Commissioner of the Metropolitan Police on 3 August 1987, took up the cause six weeks after his appointment when he told the International Police Exhibition at the Barbican in London: 'It is a puzzle to me how a privilege against self-incrimination, for that is what it really is, ever gained any sort of respectable place in English legal tradition.' He added that its removal would be 'the most important step legislators could take to control and reduce crime', for if society was serious about deterring people from committing crimes, it had to increase the prospects of convicting them. Instead, he said, a situation should exist where a court was able to comment on, or draw inferences from, the fact that a defendant had been silent when questioned by police.

To support his case, he quoted the nineteenth-century

British social reformer Jeremy Bentham, who had called the right 'one of the most pernicious and irrational rules that ever found its way into the human mind. If all the criminals in every class had assembled and framed a system after their own wishes, is not this rule the very first they would have established for their own security?' And Imbert quoted Sir Robert Mark as saying, 'The right of silence might have been designed by the criminals for their especial benefit and that of their professional advisers. It has done more to obscure the truth and facilitate crime than anything else in this century.'

The call was promptly endorsed by the Association of Chief Police Officers and Lord Lane, the Lord Chief Justice.

Critics of the proposed change to the law included the Law Society, which said, 'We feel strongly that the right of silence should stay. We do not believe that the principle that a person is innocent until proven guilty should be abandoned.' Leon Brittan, a former Home Secretary, said that to remove it would substantially alter the burden of proof in criminal cases, and the chairman of the Criminal Bar Association, David Cocks, said, 'It cannot be proper to tack on to the coat-tails of the Criminal Justice Bill a provision so fundamental to the English criminal trial and seek to make it law with the minimum of debate and consultation.' As late as December 1987, however, government ministers were still determined to change the law to allow the prosecution in a criminal case to comment on a suspect's remaining silent, although a rough passage was expected for the Criminal Justice Bill through the House of Commons.

While the debate continued, solicitors acting on behalf of the insurance brokers who had paid out over the Brink's-Mat haul were quietly going to unprecedented lengths, through the civil courts, to regain their money. For with the exception of the eleven bars of gold found at Hollywood Cottage, two bars found at Palmer's residence and a further twenty-seven bars that had been sold on, none of the gold had been recovered.

By December 1987 more than fifty defendants, ranging from

banks and companies to private individuals, had received writs regarding their involvement in the Brink's-Mat case. Those found guilty of handling the cash proceeds, and even some of those acquitted, had their assets frozen pending the hearing of civil cases in which the money was sought. In the case of those acquitted, the insurers were making full use of a subtle distinction between criminal and civil law. In criminal cases a defendant's guilt has to be established 'beyond reasonable doubt' before a conviction ensues. In civil cases the law is not so stringent: guilt can be established on a 'balance of probabilities'. In some cases wholly innocent parties were served writs based on claims in equity law that their innocence did not mean that they should not forfeit the money they had obtained. In other cases financial institutions were served writs aimed at forcing them to make their records available to investigators trying to trace financial transactions based on the gold.

Similar proceedings were started in Jersey, the Isle of Man and Ireland.

Nineteen eighty-seven was not entirely given over to court cases, points of law and political decision making. Out on the streets the hunt for the gold continued. And in a Rotherhithe back street, on a cold November morning, it became evident that the hunt was as dangerous as ever when detectives from the task force spotted a man long suspected of having handled some of the bullion. The man, son of a south London bookmaker and director of a firm of building developers, had been in hiding for nearly a year after leaving his £1 million Tudor mansion in Kent, where the curtains alone cost £60,000 and the four bathrooms had gold fittings, when he knew police were after him.

The detectives were on one of their routine checks of addresses to which they thought the man might return when he was spotted in a car with his son. A police officer moved fast, reaching in through the car window to grab the keys, but not fast enough. The car shot forward, carrying the officer for some distance on the bonnet before he was thrown off into the gutter. Eventually, after a chase, the fugitive's son was arrested, but of the wanted man there was no trace.

The Brink's-Mat case had gone full circle. Countless hours had been spent in courtrooms; links with sophisticated international criminals had been established; corruption allegations had been made; and the politicians had been forced to sit up and take notice. But on the streets of south-east London it was business as usual – police officers pitting their lives against men to whom life was cheaper than 'easy' money.

A CHOICE OF PENGUINS

An African Winter Preston King With an Introduction by Richard Leakey

This powerful and impassioned book offers a unique assessment of the interlocking factors which result in the famines of Africa and argues that there *are* solutions and we *can* learn from the mistakes of the past.

Jean Rhys: Letters 1931–66
Edited by Francis Wyndham and Diana Melly

'Eloquent and invaluable . . . her life emerges, and with it a portrait of an unexpectedly indomitable figure' – Marina Warner in the *Sunday Times*

Among the Russians Colin Thubron

One man's solitary journey by car across Russia provides an enthralling and revealing account of the habits and idiosyncrasies of a fascinating people. 'He sees things with the freshness of an innocent and the erudition of a scholar' – *Daily Telegraph*

The Amateur Naturalist Gerald Durrell with Lee Durrell

'Delight . . . on every page . . . packed with authoritative writing, learning without pomposity . . . it represents a real bargain' – *The Times Educational Supplement*. 'What treats are in store for the average British household' – *Books and Bookmen*

The Democratic Economy Geoff Hodgson

Today, the political arena is divided as seldom before. In this exciting and original study, Geoff Hodgson carefully examines the claims of the rival doctrines and exposes some crucial flaws.

They Went to Portugal Rose Macaulay

An exotic and entertaining account of travellers to Portugal from the pirate-crusaders, through poets, aesthetes and ambassadors, to the new wave of romantic travellers. A wonderful mixture of literature, history and adventure, by one of our most stylish and seductive writers.

FOR THE BEST IN PAPERBACKS, LOOK FOR THE 

A CHOICE OF PENGUINS

A Fortunate Grandchild 'Miss Read'

Grandma Read in Lewisham and Grandma Shafe in Walton on the Naze were totally different in appearance and outlook, but united in their affection for their grand-daughter – who grew up to become the much-loved and popular novelist.

The Ultimate Trivia Quiz Game Book Maureen and Alan Hiron

If you are immersed in trivia, addicted to quiz games, endlessly nosey, then this is the book for you: over 10,000 pieces of utterly dispensable information!

The Diary of Virginia Woolf
Five volumes, edited by Quentin Bell and Anne Olivier Bell

'As an account of the intellectual and cultural life of our century, Virginia Woolf's diaries are invaluable; as the record of one bruised and unquiet mind, they are unique' – Peter Ackroyd in the *Sunday Times*

Voices of the Old Sea Norman Lewis

'I will wager that *Voices of the Old Sea* will be a classic in the literature about Spain' – *Mail on Sunday*. 'Limpidly and lovingly Norman Lewis has caught the helpless, unwitting, often foolish, but always hopeful village in its dying summers, and saved the tragedy with sublime comedy' – *Observer*

The First World War A J P Taylor

In this superb illustrated history, A. J. P. Taylor 'manages to say almost everything that is important for an understanding and, indeed, intellectual digestion of that vast event . . . A special text . . . a remarkable collection of photographs' – *Observer*

Ninety-Two Days Evelyn Waugh

With characteristic honesty, Evelyn Waugh here debunks the romantic notions attached to rough travelling: his journey in Guiana and Brazil is difficult, dangerous and extremely uncomfortable, and his account of it is witty and unquestionably compelling.

A CHOICE OF PENGUINS

Castaway Lucy Irvine

'Writer seeks "wife" for a year on a tropical island.' This is the extraordinary, candid, sometimes shocking account of what happened when Lucy Irvine answered the advertisement, and found herself embroiled in what was not exactly a desert island dream. 'Fascinating' – *Daily Mail*

Out of Africa Karen Blixen (Isak Dinesen)

After the failure of her coffee-farm in Kenya, where she lived from 1913 to 1931, Karen Blixen went home to Denmark and wrote this unforgettable account of her experiences. 'No reader can put the book down without some share in the author's poignant farewell to her farm' – *Observer*

The Lisle Letters Edited by Muriel St Clare Byrne

An intimate, immediate and wholly fascinating picture of a family in the reign of Henry VIII. 'Remarkable . . . we can really hear the people of early Tudor England talking' – Keith Thomas in the *Sunday Times*. 'One of the most extraordinary works to be published this century' – J. H. Plumb

In My Wildest Dreams Leslie Thomas

The autobiography of Leslie Thomas, author of *The Magic Army* and *The Dearest and the Best*. From Barnardo boy to original virgin soldier, from apprentice journalist to famous novelist, it is an amazing story. 'Hugely enjoyable' – *Daily Express*

India: The Siege Within M. J. Akbar

'A thoughtful and well-researched history of the conflict, 2,500 years old, between centralizing and separatist forces in the sub-continent. And remarkably, for a work of this kind, it's concise, elegantly written and entertaining' – Zareer Masani in the *New Statesman*

The Winning Streak Walter Goldsmith and David Clutterbuck

Marks and Spencer, Saatchi and Saatchi, United Biscuits, G.E.C. . . . The U.K.'s top companies reveal their formulas for success, in an important and stimulating book that no British manager can afford to ignore.